SOCIAL EXPERIMENTATION AND ECONOMIC POLICY

CAMBRIDGE SURVEYS OF ECONOMIC LITERATURE

Editors:
Miss Phyllis Deane, University of Cambridge
Professor Mark Perlman, University of Pittsburgh

Editorial Advisory Board:
Professor A. B. Atkinson, London School of Economics and Political Sciences
Professor M. Bronfenbrenner, Duke University
Professor K. D. George, University College, Cardiff
Professor C. P. Kindleberger, Massachusetts Institute of Technology
Professor T. Mayer, University of California, Davis
Professor A. R. Prest, London School of Economics and Political Science

The literature of economics is expanding rapidly, and many subjects have changed out of recognition within the space of a few years. Perceiving the state of knowledge in fast developing subjects is difficult for students and time consuming for professional economists. This series of books is intended to help with this problem. Each book will be quite brief, giving a clear structure to and balanced overview of the topic and written at a level intelligible to the senior undergraduate. The books will therefore be useful for teaching, but will also provide a mature yet compact presentation of the subject for economists wishing to update their knowledge outside their own specialism.

Other books in the series
E. Roy Weintraub: Microfoundations: The compatibility of microeconomics and macroeconomics
Dennis C. Mueller: Public choice
Robert L. Clark and Joseph J. Spengler: The economics of individual and population aging
Edwin Burmeister: Capital theory and dynamics
Mark Blaug: The methodology of economics

Social experimentation and economic policy

ROBERT FERBER

Former Research Professor of Economics and Business Administration
and *Director, Survey Research Laboratory,*
University of Illinois

WERNER Z. HIRSCH

Professor of Economics, University of California, Los Angeles

CAMBRIDGE UNIVERSITY PRESS

CAMBRIDGE

LONDON   NEW YORK   NEW ROCHELLE

MELBOURNE   SYDNEY

Published by the Press Syndicate of the University of Cambridge
The Pitt Building, Trumpington Street, Cambridge CB2 1RP
32 East 57th Street, New York, NY 10022, USA
296 Beaconsfield Parade, Middle Park, Melbourne 3206, Australia

First published 1982

Printed in the United States of America

Library of Congress Cataloging in Publication Data
Ferber, Robert, 1922–
Social experimentation and economic policy.
(Cambridge surveys of economic literature)
Bibliography: p.
Includes index.
1. United States – Economic policy – 1971–
– Evaluation. 2. United States – Social
policy – Evaluation. 3. Public welfare – United
States – Evaluation. I. Hirsch, Werner Zvi,
1920–   . II. Title. III. Series.
HC106.7.F47   338.973   81–6146
ISBN 0 521 24185 5 hard covers   AACR2
ISBN 0 521 28507 0 paperback

CONTENTS

TABLES AND FIGURES

PREFACE

Although there has been much experimentation – and information about experimentation – on issues in other fields of endeavor, especially education and psychology, there has been little work of this type in economics and even less information. Not until the past dozen years, in fact, have we seen any appreciable social experimentation on economic issues with real populations. Nevertheless, the growing interest in evaluating the effectiveness of social programs makes it likely that this type of experimentation will increase in the future. For those social experiments in economics that have been carried out, a fair amount of technical material has been published, but hardly any material of a general evaluative nature has appeared except for the survey articles by the authors of the present volume.

The objective of this volume is to provide an overview and a synthesis of the social experiments in economics, based on these review articles. The level of presentation is relatively simple and requires only a knowledge of elementary microeconomic theory and some statistics. Hence, this volume should be of use not only to professional economists and graduate students in economics but also to policymakers and to undergraduates majoring in economics. For those interested in investigating particular social experiments in greater detail, the references cited in the chapters dealing with those experiments should be very helpful.

The authors would like to thank Mark Perlman and Robert Lampman for very useful comments on earlier drafts. Finally, they would like to express their appreciation to Bernita Fruhling, Bette Hulmes, and Rosemary G. Rees for typing and retyping the various drafts of this manuscript. Though the authors would like to dodge the responsibility, they must admit that any errors or mistakes in this volume are of their own making.

ROBERT FERBER

WERNER Z. HIRSCH

It is with deep sadness that I must add a lonely postscript to this Preface. Bob Ferber died on September 8, 1981, after a brief illness, and after having corrected proofs but, sadly, before having seen the book in print.

He will be missed – not only by his wife Marianne, son Don, and daughter Ellen, to whom he was devoted, but also by myself and many others for whom he was colleague, teacher, collaborator, and friend. His warm, self-effacing personality and wry humor were special, endearing qualities.

The profession respected Robert Ferber for his contributions to statistics and survey methods, research on Latin America, and consumer expenditure research. His contributions were many, including those as editor of the *Journal of the American Statistical Association*, the *Journal of Consumer Research*, and the *Journal of Marketing Research*. Moreover, he wrote or collaborated on more than 17 books and 160 articles.

I feel privileged to have been Bob's collaborator on this volume.

September 28, 1981   WERNER Z. HIRSCH

1

Introduction

Economists have long faced the problem of how to measure the effect of changes in policy variables on the behavior of economic units and particularly of changes that have been merely contemplated. How low-income households will use cash subsidies for housing, for example, and what effect these subsidies will have on the quality and price of housing are key questions that would help to determine whether such subsidies are desirable.

A variety of techniques have been used for estimating such effects in the past, including econometric models, surveys of past and present behavior, simulation models of artificial populations, surveys with questions about behavior under hypothetical conditions, and demonstration projects. Each of the methods yields estimates of these effects.

Because the true response remains unobservable until the policy under consideration is actually put into effect, the accuracy of these estimates remains an unknown quantity, especially on a micro basis. That it might be possible to measure these effects directly by the use of controlled experiments, as is so frequently done in such fields as biology and agriculture, seemed too farfetched to merit serious consideration.

Social experimentation, however, does just that. It seeks to measure the effects of changes in policy variables by applying these changes to human populations under conditions of controlled experimentation similar to that used in the physical and biological sciences. Whereas controlled experiments in the physical and biological sciences are usually designed to test the effects of particular substances, social experiments are designed to measure the effects of new or potential social programs. By testing different policies on human populations with experimental controls, or by testing variations of the same policy (such as different amounts of housing subsidies) with experimental controls, a great deal of information is obtainable on the effects of these programs that may then serve as a basis for informed policy formation.[1]

What differentiates the economics experiments from those in the physical and biological sciences is the use of the real world as a laboratory; this introduces a major new dimension to the methodology of experimentation because humans, unlike other animate or inanimate objects, are very likely to react to the conditions of the experiment and thereby confound the results. For this reason, social experimentation, especially in economics, faces a very different set of problems from other types of experimentation, problems that may be so severe as to vitiate many of the advantages of this approach, as is discussed at length in the later chapters.

Expectations about the usefulness of social experimentation have been so great that in the past 10 years in the United States hundreds of millions of dollars have been spent or committed on them (they have been of interest in other countries but have been used there to a lesser extent).[2] Although these are huge sums in terms of economic or any other type of social research, the justification is that the results are to serve as the basis for national programs that will ultimately involve hundreds of billions of dollars, not to mention their political and social risks. Hence, even these seemingly large research outlays are small if they help policy makers to avoid errors in the later implementation of the national programs.

Still, the experience with these social experiments has exposed many problems relating to design, implementation, and interpretation of the results. It has led to many questions about the validity and the value of these experiments, and the controversy is likely to continue for many years to come. This is particularly so because only in the last few years have the first few social experiments been completed and the data become available for study and reflection. For this reason also, this would seem to be a propitious time to evaluate this emerging analytical tool of economic analysis and to consider its implications for economic research and for public policy. The considerable material that is just now beginning to become available makes it possible to conduct such an evaluation, to place social experimentation in proper perspective and provide a fairly good idea of what it can do for economic policy making.

For the purposes of this evaluation, this book is organized into three major parts. The first part, Chapters 1–3, provides a general introduction to what social experimentation is all about and how it operates. Chapter 2 outlines what is meant by a social experiment, discusses the rationale for having social experiments, and considers how they differ from other tools of economic analysis and to what extent these other tools may serve as alternatives to social experiments.

An overview of the problems encountered in the planning and conduct of social experiments is provided in Chapter 3. Also considered in that chapter are ethical and moral questions that arise in the experimental manipulations of human populations, as well as the problems of planning and administering such experiments.

The second and largest part of the book, Chapters 4–9, is devoted to a review of the principal social experiments that have been conducted or are currently underway in economics, mainly in the United States. This includes the four sets of income maintenance experiments, the experiments on supported work, the Health Insurance Study, the experiments with electricity pricing, and the cash housing allowance experiments. For each of these experiments, information is provided on the rationale for the experiment; its basic design, from both an experimental and a survey point of view; the manner in which it was implemented; and the nature of the results obtained so far. In addition, the discussion of each experiment closes with an evaluation that considers how well it seems to have been carried out and how well it seems to have met the original objectives of providing a firm basis for the formulation of economic policy.

The final part of the book, consisting of a single chapter, returns to the questions raised at the outset of this section and considers the value of social experimentation as an economic tool in the light of the experiences and the results obtained so far through its use. In effect, based on these experiences, we ask what has been learned about social experimentation both as a research approach and as a tool for economic policy. A set of recommendations on the conditions under which social experimentation might or might not be used and on ways in which further evaluations might be made of this tool close out this book.

2

Nature of social experimentation

What are social experiments?

Social scientists can choose from a large menu of research alternatives, one of which is the social experiment. It is akin to the controlled experiments used for many years by physical and natural scientists as well as medical researchers and agronomists. They have in common reliance on a careful statistical design that seeks to isolate the effect of a single factor or group of factors – often referred to as treatment variables – on specified outcomes. Thus, the statistical design makes possible estimation of this effect distinct from other factors.

Chemists' test-tube experiments are perhaps the best-known controlled experiments. For a long time, also, agronomists have carried out experiments that apply different amounts of water or fertilizer to specified crops under controlled circumstances. Medical researchers, too, particularly those in the field of public health, have often engaged in controlled experimentation with humans as their subjects. Whereas these experiments on humans have focused on health matters, social scientists more recently have undertaken controlled experiments on humans to learn about their behavior. Such social experiments have been defined by R. F. Boruch as requiring "that experimental units are assigned randomly to one or more treatment conditions, that one or more outcomes are measured, and that relative differences in outcomes form a basis for making evaluative judgments about the effectiveness of the treatments."[1]

Among the first to carry out social experiments were psychologists, and indeed the literature of psychology is replete with reports of such experiments. One of the most notable is that done with factory workers in 1928 at Hawthorne, New Jersey. This famous experiment has been of particular interest because of its substantive bearing on social experimentation. It brought out that the mere fact that people know they are being experimented upon can have an effect in itself independent of the nature of the treatment.[2] This so-called Hawthorne effect has important ramifications for all sorts of experiments, including social experiments.

Experiments with human subjects are legion in various other social sciences and related fields – for example, experiments with teaching practices in education and experiments on the effectiveness of different advertising and communications media carried out often on broad (and sometimes undefined) segments of the population. The latter type of experiment, especially those carried out in the last decade in other countries to promote the adoption of birth control methods, comes very close to the social experiments covered in this paper.

The social experiments in economics may be said to have two broad objectives: to contribute to knowledge about a question of interest to economic theory; and to furnish a basis for evaluation of the desirability of a proposed social program. Although the funding agencies are obviously more concerned with the second objective, considerations relating to the first play a major role in the design of the experiments and the resulting analysis. In either event, what distinguishes the social experiments in economics from others is the focus on aggregate economic and social effects of changes in certain policy variables and the long time needed for measurement. The time element is of key importance in view of the fact that people do not adjust instantaneously to changes in the economic environment. Such adjustments require considerable time, not only for this reason but also because adjustment is not likely to be the same when the change is temporary as when it is permanent. Thus, a family's consumption responses are not likely to be the same if it knows that its income will be supported at a minimum level for one year as if it knows that the income support will last for ten years.

The type of social experiment being carried out in economics may be defined as a publicly financed study that incorporates a rigorous statistical design and whose experimental aspects are applied over a period of time to one or more segments of a human population, with the aim of evaluating the aggregate economic and social effects of the experimental treatments.

Certain elements of this definition should be stressed. One is the rigorous design feature, meaning that certain treatments are to be applied to one or more human populations, making full use of the principles of statistical experimentation. In other words, allowance has to be made for control groups, for randomization in the selection of subjects, for measurement of sampling errors, for provision for adequate sample sizes to detect effects if they exist, for detection and correction of bias due to the experiments, for control of the process through time, and for collection of the necessary data.

It seems needless to say that the populations covered in these experiments are those that would be directly affected if the particular treatments were adopted as national policy. Still, for example, one of the major criticisms of the New Jersey Negative Income Tax Experiment was that its eligibility requirements were so narrow as to exclude the majority of low-income families who would be beneficiaries of such a negative income tax plan.[3] The remedy in this case was to launch other experiments covering other types of families, a remedy that may be unavoidable in many of these instances.

One other key aspect of the definition of these experiments is the *search for information* to serve as a basis not only for economic policy but for social policy as well. It is here that economics has to interact with other social sciences, for there is no question that broad policy measures such as a guaranteed annual income or housing allowances affect not only behavior in the labor markets or with regard to housing but many other aspects of life as well. Thus, if a low-income family uses housing allowances to obtain living quarters with adequate heat, sickness may be reduced and the children might then attend school on a more regular basis. In other words, a social experiment has to be designed to measure not only direct economic effects of the particular treatment but also numerous indirect effects, which could conceivably have ramifications as important as the direct effects themselves. Thus, ideally, the economist should use a general model that allows for the direct and indirect relationships among all relevant variables rather than a partial model that focuses on only the direct response effects on the key variables.

It should be stressed that the focus of this volume is on social experiments having implications for broad changes in economic policy. In other words, we exclude those types of experiments, though they also are social in nature, that do not focus on providing direct economic benefits. An example is the 1972–3 experiment in Kansas City, Missouri, to ascertain the effect on crime, and on the perception of crime, of the use of marked and unmarked police patrol cars.[4]

Expenditure of public money is the only means of carrying out social experiments in view of the very substantial amounts that are involved. The total cost of all the negative income tax experiments, for example, was reported in 1975 to be already approaching $70 million[5] and has since exceeded $200 million.

Large public funds are needed because the cost per experimental unit tends to be so high. In the Denver–Seattle Income Maintenance Experiment, for example, the average cost per experimental family was about $3,000 per year. Even the cost of a control family was about $1,000 per year.[6] One of the experiments currently underway, the Health Insurance Study being carried out in six areas of the country with field work varying from three to five years, is estimated to cost approximately $63 million by the time it is over; and the housing allowance experiments were estimated to amount to about $200 million over their expected duration.[7]

In view of these amounts, it is clear that only government, probably only the federal government, can afford research of this magnitude. This serves to place policy makers in a unique position with regard to social experimentation, because they are the ones who can choose what policies are to be subjected to this type of experiment and in what manner. Given the fact that even with these huge outlays social experiments are of limited size and tend because of various design features (noted in Chapter 3) to lend support to the null hypothesis of lack of appreciable effects, this places a powerful weapon in the hands of a politically astute policy maker.

Why social experiments?

Given the long time and substantial funds involved and the many unresolved technical issues, one may well ask why social experiments of this type should be undertaken at all. From a theoretical point of view, the answer is clear. If a fundamental policy change is under consideration, and if there is no clear basis for estimating a priori the effect of this policy on economic behavior, then the only way to obtain this information is to put the policy into practice on a limited scale and see what happens. This is especially so if there is reason to believe the policy change could have strong negative as well as positive effects.

The question that led to the negative income tax experiments, for example, is how labor force participation would be influenced by a guaranteed minimum income. The fear was that such an income floor might reduce substantially the work incentives and behavior of the participants. As there was no way to answer this question without making some highly controversial and untested assumptions, it was felt that an experiment to obtain this information was crucial for deciding whether such a policy should be implemented.

Aside from the obvious intent to measure the economic effects of alternative policies, two other principal reasons might be cited in favor of social experimentation. One of these, alluded to earlier, is that with proper design a broad range of social effects can be monitored that could be obtained in no other way and that interrelate with economic variables. These include, for example, in relation to income maintenance experiments, education (both adult and child), labor force participation of secondary members, health, life style, and outlook on life.

Second, a social experiment provides, as a by-product, an invaluable opportunity to obtain information on the administrative aspects of the policies under consideration. In particular, it helps to highlight types of situations involving the treatment variables where special problems of an administrative nature may arise. Thus, the New Jersey Experiment brought out not only that administrative costs had been underestimated but, in addition, that there was need for auditing of income reports to check for underreporting, especially among the families most eligible to receive benefits.[8]

Alternatives to social experiments

Social experiments have certain advantages, as mentioned in the preceding section, but they are not devoid of shortcomings, as will be shown in the following chapters. But what are the alternatives?

There are a number of alternatives, the principal ones being use of theory, econometric analysis, and a demonstration project. Each of these is discussed in this section. Several other alternatives are also discussed, namely, simulation models, analysis of secondary data, or a specially designed survey.

Use of economic theory

In some instances, a theoretical model of response behavior will provide a basis for deducing the effect of a new policy. This can be illustrated with reference to the basic question in the negative income tax experiments of the effect on labor supply of a guaranteed income. A basis for this analysis was the application of a static theory of choice between work and leisure as presented by Albert Rees and as reproduced in Figure 2.1.[9] This figure depicts a hypothetical worker at an equilibrium point, X, on the indifference curve I_0. This equilibrium point is the tangent of the indifference curve, I_0, and the budget line OA, which represents the various combinations of income and leisure available to this worker. It is downward sloping because hours of work decline as one moves from left to right, the line showing that the worker has a choice between working 80 hours a week at $4 an hour, with no leisure (other than time for necessities) but earning $320 a week (point A), and not working at all, thereby being free completely but receiving no income. At the equilibrium point, X, the worker has reached the maximum combination of work and leisure,

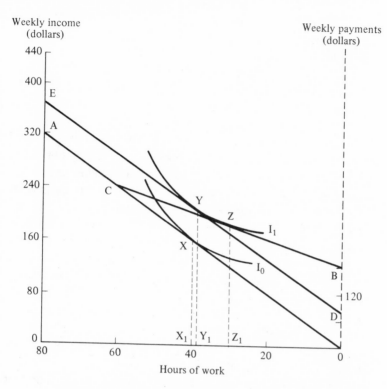

Figure 2.1. Hypothesized impact of an income maintenance plan. *After*: Albert Rees, "An Overview of the Labor Supply Results," in Watts and Rees, *Final Report*, 2: 5.

given his indifference curve; he is working 40 hours a week, earning $160, and has 40 hours of leisure time.

Suppose, now, that he becomes a member of an income maintenance plan whereby he is guaranteed $120 a week if he does not earn any income, but this subsidy is reduced by 50 percent for each dollar that is earned. The worker's constraint is now depicted by the line *BCA*, because with no work he would receive $120 a week (point *B*), whereas if he worked 60 hours a week his income would be the same as if there were no subsidy, namely, $240, at point *C*; to the left of this point the original budget constraint remains in effect.

Under these new conditions, the worker will seek to adjust his allocation of time to reach the highest indifference curve that is tangent to the new budget constraint. This is shown in the diagram as point Z, at which the indifference curve I_1 is tangent to BCA. At this point, he has managed to decrease his hours of work to 30 but has increased his income to $180 per week, representing earned income of $120 plus the benefit payment of $60.

This shift in preference can be divided into both an income effect (brought about by the higher income) and a substitution effect (brought about by the movement along the same indifference curve to keep utility unchanged). Graphically, this is accomplished by drawing the line, DE, parallel to OA and tangent to the indifference curve, I_1. The horizontal distance between this point of tangency, Y, and Z reflects the substitution effect, because both points are on the same indifference curve. Correspondingly, the horizontal difference between points X and Y represents the income effect of the subsidy because the wage rate at both points is the same.

In this instance, both the income and the substitution effects act to reduce the worker's labor supply. This would be expected, given the convex shape of the indifference curves and the assumption that leisure is not an inferior good. In practice, however, this need not necessarily be the case. Thus, a more sophisticated model, one that incorporates more real-life characteristics, may contradict this unequivocal deduction of the static model. A person whose work is physically hard and at inconvenient hours, for example, may seek a more pleasant job once a minimum income is guaranteed. Rather than work fewer hours, he may prefer to work at lower wages at a more pleasant job. He may even work longer hours than before in this new job.

The duration of a guaranteed minimum income program as perceived by workers is also an important issue. Should workers decide that such a program is very likely to be terminated after a few short years, this expectation may influence many of them not to get used to shorter hours; or, some workers may use the period during which the program is in existence to search for a better job and even undertake training for such a job. Finally, existing welfare programs in certain states may reduce the attractiveness of a guaranteed income program, possibly to such an extent that willingness to work is basically unaffected.

This discussion makes it clear that microeconomic theory does not permit the unequivocal deduction that a guaranteed minimum income will always reduce work incentives. Moreover, and this is most important, such a research strategy does not allow for the estimation of the precise size of the labor supply response under specific income maintenance programs. Yet it is essential for policy makers to select the most promising program in terms of the guaranteed income level as well as income tax treatment.

Econometric analysis

A second major alternative is to use ex post data and attempt to estimate effects of a new policy in terms of changes in the dependent variables brought about by changes in policy variables that are part of the explanatory model. This approach is most likely to be feasible if data are available for periods in which major changes took place in terms of these policy variables.

As an example, let us once again focus on the effect of a guaranteed minimum income policy on labor supply. In addition to the availability of appropriate econometric methods, this alternative requires availability of relevant data. In the absence of experience with such a program in the United States, one could possibly work with data from countries that have instituted such a program, except that none has done so; but one would do so only at the considerable risk of being unable to properly account for cultural and other basic differences between the two countries.

Another way to apply econometric methods would be to undertake some empirical studies using the best available U.S. data, as was done in the late 1960s and early 1970s.[10] Estimation of labor response functions became possible in the late 1960s when data from the Survey of Economic Opportunity and from the National Longitudinal Survey became available relating to hours worked, nonlabor income, and wage rates. As a result, there exist at least seven econometric studies that attempt to estimate a labor supply function using basically similar analytical frameworks and types of data, that is, cross-section data for 1967. All these studies have in common an attempt to estimate the effect of income changes as well as of other variables on the quantity of labor supplied by workers.

One of the most significant parameters estimated by these econometric techniques is the total-income elasticity. Thus, for example, a study by Orley Ashenfelter and James Heckman yielded a total-income elasticity of − .27. For each 1 percent increase in total income, that is, of labor and nonlabor income, the worker reduced on the average his labor supply by 0.27 percent. All seven econometric studies, however, though they use similar data, often from the very same survey, similar time periods, and very similar populations, produced distinctly different elasticity coefficients.[11]

In addition to the total-income elasticity, the substitution elasticity, that is, the tendency to substitute leisure for working time in response to a higher tax rate, wages fixed, was estimated. It is expected to be positive on the basis of economic theory. The variation of the substitution elasticities in the various econometric studies was even greater than that of the total-income elasticities. The range was from near zero for all able-bodied husbands, 25 to 61 years old and in the labor force, to .86 for white males, 24–61 years of age, with income below $8,500 for nonwhites.[12] Consequently, Cain and Watts conclude "that the range of reductions in the labor supply implied is too large to be useful to the policymaker."[13]

The effect of a guaranteed minimum income program on the supply of labor was estimated using the income and substitution elasticities in a simulation of a specified program. Three of the econometric studies made such estimates with very different results:

> Kalachek and Raines predict that an income-maintenance plan providing a $2,400 annual guarantee (for a family of four) and a 50 percent "tax" on earnings would produce a 46 percent reduction in the labor supply of the eligible population. (Male family members would reduce their labor supply by 37 percent.)
>
> Greenberg and Kosters predict that a $2,400 guarantee

and a 50 percent tax would cause a 15 percent reduction in the labor supply of male heads of covered families.

Garfinkel predicts that a $3,000 guarantee and a tax rate of 50 percent would reduce the labor supply of prime-age, able-bodied husbands under the plan by anywhere from zero to 3 percent.[14]

The wide range of these estimates reflects three major problems associated with using econometric methods to guide policy making on this topic. First, there are definitional problems. Because the focus is on "poor" people, for example, we face the difficulty of effectively separating, in the data, poor from nonpoor people. Unless designed for the purpose, survey data do not readily allow identification of the "permanently" poor as distinct from the "normal" nonpoor, those who in a particular year had an unusually low income.

There is also the problem of specification of the response variable in the labor supply function. Should labor supply be measured in terms of an "offer" function, which combines time spent at work with any periods spent looking for work? If the answer is positive, we have a labor force participation concept. If the answer is negative, we are dealing with the concept of gainful employment.

Second, there is the problem of specification of income and wage variables as well as other "control" variables. Such specification raises at least three difficult econometric problems: possible omission of important variables, errors in variables, and simultaneity, not to mention possible differences due to different estimation procedures.

A third class of problems relates to the difference between what actually happens when a guaranteed minimum income has been instituted and the situation in the absence of such a program. There exist great difficulties in attempting to use survey data from workers who live in a world with no guaranteed minimum income and infer from these data a supply response should such a policy be enacted. It is virtually impossible to generalize from existing, relatively low positive tax rates to the combined effects of high tax rates and direct income transfer payments under a guaranteed minimum income program. These two worlds generate distinctly different incentives for workers to supply labor and, without actual experience, one can only speculate how different types of low-income families will react to myriad alternatives of a guaranteed income plan.

Econometric methods are most useful when data very similar to those of the proposed new program are already available. A good deal of information is available, for example, on the manner in which the consumption of electricity varies with price variations for different types of customers. Such information could be used as a basis for electricity rate studies to guide load management and to estimate to some extent the effect of a peak pricing policy for electricity rates.

Econometric analysis is perhaps best used even in this area in conjunction with the data generated from a social experiment, because these data provide a wealth of material for estimating response functions.

Demonstration projects

In the absence of previous experience with a particular policy, a demonstration project is an important alternative to a social experiment. Though demonstration projects are, as their name implies, designed to show that a particular treatment can be administered to a given population – that is, they are organized tryouts – they tend to produce a host of data, many of which are of great significance. Yet in the absence of controls no scientific inferences are possible.

A public school voucher demonstration in the early 1970s at the Alum Rock Union Elementary School District in San Jose, California, is a good example. About half of the schoolchildren in Alum Rock were Mexican-American, 40 percent were Anglo, and 10 percent were black. Most were from lower-income classes, lived in single-family residences without segregation, and were highly transient, with a 30 percent annual residential turnover.[15]

The Alum Rock demonstration was designed to create an educational "marketplace" within the public schools by introducing a voucher system. It started in 1970 with a two-year mobilization phase that sought to generate support for the program. This was followed by a three-year experimentation phase, during which the school district tried to implement its proposed policies in the voucher schools. Two years of an incorporation phase followed, during which the district began to prepare for the end of federal funding in support of the demonstration.

During the experimentation phase, minischools were created that had the freedom to set their own curricula and staffing and to make resource-use decisions. Each voucher school offered between two and five educational programs determined mainly by teacher interests, with principals and parents playing a minor role. As compared with the situation before this demonstration, there was a distinct increase in the influence of teachers, yet no significant increase in parent involvement. The cooperation among teachers in making educational decisions was greatest in small minischools. Parents did exercise their right to choose programs for their children, thereby influencing minischool enrollment. This furnished incentives for these schools to work toward satisfying the parents (the education customers), thereby preventing an enrollment decline. The competition was not only for enrollment but also for resources, for the principal's favor, and for status vis-à-vis other programs. In spite of constraints due to state and federal laws and regulations, the voucher program, in the opinion of the teachers, created a diversity of education programs.

In many respects, the voucher program was a flawed demonstration, if for no other reason than that after the Office of Economic Opportunity authorized three such demonstrations only a single school district agreed to participate. Moreover, serious opposition in the Alum Rock district restricted the extent and scope of treatment.

Although the demonstration permits some comparison with conditions prevailing before the project was initiated, the absence of controls and of continuity over time precludes any inference about voucher programs. Moreover, because only a single voucher program was included in the demonstration, nothing was learned about alternative voucher programs.

There are some positive considerations, however. Although a demonstration project cannot hope to do what a good social experiment can accomplish, it offers great flexibility. Its major advantage derives from the possibility of carrying out demonstration projects over a number of years. Thus, it becomes possible to learn from the first-period experience and to modify the design to be used in subsequent periods. This is quite feasible because, unlike a social experiment where early agreed-upon controls must be continued, modifications are possible at little cost and little inconvenience.

It is possible to carry out a demonstration project in conjunction with a social experiment, as was done in the Experimental Housing Allowance Program. This project sought information about the housing supply effect when housing allowances were applied on an area-wide basis. Because such a saturation experiment is very expensive and has difficult technical aspects, the supply side of the study was basically carried out as a demonstration project.

A demonstration project can ascertain the operational feasibility of a particular policy; its great shortcoming is the lack of control over who participates in the program and who does not. Because the project is invariably carried out on an areawide basis and there is no control group comparable to the subjects, there is no way of rigorously measuring the effect of the new program.

Moreover, if the demonstration project is carried out for a brief time period, as is often the case, this in itself tends to rule out measuring effects of the policy because these effects may not be manifested until several years have passed. If consumers are faced with a new pricing schedule for electricity, for example, by which they are charged much higher unit costs in key periods of the day than at other times, it will take them several years to adjust their stock of appliances and their electricity consumption patterns to these new rates.

A demonstration project can be useful not only in itself but also as a prelude to a social experiment in indicating the types of operational problems that need to be overcome in implementing the later social experiment. This is especially so because, as will be shown in later chapters, serious unanticipated operational problems have been encountered in every social experiment conducted so far. A prior demonstration project would have almost certainly uncovered these problems and made the later social experiment far more effective. Such an approach, however, is not always feasible for political reasons, because when the opportunity to undertake a social experiment arises administrators are loathe to delay lest the "urge" disappear.

Other alternatives

A further alternative is to deduce response effects from comparison of relevant past and present behavior survey data, if such data are available. This "if" is the major problem with this approach, as the proper data are hardly likely to be available. At best, such estimates regarding a proposed new policy would have to be indirect, because data on behavior under this new program would by definition not be available. Even if roughly comparable data are available, perhaps for similar programs, there is the further problem of the comparability of the different surveys. Unless the analysis can be restricted to a carefully designed set of panel data, any attempt to compare data from surveys taken at different times tends to raise knotty questions of comparability with regard to sample design, selection of sample respondents, question wording and questionnaire format, field operations, and definitions of key terms. Even with sophisticated econometric and other analytical methods, the necessary data are usually not available to permit proper adjustments to be made for these different sources of lack of comparability, as noted by the different elasticity estimates derived by econometric methods for labor supply response to a guaranteed minimum income program.

Still another alternative involves simulation models of artificial populations. To estimate the effect of a new policy on economic behavior, however, such models require information about response to various alternative treatments, which is in fact nonexistent for otherwise the study would not be necessary. Simulation can be used, however, to introduce a wide range of assumptions of these response effects and thereby trace the effect on the economy (or on any other entity) of such treatments. Such a sensitivity analysis can be very useful for providing some idea of the nature and the range of the effect of the proposed new policy on a number of aspects of economic and social behavior. The ranges obtained in this manner, however, will very likely be too broad for policy determination.

The simulation approach is in fact likely to be more useful after empirical information has been obtained on response to alternative treatments. With this information as a key input into a simulation model, the macroeffects of a particular policy can be evaluated far more precisely than is otherwise possible. Indeed, this is exactly what is being done in the case of the cash housing allowance experiments, as discussed in Chapter 9.

Yet another alternative to estimating response effects is to conduct a survey of the target population and ask questions about response under hypothetical conditions that encompass the proposed policy. The problem with this approach is that the answers also may be quite hypothetical, and there is no assurance that they are a valid indication of the actual behavior of the subjects if that policy were put into practice.

Classification of social experiments

Although many social experiments have been carried out in this country,[16] relatively few have focused on economic policy. This is understandable in view of the substantial time and cost these studies involve. Even so, in order to place them in proper perspective, some sort of classification system for such studies would seem desirable.

There are many ways to classify these studies, such as by the specific types of economic policy, by the sector of economic activity being studied, by the design features of the experiment, and others. The only systematic attempt to classify experiments from an economics viewpoint was made by Alice Rivlin. She classified social experiments into four groups by the type of effect or response being measured as a result of a change in economic incentives. The four categories are the response of microunits (as in the negative income tax experiments); the response of entire markets (such as the housing allowance experiment to measure market supply); the change in the production function of a public service (such as the experiments in education, like Head Start, designed to alter the productivity of the educational process); and the response to a particular type of service (such as using education vouchers to give parents a greater choice of schools).[17]

As Rivlin points out, only the first two types of experiments seem to be presently feasible, the latter two being so complex that it is not clear whether they are amenable to the necessary experimental controls. For the purpose of reviewing the present status of social experimentation in economics, a somewhat simpler classification system seems appropriate. If we focus on Rivlin's first two categories, it is possible to classify social experiments according to whether direct response effects are sought on the supply side, on the demand side, or on the institutions providing that service. The negative income tax experiments, for example, relate mainly to the supply side, as the focus is to ascertain the effects of the experimental treatment on the supply of labor offered in the marketplace.[18] The Health Insurance Study is a social experiment focusing on the demand side, as it seeks to explore the effect of better health coverage on the demand by families for health care.

Sometimes an experiment may focus on two or all three of these components, as is true of the Experimental Housing Allowance Program. That experiment had three components, each carried out in different areas. One experiment sought to test the effect of housing allowances on the demand of low-income families for housing, a second the effect of these allowances on the supply of housing in a particular area, and a third the effectiveness of different institutional arrangements for implementation of the program.

When an experiment seeks to estimate the supply effects of economic actors who are not direct participants in the specific experiment, great difficulties arise that can be overcome only at enormous costs. Thus, for example, in the Housing Allowance Program, where low-income tenants were subsidized, the Supply Experiment sought to learn the housing supply response of landlords, and in a health insurance program where the health insurance of the poor is subsidized, the supply experiment would seek to estimate how health service providers (for example, hospitals and physicians) respond to the income transfer. Such supply experiments require saturation sampling to capture the response of this market. Saturation sampling requires inclusion in either the treatment or control group of, it is hoped, all members of the population meeting the agreed-upon criteria. This is an enormous undertaking, which so far has proven to be unmanageable. As a result, the Health Insurance Study does not include any supply experiment, and the Housing Allowance Program investigated the supply issue at only two sample locations and without any control groups; that is, it was not an experiment in the sense of measuring response effects applying certain stimuli to some groups but not to other statistically matched groups.

3

Challenges posed by social experiments

Although social experiments offer a unique set of advantages, they bring with them a host of problems, which are frequently serious enough to vitiate these advantages. An overview of these problems is provided in this chapter. No attempt is made to go into detail, because these details are best considered in conjunction with a review of the individual experiments, as given in Chapters 4 to 9.

We begin with a discussion of the general problems involved in planning a social experiment and then proceed to consider some of the more technical problems that arise in its planning and implementation, with the primary focus on some of the key statistical problems. Moral and ethical aspects of social experimentation are then considered, followed by a discussion of some of the critical issues that arise in the administration of a social experiment.

Some general problems

A social experiment is a massive undertaking by almost any research standards. In terms of the time involved, there are one to two years of advance preparation, anywhere from two to ten more years for the conduct of the experiment in the field, and from one to three years after that for the analysis of the huge amount of data that have been collected. Even preliminary results may require four to five years of work from the time the experiment is authorized.

This time element is a major problem for social experimentation.

Because of it, special attention is needed to possible environmental changes beyond the control of the experimenter. Such changes, exogenous to the experiment, fall under two categories: societal and governmental. Control of the former can be only partial in social experiments, unlike the case of many physical experiments, because the experiments have no way (or authority) to control economic conditions or sociodemographic changes in the areas in which they are working. If such changes can be foreseen, attempts can be made to control them in the experiment by suitable allowances in the statistical design. More often than not, however, unforeseen societal changes also take place, and one can only hope to segregate the treatment effect from their influence by suitable types of multivariate analysis.

Governmental action is a very different type of uncontrollable force that may devastate a social experiment. Thus, there is always the possibility that a swing in the political winds may lead to curtailment of the initial agreed-on budget to carry out the experiment over the years. The exogenous forces that can produce unforeseen fluctuations in the research budget, to say nothing of the legislating of a premature cutoff, can play havoc with the experimental effort.

There is also the frequent impatience of policy makers. Will they appropriate funds for a five-year social experiment and then be content to wait that long for the results? Indeed, is it feasible to fund such projects over many years, given the vagaries of the funding agencies and the frequent turnover of top-level personnel in the federal government? The paradoxical fact is that the very conditions that lead to the initiation of a social experiment of a particular policy may also lead to action that can vitiate the need for that experiment. Within two years after the start of the New Jersey Income Maintenance Experiment, for example, President Nixon was proposing to Congress a bill for a guaranteed annual income. Had that bill passed, the New Jersey Experiment, and the others that followed it, would have been redundant.

The time required for a social experiment also makes it more likely that background or other external conditions will change and that it will be more difficult to measure response effects. Careful monitoring procedures, therefore, have to be incorporated in the study design and appropriate adjustments made in the analysis of the data. Sometimes such changes may be completely unanticipated. Shortly after the income maintenance experiment started in New Jersey, for example, that state liberalized the welfare laws to the extent that families in the less generous experimental treatments would have been better off under the welfare system. As a result, the experimental design had to be modified to deal with the new situations.

Although these costs can be justified, the fact remains that they are huge. Hence, the justification has to be not only in terms of the actual expenditures but also in terms of the additional benefits that would accrue by undertaking a social experiment. Ideally, the choice between a social experiment and the alternatives should be made on the basis of the approach that promises the largest expected net benefits.

Where to conduct a social experiment is a third general problem. All the social experiments carried out to date have been concentrated in particular geographic areas. The justification has been that this is the only cost-effective approach, given the need for an intricate transfer payments system and the huge amounts of data that have to be collected from the participants. For these reasons it is argued that the usual survey approach of a nationwide probability sample is not feasible for such an experiment, even though this is the only basis on which valid statistical inferences could be made for the entire eligible population.

Though the judgmental selection of geographic areas may be cheaper, it introduces all the biases of purposive sampling and has led to considerable controversy over the applicability of the results of these experiments to the national population.[1] Such questions are especially relevant because many of the social experiments have been conducted in only two areas and many of the sites had to be selected more on the basis of convenience than anything else. Under these circumstances, one might argue whether any extra cost of carrying out these studies on a national probability basis would not be worth it in terms of the extra validity imparted to the results (assuming of course that the probability design is not vitiated by difficulties in obtaining the necessary cooperation).

Regardless of the area in which the study is carried out, a decision has to be made as to the sort of population that will be covered in the social experiment. Such a decision invariably involves a trade-off between reliability of the information and breadth of coverage. Because the sample size is invariably limited to at most a few thousand households, frequently only one to two thousand households, if a broad coverage of a population is sought a great deal of heterogeneity is introduced, so that study of the behavior of any particular subgroup has to be based on a relatively small number of observations. In evaluating the effect of a negative income tax on poor people, for example, it is desirable from a broad policy point of view to cover all the different parts of the welfare population that may be eligible. Past study, however, suggests very strongly that the effect of such a tax on labor market behavior will vary depending, among other things, on whether the family is intact or not, whether small children are present, whether the main wage earner is in good health, whether the main wage earner presently has a job, whether the family lives in an urban area or a rural area, and probably also the background of the family and the age of the main wage earner. To include in a social experiment a sample large enough to have an adequate basis for analysis by all of these different characteristics is hardly feasible, especially so if we keep in mind the need to have each subgroup large enough so that random segments can be assigned to the various experimental treatments and also to the one or more controls that will be used. As we shall see, many of the social experiments have sought to resolve this problem by focusing on particular subgroups of the eligible population, and even then it is not clear that these eligibility requirements were not spread too thin.

The last general problem to be discussed in this section is in some ways the most important, namely, whether the proposed treatment variables are amenable to social experimentation. In some instances, this is a matter of ascertaining whether the appropriate institutional and legal barriers can be relaxed for the purpose of the experiment. In an experiment designed to make drug addicts more employable, for example, arrangements have to be made with the appropriate authorities for such people to be available for the term of the experiment and for the custody of these people to be taken over by the agency administering the experiment.

More basically, a social experiment can be carried out only if the necessary design features can be incorporated within the legal and institutional constraints within which society operates. This means, for example, that people cannot be deprived for purposes of the experiment of certain benefits they already have. Thus, in an experiment on cash housing allowances, one cannot set up a control group by taking away housing assistance programs already available. In other words, a social experiment can be carried out only if it is feasible to give something to people who already do not have it and also to have a control group that not only does not receive these benefits but is not contaminated by the fact that certain other groups are receiving these additional benefits. This is by no means an easy task, especially in the case of an experiment that involves replicated random samples in the same areas for both treatment and control purposes. In the case of the Health Insurance Study, for example, the problem had to be solved by actually "buying" a control group in the sense of offering it certain services (membership in a health maintenance organization [HMO]) so that a matching sample could be obtained to compare with other groups that received the full range of benefits offered by the experiment.

Social and public relations constraints are another consideration. Thus, families living next to each other cannot be assigned to different treatments on a random basis because such differential actions will certainly become known to these families and will very likely offset their subsequent behavior. Furthermore, because of public relations aspects it would be hardly feasible to conduct a social experiment on the effect on saving practices of removing the capital gains tax. The public outcry over having several hundred families excluded from the provisions of that tax would be so great as to seriously influence the behavior of those people, if not to result in cancelation by the federal agency of the funding for the experiment. Even in the case of the New Jersey Negative Income Tax Experiment, the publicity about the experiment was such as to raise the question of whether people's behavior might not have been influenced by it.

Some technical problems

Aside from the usual statistical and other technical problems that arise in the conduct of an experiment, certain additional problems are encountered that are unique to this particular type of approach. The principal such problems include specification of treatment variables, measurement of response effects, allocation of the sample given the later analysis needs, operating problems relating to the longitudinal nature of the experiment, assurance of the quality of the data, and biases to be watched out for in the study design. Each of these is reviewed briefly in this section.

Treatment variables

Invariably, the objective of a social experiment is to test the effect not of one particular treatment but rather of a range of treatments. Thus, a major objective of the cash housing allowance experiments was to ascertain the effect on the demand for housing when low-income families are subsidized by varying percentages of the cost of housing, as there is no basis for inferring that one percentage may be more effective than another. The allowable range is invariably set on the basis of political and fiscal feasibility and may include, say, anywhere from 10 percent to 30 percent of the cost of adequate housing. It is the duty of the experimenter to then select various alternatives within this range. The selection of these alternatives is best guided by a theory that specifies a functional relationship between the response on the one hand and the treatment variables on the other hand, including also as independent any other variables that may affect this particular behavior. In selecting these alternatives, consideration has to be given to the possibility that the functional relationship between response effect and treatment may not be linear.

Given these constraints, it is the duty of the experimenter to select enough alternative treatments to blanket this range and provide reliable estimates of the response function and, at the same time, to have a small enough number of treatments so that the response effect can be estimated for each treatment with enough reliability. Some highly innovative work in solving this problem has evolved from the social experiments, involving the use of mathematical models to optimize the error variance subject to cost and other constraints, as is illustrated in later chapters.

A key step is the initial step, namely, specification of the functional relationship and the variables that enter into it. In particular, the sample sizes allocated by these models to various treatments will vary substantially with this specification of the model. Thus, the objective of optimizing the results invariably leads to a large proportion of the total sample being allocated to the control groups and to the experimental treatments that involve small transfer payments.

Although this is fine for economizing on the cost of the experiment, it serves to provide much less reliable information on the response effect of the higher-cost treatment variables, which in some instances may be especially important from a policy point of view. These high-cost treatment variables may include, for example, families that have no income whatsoever and to whom the subsidy may be especially important, both to them personally and to improving living standards generally. The results of these models, therefore, frequently have to be modified on the basis of subjective considerations, which may include assigning "importance weights" to particular treatment combinations or imposing the constraint that no treatment combination should be applied to less than a certain number of families.

Response effects

A very different set of problems with regard to treatment effects relates to the nature of the response variables. Virtually by definition, the type of policy tested in a social experiment will affect not only the response variables of immediate interest but a wide range of other social behaviors as well. An experiment that seeks to vary the price of electricity by the time of day, for example, may affect not only the stock of durables owned by the family but the way it spends its leisure time. An income maintenance program may affect not only the work response of the members of the household but also their consumption pattern, their type of housing, their nutrition, and the school attendance of the younger members. Moreover, these effects are clearly not independent, and therefore study is needed of the interrelationship of such effects.

Growing recognition of these indirect influences has led to substantial expansion of the data collection and analytical efforts of the social experiments. It has also led to the adoption of a more interdisciplinary approach to the analysis of the data, although in the social experiments that have been reported so far the approach has been more multidisciplinary than interdisciplinary – economists work on one topic, sociologists on another, and so forth. The task of relating indirect response effects to direct response effects in an interdisciplinary framework has still to be carried out.

The measurement of response effects is one of the most critical, and difficult, aspects of a social experiment. The basic problem is that these response effects will be affected not only by the treatment variables but also by the characteristics of the participating households, by their previous behavior relevant to these response variables, and by the institutional environment in which the experiment is carried out, not to mention changes in this environment over time. As noted previously, moreover, response effects are not independent of each other, so that account has to be taken of this interdependence in any measurement approach.

The problem is further complicated by the fact that many treatments are not single variables but combinations of variables. All the treatments of the negative income tax experiment, for example, have been combinations of a minimum guaranteed income and a tax rate by which benefits are reduced in some proportion to earned income; and some such experiments have introduced other treatments as well, as noted in Chapter 5. To be most meaningful, the estimation of the treatment effect should seek to establish not so much the effect of the combination of these variables as the separate effects of the level of guaranteed minimum income and of the tax rate. Doing so, however, introduces nonlinearities into the measurement procedures and can make the estimates of these effects both more difficult to obtain and less reliable.

The general approach to dealing with this problem has been to apply econometric methods, specifying an a priori model relating each response variable to two sets of influencing variables: the variables that would be expected to affect this response variable under any circumstances; and a set representing a parameterization of the treatment variables. Thus, in a negative income tax experiment, the labor force participation of the main wage earner may be specified as a function of, on the one hand, age, occupation, education, income level, and current labor force participation, plus, on the other hand, the level of guaranteed minimum income, the tax rate, and the ratio of current family income to the level of guaranteed minimum income. The last set of variables is clearly meant to measure the response effects of the treatment variables, the very last variable reflecting the "incentive" of the main wage earner not to continue working in the face of a guaranteed minimum income. The variables entering into the first set are selected on the basis of theoretical considerations and previous studies. This set may also include other response variables, with the different types of responses linked to each other in a system of interdependent equations.

A major innovation has been the use of such a specification not only for analysis but also as the basis for estimating the optimum total sample size for the given resources and the allocation of the sample among different treatments. Though this approach raises certain problems, as noted in the "sample allocation" section below, it does serve to make clear what sort of results can be expected from the experiment, in terms of sample sizes and data availability for different types of analysis.

Sample allocation
In most experiments sample members are allocated randomly, and usually in equal numbers, to the various treatment groups as well as to the one or more controls that are incorporated. In a social experiment, the problem is more complicated because the cost of maintaining a sample member in the study will vary appreciably according to whether that unit is in one of the treatment groups or is in the control group. Moreover, this cost may also vary with the income level and the characteristics of the unit, depending on the type of treatments being administered. Families in the cash housing allowance experiment, for example, received monthly subsidies to help them pay their housing costs if they were in one of the treatment

groups, subsidies that varied with their income level. Hence, the cost of maintaining a family in this program is not only that of data collection but also that of these subsidy payments, which vary from one experimental group to another and also, clearly, with the income level and the size of the family. Over the 5 to 10 years in which the family might be kept in the study the cost of maintaining families in some experimental treatments will turn out to be many times the cost of maintaining families in other treatments and many, many times that of the control families.

The necessity therefore arose of modifying the usual sample allocation procedures to take account of this phenomenon, to maximize the efficiency of the sample design, given the resource constraints. The Conlisk–Watts model originally developed for this purpose, in connection with the New Jersey Experiment, was based on the a priori specification of the response function mentioned earlier, hypothesizing the manner in which the experimental treatments, plus other economic and behavioral variables, would affect the dependent variable, a measure of labor market participation. The research strategy was to minimize the variance of this function subject to the estimated costs of maintaining families with given characteristics in various experimental conditions.[2]

As it turns out, although this model fully satisfies the basic condition of yielding minimum overall variance within the resource constraints, it does so by assigning inordinate numbers of families to the control groups and to those treatment levels where the anticipated welfare payments will be very low. This is a logical approach from the point of view of cost minimization, but it conflicts with a major objective of a social experiment, which is to obtain reliable estimates of the treatment effects. Moreover, with so many observations concentrated in the control and the low-cost treatment groups, such a model tends to load the dice in favor of the confirmation of the null hypothesis of no effect of the treatments. In particular, it is less likely that a high-cost treatment will be found to have a particular effect because of the very small sample sizes in those groups.

There is the further pitfall that the treatment effects may be confounded with the characteristics of the sample members, to the extent that the cost-minimization approach tends to concentrate higher-cost families in the low-cost conditions. In the case of cash housing allowances, for example, this approach would assign many more large-size eligible families to a low-subsidy treatment (say, a treatment that offers only 25 percent of the gap between ability to pay and housing needs) and many more small-size families to a high support level, because the amount of support offered in the experiment varied with family size.

These problems can be, and have been, dealt with in various ways, ranging from arbitrary adjustment of the results of the allocation model to use of such variables as income and family size as covariates in the study of response effects. The fact remains, however, that as a result of problems of this type, which are frequently compounded by problems of panel mortality, the base for analysis of the treatment effects is greatly weakened.

Longitudinal headaches

As noted earlier, a social experiment involves all the well-known headaches of the panel type of operation – recruitment, attrition, conditioning effects – and there is no need to go into the details here.[3] Two points deserve emphasis, however. One is that recruitment of families for participation in a social experiment is generally more frustrating than in the usual panel study. A primary reason is that a social experiment usually focuses on a group with a well-defined set of characteristics (such as intact families, one to three children, at least one member in the labor force, main wage earner between the ages of 21 and 58, income under $7,500 per year) and the problem therefore becomes tantamount to sampling a rare population. Moreover, if the estimates of the size of this population are very inaccurate, the validity of the entire experiment may be affected. Such was the case with the New Jersey Experiment, where it was impossible to find enough families with the particular characteristics in the cities to be included in the experiment in New Jersey, with the result that the experiment had to be extended to Scranton, Pennsylvania.

Perhaps the most striking example of the difficulty of locating eligible families occurred in one of the cash housing allowance experiments, where the contracting agency had to contact on the average approximately three hundred households in order to get one eligible household into the sample. This remarkably low fraction represents problems not only of locating eligible families but also of convincing them to participate once they were located. In this respect, the experimenters have not had notable success, occasionally getting not much more than half of the eligibles to finally enroll. Although this is no worse and in some ways much better than the commercial panel operations, the fact remains that such results raise serious questions about the generality of any results that may be obtained from these data.

Second, there is the danger of bias due to attrition, namely, the likely interaction between attrition and membership in an experimental group. Although there are ways of dealing with this problem analytically,[4] the problem is nevertheless a serious one because the attrition in some of the experimental groups may be so large as to leave a very thin base for analysis. Attrition tends to be much higher in the control groups and in the lower-benefit treatments, which over time leads to increasing doubts about the representativeness of the remaining families of the original group.

Data quality

Because a social experiment usually seeks highly sensitive information from the participating families – income, assets, medical condition, and so on – many precautions are needed to assure that the data provided are accurate and complete. The problem is compounded by the fact that the subjects of the experiments are invariably poorly educated people who usually have little understanding of, or interest in, financial and economic terms and who may not be inclined to be too precise in any event.[5] As a result, extra efforts have to be made to explain these terms to the participting households, to make sure that they understand them.

Even so, it is not clear that many of the participating households understood either the terms or the various ramifications of the experimental treatments to which they were subject. Hence, the extent of information under which these families were operating both in providing data and in reacting to the treatment variables is another source of variation.

In addition, partly to ascertain that families are providing the requested information and are doing so accurately, an integral part of every data collection operation has been a periodic audit to verify key items of information, especially income and assets. Though this type of audit helps materially to increase the reliability of the data, it also serves to raise the cost of the experiments. Moreover, even then questions can be raised about the accuracy of information that cannot be audited, such as nonwage income. The fact remains that there is little doubt that much of the data collected in these experiments are subject to error, and so far the analytical models seeking to measure the response effects have not attempted to incorporate any allowances for such errors. If they were to do so, the results very likely would be even further influenced toward confirmation of the null hypothesis, as there is ample evidence that especially the financial data are subject to considerable error.[6]

Biases

A number of different biases have to be considered in the planning of a social experiment. Perhaps the most well-known is the *Hawthorne effect*, discussed in Chapter 2. To what extent do families alter their behavior not because of the type of benefits they receive but because of their awareness of being in an experimental plan and of being continuously under observation?[7]

As an example, in the Health Insurance Study all the families in the plan were to be given a medical examination when enrolled, and the family's physician was to be notified of problem conditions. In such cases, families may be much more likely to utilize health services than would otherwise be the case. If this phenomenon were uniform, it could be corrected for from the data for the control families. There is good reason to suspect, however, that families under the more generous plans would be even more likely to utilize health services than otherwise, given this additional information.[8]

Second, a *dowry effect* can exist if persons eligible for experimental treatments can extend their eligibility to ineligible persons. In the

Denver–Seattle Income Maintenance Experiment, for example, men marrying eligible women become eligible for income maintenance payments and "manpower" options.[9] Consequently, women enrolled in the experiment have an "extra added" attraction to a potential husband over other women, depending on the man's income; if he has little or no income, there is a financial incentive for marriage.

A third bias relates to *community effects*, which may arise if individual conduct is conditioned by social norms that either discourage or reinforce particular behavior. An example is "work ethics," which by and large are culture conditioned and which may change in the presence of a nationwide income maintenance program. Individual labor supply responses derived from an experiment using selective enrollment may be biased downward because they are based on attitudes toward work in communities lacking an income maintenance system.

Fourth, there are *time horizon effects*, namely, the possible influence of the length of the experiment on the responses of the families. Thus, how well do responses of families to guaranteed minimum incomes for three years represent what their behavior would be if this same program were permanent?[10] To answer this question, some of the more recent experiments have incorporated different time horizons into the experimental treatments, as is discussed in Chapters 7 and 9.

In the case of income maintenance, there is a downward bias in the income effect because the support available in a finite experiment has a lower capitalized present value than a support guarantee available indefinitely. There is also an upward bias in the substitution effect because the wage rate, which is lowered by the tax rate imposed in the experimental program, can be expected to return to the higher pre-experimental level after the experiment terminates.[11]

Fifth, there is *attrition bias*, resulting from the interaction between treatment effects and dropout rates of different parts of the samples. As noted earlier, families in the control groups are more likely to drop out than families in the treatment groups, and families in the less generous treatment combinations are more likely to drop out than those in the more generous combinations. If the probability of attrition depends linearly on either treatment or exogenous variables included in the response equation, its existence will not affect the expected values of parameter estimates. If attrition depends, however, on some interaction between the treatments and exogenous variables erroneously excluded from the response equation, the expected values of the parameter estimates will be affected by the presence of attrition.[12]

Attrition may also depend on the response to the experimental treatment. In a health insurance experiment, for example, control subjects may drop out of the program at one rate and experimental subjects not needing or making use of medical services may drop out at a lesser rate, whereas experimental subjects who actually alter their behavior and make use of medical services might not drop out at all.

Sixth, there is the possible bias from *spillover effects*, which can blur the distinction between treatment and control groups and thereby violate the validity of the comparisons. To fully separate treatment from control groups is a continuous challenge, because contamination of control groups is hard to prevent in the light of physical contacts that may take place between members of these groups and in view of the large amount of local publicity that these experiments frequently receive. Even without personal contact, sufficient publicity about an experiment can influence people receiving different treatments to act in the same manner.

Seventh, there is the possibility of bias from *contamination of the treatment process*. Thus, political, social, and even other research programs may affect the behavior of participants in the social experiment, particularly if their anonymity is not scrupulously maintained. The introduction, for example, of a greatly liberalized program of Aid to Families with Dependent Children after the Negative Income Tax Experiment in New Jersey had gotten underway wiped out some of the differences between the treatment groups and the control families.

Ethical and moral issues

Because social experimentation may involve the manipulation of people's resources and even life styles, ethical and moral aspects must be examined closely. This is particularly true for the groups subjected to the experimental treatment, though some problems exist also for the control groups.

The basic problem of social experiments is that treatment groups are offered certain benefits or incentives that may cover a period lasting anywhere from 3 to 10 years. On the surface, this would seem to be all to the benefit of the families in the experiment, who clearly are not being made any worse off financially as a result. The fact remains, however, that they are being placed in an exposed position as a result of the experiment and, regardless of what they are told, they may be misled into taking actions detrimental to their welfare. In the housing allowance experiments, for example, although some participants were told that their supplemental payments would be continued for only five years, after two or three years they may have begun to consider these payments permanent and to act accordingly. From an analytical point of view, this would appear highly desirable as it would then yield a measure of the permanent effect of such a treatment. From a moral point of view, however, this state of mind could have led the family to commitments that left it exposed to unpleasant consequences when the experiment ended. The family may have moved into more expensive housing, for example, which it would be unable to afford when the supplemental payments ceased. The resulting readjustment could be far more painful than if the more expensive housing had not been obtained in the first place.

A very different ethical problem arises from the income and other reports that families have to file to continue in the plan. Because many of these families are eligible for other welfare benefits, these reports may be sought by welfare agencies as a means of supplementing or checking their own records, and such attempts were indeed made during the course of the New Jersey Experiment. Although the confidentiality of these reports has so far been preserved from public investigation, the matter has never been fully tested in the courts.

The moral and ethical problems relating to the control families are of a somewhat different nature. Because the control families receive no benefits from the experiment (except for nominal payments for providing the same information as the experimental families), there is no danger that their hopes and aspirations will be raised artificially. Still, the data they provide make them as vulnerable as the experimental families to possible attempts by welfare agencies to obtain this information. In addition, they, as well as nonparticipants, could actually be worse off because of the experiment. The major objective, for example, of the Supply Experiment on housing allowances was to ascertain market effects of providing an appreciable proportion of the low-income population with funds for improving their living accommodations. If the effect were higher prices rather than more or better housing, the control families as well as others in the area might have to pay more for housing and thereby would be worse off.

In theory, this should not happen if the housing Supply Experiment is undertaken in areas that initially have excess housing capacity. Yet, for experimental reasons, one of the two areas in this experiment was not of this type (Brown County, Wisconsin). Moreover, in an experiment covering 10 years, as with the Supply Experiment, economic conditions in any area can change sharply.

A very different sort of issue arises from the varied treatment given to different groups of experimental families. Such variation is an integral part of the experiment and is clearly unavoidable. Unavoidable also, however, are some of the moral issues that arise. In the Health Insurance Study, for example, to deal with the possibility that an initial medical examination would in itself lead people to seek medical care, a certain proportion of the families being enrolled were not given this health examination initially. Experimentally, this is sound; but is it sound morally? Conceivably, a person whose examination is postponed has a condition in which early detection would save a great deal of trouble or even his life. Of course, if the individual were not in the experiment there would be no free medical examination anyway. Still, the individual might reason that, being in the experiment and expecting a free examination within six months, he might as well wait even though he may not currently be feeling well. By then, it might be too late.

In fact, the act of participation in a social experiment raises an ethical dilemma, for despite any guarantees of anonymity that may be given to the participants their participation exposes them to disclosure regardless of what the experimenters may do. In order to interview participants to document a story on the Denver–Seattle Income Maintenance Experiment, for example, *New York Times* reporters located participants by placing advertisements in Seattle-area newspapers.[13] To be sure, those who responded did not have to do so (and it is doubtful that the respondents were typical of all participants), but the fact remains that techniques similar to this could be used to locate participants for purposes that might be detrimental to them.

A different type of threat to confidentiality stems from the belief on the part of some government officials that all aspects of every federally funded contract should be audited periodically, including the field operations of any survey. Because of this feeling, there have been attempts by the U.S. General Accounting Office (GAO) not only to audit the financial statements of the agencies conducting the social experiments but also to verify the interviewing procedures and to make sure that they were carried out properly. To perform such an audit, the GAO has in the past requested the names and addresses of participants in these social experiments, and is known to have been successful in at least one instance. From an administrative point of view, one could argue that the GAO is justified in conducting such reinterviews because its task is indeed to monitor the manner in which government funds are being spent. In terms of assuring respondent privacy and confidentiality, however, this clearly raises some very knotty questions, as the research agency can hardly assure complete confidentiality if the names and addresses of the participants are to be provided to a government agency at a later time.[14]

Essentially, there are two major schools of thought among social scientists on the ethics of research. The consequentialists (sometimes called utilitarians) hold that the rightness or wrongness of any act, such as a social experiment, can and must be judged by its results. This attitude relies on an implied or explicit benefit–cost framework, one that is by and large accepted by federal granting agencies. In this view, certain apparently immoral practices can sometimes be justified on the grounds that they provide a large benefit compared with their cost.

The deontological school of thought, on the other hand, is nonconsequential; its philosophy is based on absolute moral values and is fundamentally more conservative. An extreme deontological position could be that deception of those participating in a social experiment can never be justified, regardless of the potential benefits of the research. The deontological view appears to be founded on the categorical imperative philosophy of Immanuel Kant, which views human beings as ends rather than means.[15]

Changes in both values and technology heighten today's concern with ethical considerations of social experimentation. Throughout the world, individuals are demanding equality of treatment as well as the right to be informed about and to participate in decisions affecting them. Technology, including that of communication, makes it possible not only to involve large numbers of participants in social experiments but also to provide information about the experiment almost instantly to the entire country. The latter aspect makes it impossible for investigators to hide the implications for participants, or for the general public.

Social experimentation may follow the same course as in the medical field, where in 1966 the federal government moved to protect human subjects. Since then, the National Institutes of Health, the Food and Drug Administration, and the Department of Health, Education, and Welfare have issued increasingly detailed regulations governing experimentation with human subjects that is financially supported by them; and in 1974 a National Commission for the Protection of Human Subjects of Biomedical and Behavioral Research was set up as advisory to the Department of Health, Education, and Welfare.[16]

In medicine, because of the seriousness of possible consequences of treatment or lack of treatment, government funding agencies and most institutions have instituted regulations that require that the human subject included in an experiment (or his guardian, in the case of small children and mentally incompetent patients) be made to comprehend the fact that part of the treatment is given for reasons other than immediate therapeutic ones. Most important, the participant or his guardian must be given complete information about any risks and must give consent voluntarily.

The grave ethical concerns that have been voiced about social experiments center around the issues of informed consent and deception. Informed consent is a most difficult and yet crucial concept in all experimentation involving human beings.[17] The concept is troublesome because the extent to which a person is to be informed is relative and so is the degree of consent. Researchers often benefit from providing a relatively small amount of information and accepting a relatively low level of consent. Under those circumstances, investigators have a better chance of ending up with enough subjects who, from the investigator's point of view, perform better. On the part of subjects, underemphasis of ethical concerns is likely to exhibit a high correlation with low income, nonwhite race, and low education. Informed consent among minority groups with low incomes and low education levels often appears to involve relatively low levels of information.

The issue of deception is closely related to that of informed consent. Deception can take the form of an incorrect statement to or a withholding of information from participants. Researchers in social experiments are naturally tempted to convey the impression that the treatment will last a long time, usually longer than it is scheduled to last, in order to obtain better measures of long-run impacts. This may be done by offering misleading information, withholding information, or both. It is through such forms of deception that informed consent is corrupted, even though such actions are invariably unintentioned.

The trade-offs between these costs and benefits are important in an individual's decision to participate in an experiment. The costs fall into three classes: First, there is the cost to the patient who does something that he otherwise would not do; this includes habit formation that otherwise would not occur. A second cost is particularly germane to those in the control group and involves missed opportunities; they may not be given a treatment that they otherwise could, and possibly would, obtain. A third cost is associated with possible manipulation and deception accompanying the treatment or nontreatment; if participants feel they have been duped, they may lose confidence in social experiments in particular and the political system in general. In a world in which trust is in short supply, further deterioration can be disastrous.

On the other hand, there are benefits associated with social experiments: First, there are direct benefits accruing to those participating in the experiment; for example, in the housing allowance experiment, participating families received rent subsidies that enabled them to live in better housing. Additionally, there are indirect benefits, admittedly often quite small, affecting all or many members of society as a result of improved policies based on these experiments.

These trade-offs should be no less important to the researcher in his determination of the proper level of informed consent that should be applied. Successful experimentation with human subjects in the field of medicine can often produce much greater societal benefits than experimentation with regard to housing, electricity pricing, and so forth. The reasons for relatively low benefits from many social experiments relate less to the nature of the service investigated than to the roles played by political factors. Though the probability is high of successful medical results becoming widely used, it is not so for social experiments. For the latter, congressional approval and funding are required, and often political factors overshadow scientific ones.

Administration

Administering a social experiment is a large order. Indeed, some students of social experiments feel that the problems of administration and implementation are far more important than those of design or measurement.

> What is increasingly evident is that conventional methodological problems of sample design, outcome measurement reliability and validity, and the appropriateness of statistical tests – the topics generally covered in books or courses on statistics of experimental design – are not the main barriers to doing better experiments. The primary obstacles

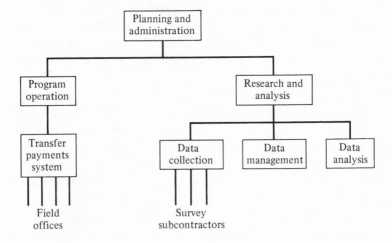

Figure 3.1. A simplified sketch of the administration of a social experiment involving transfer payments.

are weaknesses in organization and personnel – in foreseeing the need for an experiment soon enough to meet decision-making demands, designing the experiment, getting it into the field, and determining if it is working well enough to provide a valid basis for testing the experimental hypothesis. The hard truth is that we did not know how to put an experiment into the field so that it corresponds reasonably well to the drawing board plans.[18]

Whether one agrees with this statement or not, there is no question that proper implementation of a social experiment is indispensable to its success. Recognition of this fact led in the case of housing allowances to a separate social experiment focused solely on the administrative aspects of such a program, as discussed in Chapter 9.

As shown by the simplified sketch in Figure 3.1, at least two distinct administrative organizations are needed, one for the operation of the transfer program and one for planning the research and analyzing the data. For administrative reasons as well as for sound experimentation, these two organizations (sometimes sets of organizations) have to be kept distinct, though they also have to work with each other as problems arise. If, for example, the rate of cooperation obtained for particular treatment cells is much less than anticipated, the researchers may have to develop a different payments plan or a different approach, the feasibility of which has to be considered by the program people; or, the researchers may want very detailed information on, say, work histories, which the program staff may feel would interfere seriously with the willingness of participants to remain in the program.

To keep these two aspects separate, the general practice has been to have the transfer payments system operated by a separate organization. In some instances, this may be a subsidiary organization of the principal contractor, and in other instances it may be an existing welfare agency or other organization with experience in making these types of payments. The research and analysis aspects remain the responsibility of the principal contractor, but even part of this work may be subcontracted. This is especially true for the data collection, which can be a substantial operation in itself and involves highly specialized resources. Even where the data collection is carried out by the principal contractor, a subsidiary organization may be created to focus on these aspects. More usually, however, the data collection operations have been subcontracted.

A separate corporation to handle transfer payments is also highly desirable for legal reasons. Numerous agreements have to be negotiated with local governments, such as the waiver of rights of the participants to the more usual welfare payments in exchange for those in the experimental program. Moreover, legal and financial problems frequently arise in dealing with the participants or in dealing with intermediaries, and these are best left to a separate corporation that can specialize in these problems.[19]

In some ways, the problems faced by this separate corporation are not much different from those faced in the administration of many welfare programs. Indeed, this may turn out to be one of the major findings of at least the negative income tax experiments, namely, that the administrative headaches in carrying out this program may not be much less than for Aid to Families with Dependent Children (AFDC) or some of the other current welfare programs. Though income maintenance does not require a "means test," it does require a monthly report of income and a system of continuous surveillance to ensure the accuracy of these reports.[20]

The research and analysis side of the experiment is complicated partly because of the many variables that are being studied and partly because of the huge amounts of data that are being generated and have to be digested. In the Supply Experiment of the Housing Allowance Program, for example, the measurement of supply response involves study not only of the suppliers of housing services (landlords, developers, and homeowners) but also of the behavior of market intermediaries, the behavior of the participant households, and even the behavior of the nonparticipant households. Study of the latter is important to ascertain whether any increased demand for housing by the participant households has a secondary effect on the market situation faced by the nonparticipant households. Moreover, the behavior of the participant households has to be studied not only with regard to housing demand but also with regard to many other aspects of their economic behavior and life styles in order to get a reasonably complete picture of the effect of a national housing allowance program.

Given these numerous primary and secondary objectives, it is no surprise that staggering amounts of data are needed. Thus, for the Supply Experiment just mentioned, surveys were conducted each year of landlords, tenants, and homeowners at each of the two sites in addition to periodic surveys of residential structures.

The data collection problem is even more complicated in the case of the negative income tax experiments, where in addition to survey data for research purposes, monthly reports have to be filed by the participating families on detailed sources of income. Though the primary use of these data is for the conduct of the transfer payments system, they also serve research purposes and can be used for analysis as well.

Managing these huge amounts of data is a major task in itself, a task whose complexity was substantially underestimated in the New Jersey Experiment and some of the others. Data management involves not only the merging of data but the preparation of appropriate data files for analysis purposes and the maintenance of these files for the operation of the program and for monitoring and making the transfer payments. In view of the fact that participants may be moving in and out of the program and that benefit levels in some of the experiments will be changing every month according to the financial condition of the participants, the data-processing problems become enormous. From an analytical point of view, the data management problems are conceptually no different from those of maintaining a panel operation, except that these files have to be merged with information obtained on the participants from other sources. The problems are certainly not insuperable in view of the flexibility and capacity of modern computer systems, but they are a major complicating element and cost item in any social experiment.

4

The start: the New Jersey Experiment

Background

For many years there has been great unhappiness with public assistance or "welfare" programs. Aid to Families with Dependent Children (AFDC) in particular has encompassed ever larger numbers of people and has become increasingly costly. At the same time, benefits have varied widely among states and by category of beneficiary. Most poor families headed by able-bodied, adult men were not eligible for a public assistance payment. One proposal to remedy these inequities and to minimize disincentives to work implicit in public assistance practices of reducing benefit dollar for dollar of earned income would replace state programs of public assistance with a nationwide, noncategorical "negative income tax." Early advocates of this proposal emphasized that no work test should be necessary as long as benefits were reduced only moderately for each dollar of earnings.

Under such a negative income tax plan, all families and unrelated individuals would be guaranteed a minimum income, with variations by size of family and by age of its members. The guaranteed benefit would be reduced by a certain percentage of earnings (and of other income), so that at some level of income the benefit would be reduced to zero.

Two key variables define the nature of the plan: the support level, g, and the rate at which benefits are reduced by income earned above the support level, r. Hence, the weekly payments, p, received by a family under this plan earning a weekly income, y, would be: $p = g - ry$.

As an illustration, a family of four might be assured (guaranteed) an income of $100 per week with a tax rate of 30 percent. If the family earned no income at all it would receive a "negative income tax payment" of the full $100. On the other hand, if it earned, say, $60 a week, its subsidy under the plan for that week would be: $p = 100 - (0.3)(60) = 82$.

The negative income tax payment declines as earned income rises to the point where it vanishes altogether. That point is easily found by setting the parameter p in the preceding equation equal to zero and solving for y. Doing so, we find that for this plan the break-even point is $333 a week.

As the tax rate r increases, the participant is "penalized" more for working, because a higher proportion of the benefits is taken away and the break-even point falls. If the tax rate were 70 percent, for example, benefits would be reduced by 70 percent of each dollar earned, and the break-even point would fall to $143 per week.

A central question about the effectiveness of negative income tax (NIT) plans is therefore the impact of these two key variables, the support level and the tax rate, on the labor force participation of the different members of the family. As indicated in Chapter 2, from a theoretical point of view one would expect under assumptions of rational behavior that work incentives would be lessened as the support level is increased and also as the tax rate is increased. The key question is the magnitude of these responses and how this magnitude varies with changes in the values of g and r. Attempts to estimate this effect by econometric methods yielded very different results, as discussed in Chapter 2.

A controlled experiment using real populations seemed to be the best means of finding the answer. Such an experiment was under discussion in the mid-1960s and was authorized by the Office of Economic Opportunity in 1967 to be carried out by the Institute for Research on Poverty of the University of Wisconsin.[1] It was set up as a rigorously defined study incorporating experimental treatments applied over a period of time to statistically randomly selected parts of a population, with the objective of evaluating the effect of alternative NIT plans on the work behavior of the participants.

As a matter of fact, social experimentation in economics began with the New Jersey Negative Income Tax Experiment, and much has been written about it.[2] The principal interest in this experiment was in the labor response of able-bodied men, and so the focus of this experiment was on married men in the prime working years, those between the ages of 21 and 58. In addition, to make the study more manageable from an administrative point of view and to provide better control of the key variables, the study was restricted, at least initially, to parts of a single state, New Jersey, where the authorities seemed very willing to cooperate in making the necessary arrangements.

Further, the type of negative income tax to be studied had to be defined by a fixed set of rules. These rules represented the "legislation" that would govern the administrators and participants in the experimental program. They set out in detail the operational definitions of such terms as "family," "reportable income," "income accounting period," and specified the frequency of payments of benefits and the methods of adjusting for possible overpayment of these benefits. Decisions also had to be made on whether eligibility would be affected by family ownership of wealth, living arrangements, or evidence of willingness to seek employment.

In fact, any one of these basic rules could itself be an experimental variable of some interest, but all of them were "frozen" in this experiment. Additionally, efforts were made to assure that administration of these rules was uniform across all sites and among all participants.

Treatment variables

As already noted, the two key variables for an income maintenance plan are the support level, g, and the rate at which benefits are reduced by income earned above the support level, r. In the New Jersey Experiment, four values for g were used (in addition to zero for the control group). One value was the poverty level for that family size, two others were 25 percent and 50 percent below the poverty level, and the fourth was 25 percent above the poverty level. In the New Jersey Experiment, as well as in the later NIT experiments, the poverty income of a family of four (two adults and two children) for the given area was taken as the standard, and adjustments were made for other family sizes.[3] Hence, a particular support level g is actually a vector of support levels g_i, with i referring to family size.

The rate at which benefits are reduced by income above the support level, r, is clearly not independent of the support level itself. Thus, a high rate should serve as a greater disincentive to work, especially if combined with a high value of g. Because there is no evidence to judge what the labor supply response might be to varying tax rates, three very different values of r were tested in the New Jersey Experiment – 30, 50, and 70 percent. Only 8 of the 12 combinations of g and r were actually used. The reason is that at the lower support levels it clearly does not make much sense to reduce benefits at a high marginal rate on earned income, but this may be a viable alternative for higher support levels, depending on the nature of the response effect. As a result, the tax rate r was set alternately at 30 percent and 50 percent for $g = 0.5$; at 30 percent, 50 percent, and 70 percent for $g = 0.75$; at 50 percent and 70 percent for $g = 1$; and only at 50 percent for $g = 1.25$. These combinations seemed most likely to be implemented on a national scale, and they also were felt to be likely to produce estimates of labor supply response over a fairly broad range of the treatment variables, as explained in the next section.

Sample design

As originally designed, the study was to be carried out in three urban areas in New Jersey, selected because of the cooperativeness of the state and local authorities and because New Jersey had no plan under the AFDC program that extended aid to unemployed fathers. The possibility of doing this study on a national basis analogous to an area probability sample in order to obtain estimates that could be generalized to the nation was discarded, partly because of the much higher costs that would be involved and partly because of the operational problems that would arise in attempting to administer a welfare program of this type on such a broad scale and deal with many different state and local authorities in the process.

It was felt that concentrating the study in a very few urban areas within a single state would yield lower costs and, hence, more observations. Even so, the total sample size, given the funds available, was to be only somewhere between 1,000 and 1,500 households. Because a major part of the cost of any social experiment relates to the amount of benefits paid to the families receiving the experimental treatments and the sort of experimental treatments they receive, the target sample size becomes heavily dependent on the proportion of the sample to be used for the experimental treatments and on the treatments used. In terms of minimizing costs, it is obviously best to have relatively fewer families receiving experimental treatments. From an analytical point of view, however, the preference is in the other direction, because the more families that receive experimental treatments, the more information there is on the response to the treatment, assuming a minimum number of controls to serve as a basis for the analysis. In fact, for the purposes of the analysis, it is desirable to have observations allocated to a wide range of different treatment combinations (of g and r) in order to be able to estimate labor response on a wide scale.

In the New Jersey Experiment, these diverse objectives were reconciled by means of a formal analytical model developed by John Conlisk and Harold Watts.[4] The basis for this model is the specification of a labor supply response function in terms of particular combinations of g and r and of other relevant variables. Given a criterion function of this type and given a cost function, estimates can be made of the total sample size and sample allocation that would minimize the variance of the estimates of labor supply response for alternative values of the parameters of the function.[5] This model is very different from the usual sample allocation formulas for maximizing efficiency: It does not assume independence of observations; it gives weight to observations at different treatment combinations, according to the extremity of the treatment in the set; and it seeks to estimate an entire response function rather than individual responses for particular combinations of g and r.

To be sure, a prior determination is still needed of the combinations of g and r to be tested. For this purpose, combinations are sought that will produce estimates of labor supply response over a fairly broad range of the treatment variables, with specific reference to the treatments most likely to be implemented on a national scale. These considerations entered into the selection of the eight combinations tested in the New Jersey Experiment.

This model can yield controversial results because the emphasis on obtaining a good estimate of the response function leads to allocating a very heavy proportion of the total observations to the extremes of the treatment combinations, particularly to the "cheap" cells, such as the control families and the cells with high tax rates. Although this may be the most efficient allocation in terms of estimating the national cost of such a program, it nevertheless seems anomalous to have an income maintenance experiment in which more than half the families are in the control group and a substantial proportion of the rest are in treatment groups where the support levels are so high that they receive virtually no payments. For these reasons, the Conlisk–Watts model was modified by introducing various restrictions and modifications on the conditions governing sample allocation, so that more observations were allocated to the "interior" cells, such as $g = 0.5$ and $r = 30\%$, and $g = 1$ and $r = 50\%$.[6]

The strong leaning of the model toward "low-cost" observations is brought out in Table 4.1, which compares the original sample allocation of the model with the eight different treatment combinations and with the control group (point A), the allocation finally being decided upon after much controversy. As is evident from this table, with no constraints approximately 70 percent of the observations would be in the control group and most of the remaining 30 percent in treatment combinations that have high tax rates. As a result, had the experimenters followed this allocation – taking into account the likely deterrent effects of tax rates of 0.5 or more on participation – the experiment might well have started out with less than a fifth of the total observations as participants. To be sure, there would have been many more observations overall, but at the expense of very little representation from some of the key treatment combinations.

Table 4.1. *Sample allocation by Conlisk–Watts model in New Jersey Experiment*

Design point	Tax plan		Sample allocation, no constraints	Final allocation
	g	r		
A	0.0	0.0	2,031	650
B	0.5	0.3	6	48
C	0.5	0.5	27	71
D	0.75	0.3	99	94
E	0.75	0.5	127	98
F	0.75	0.7	172	64
G	1.0	0.5	60	76
H	1.0	0.7	179	70
I	1.25	0.5	186	138
Total			2,889	1,309
Control observations as % of total			70	50

Note: Budget constraint was $1,450,000.
Source: Rossi and Lyall, *Reforming Public Welfare*, p. 36.

Administration and implementation

As noted in Chapter 3, the administration of a social experiment involves two separate operations, one a system for making and monitoring transfer payments to the participants and the other a system for planning, collecting, and analyzing the data needed for evaluation of the experiment. In the New Jersey Experiment, the Institute for Research on Poverty of the University of Wisconsin had the primary responsibility for the planning and research work, and Mathematica, Inc., looked after the field aspects of the experiment. These two operations were closely coordinated because the data collection operations had to fit in but not interfere with the filing by participants of income forms and the payments to them. To keep these operations separate both administratively and in the minds of the participants, a separate Council for Grants to Families was incorporated to handle the transfer payments and the other aspects of the transfer system. The survey work connected with the analysis of the

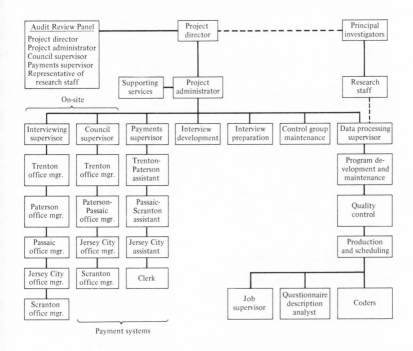

Figure 4.1. Operational aspects of New Jersey Experiment. *After*: Kershaw and Fair, *New Jersey Experiment*, p. 17.

data was subcontracted to a subsidiary of Mathematica, Urban Opinion Surveys, which was set up specifically to carry out this task.

An overall view of the organization of the work on the New Jersey Experiment is provided in Figure 4.1, which represents an elaboration of the overall concepts in Figure 3.1. Figure 4.1 shows how the payments system was separated from the data collection operation, with a separate staff for each. The payments system is represented in the diagram by the two marked columns on the lefthand side. The payments system was coordinated with the data collection operation through the project administrator. The entire operation was supervised from the Princeton office of Mathematica, with local field offices at each site to look after interviewing and payments.

How were families certified to be eligible for the program? The process involved, first, a short screening interview to determine if the family was eligible in terms of the basic criteria – intact, main wage earner between 21 and 58 years of age, family income less than 150 percent of the poverty level. When eligibility was established, a longer enrollment interview was conducted to collect base-line data on the families before they were invited to participate. When this information was obtained and the family enrolled, the family members were then interviewed as part of the research operation every three months for the following three years, in order to collect information on the labor force participation of each family member and supplementary information on consumption expenditures, health, and other aspects of family behavior.

In addition, families in the experimental treatments were required to fill out income report forms every four weeks and to provide pay stubs with these forms. If the income report form was not returned within four weeks, no payments were made to the family.

The actual payment was based on the formula:

$$p = g/52 - ry$$

where p is the weekly payment; g is the yearly dollar guarantee based on the plan assignment and the family size; r is the tax rate; y is the average weekly income, based on the income report form.

What did families receive for providing all this information? Those in the experimental treatment, of course, received in two biweekly payments the income maintenance supplement indicated by the particular plan. In addition, they received $20 for filing each income report form, and both they and the members of the control groups were paid five dollars for each interview. Members of the control group were also paid eight dollars per month for reporting their current address.

Families in the experimental treatments also received a rebate of that part of their income taxes paid to the tax break-even point, meaning that income level at which taxes would have to be paid by the family if the Internal Revenue Service were using the same tax rate as the experimental plan for that family; otherwise, families earning income above this break-even point could have experienced a decrease in disposable income. As a basis for calculating such a rebate, families were paid six dollars for furnishing a copy of their 1040 income tax form.

The process of making transfer payments proved to be a much more substantial operation than had been originally thought. Many, if not most, of the participants did not seem to fully understand how their payments were computed or other rules of the game, except for the simple question of eligibility, and considerable effort had to be made to explain to them how the system worked.

It was not clear how well the families were trained in the rules of the experiment, and apparently continual efforts had to be made to reeducate families in these rules. Particularly vexing was the fact that a large number of families initially misinterpreted the instructions and reported take-home pay instead of gross pay, with the result that much of the initial wage data had to be discarded for the analysis.

In addition, a system was needed for auditing and verifying the reports from the families, especially as employers had not been asked for information about the sample members. This system consisted essentially of two components. One involved use of external sources, in this case the Internal Revenue Service and the Social Security Administration, for systematic checks on the accuracy and completeness with which income data were reported. The results showed that the income reported was generally understated by about 4 percent, with possibly one-fifth of the families underreporting by 15 percent or more.[7]

The second component was audit of reports where there were suspicions of fraud. A panel was set up by the experiment, which audited 165 of the 1,300 families during the course of this experiment. Local welfare rolls were also checked for possible duplication, which led to audits of 138 families for receipt of overlapping benefits. There is little doubt that these figures are underestimates of the true extent of misreporting because, as the authors note, it is hardly possible in a program of this type to detect all the misreporting that may occur.

The experiment was in the field for approximately four years, from August 1968 to September 1972. In fact, the planning work began in

1968, and the final expenditures were not incurred until 1974. The total costs came to approximately $7.8 million, subdivided as follows: administration and research, $5,428,000 (Mathematica, $4,455,000; University of Wisconsin, $973,000); transfer payments, $2,375,000.

On a per-family basis, the annual administrative costs were reported to average about $90 per year.[8] In addition, there were average payments to the families of between $90 and $100 per four-week period over the period of the study, or about $1,300 per family per year. If we leave out the research and overhead costs, this means that the administrative costs of dealing with the families amounted to approximately 7 percent of the payments.[9]

Response results

The initial plan was to select the sample from three sites in New Jersey, Trenton, Paterson–Passaic, and Jersey City, the idea being to start in Trenton, gain experience there, and then select additional families at the other two sites in order to have about 1,200 families equally distributed among whites, blacks, and Spanish-Americans. The experience in Trenton and in the two other New Jersey sites, however, showed that use of the 1960 census data had led to substantial overestimates of the proportion of eligible white families. The sample in Trenton was preponderantly black, that in Paterson–Passaic preponderantly Puerto Rican, and that in Jersey City preponderantly black. To equalize the ethnic balance, the experimenters had to find a site that was heavily white, and the closest such site was Scranton, Pennsylvania. This provided the necessary ethnic balance but at the cost of intermingling site with ethnic background.

The enrollment process itself was apparently long and arduous. In each city the procedure involved listing of the housing units in randomly selected blocks within the target areas (based on 1960 census income data), followed by screening interviews, then preenrollment interviews and enrollment attempts. As is shown in Table 4.2, to enroll an initial 1,216 families involved listing 48,647 housing units and conducting 27,350 screening interviews, the latter representing

Table 4.2. *Results of sample selection process, New Jersey Experiment*

Interview stage	Trenton	Paterson–Passaic	Jersey City	Scranton	All cities
Listing					
Housing units listed	3,530	14,781	18,002	12,334	48,647
Screening interview					
Interviews attempted	3,497	14,781	18,002	12,334	48,614
Housing unit vacant	270	729	2,668	1,225	4,892
Family never home	400	2,954	3,997	1,063	8,414
Refused interview	400	2,449	3,531	1,578	7,958
Completed interview	2,427	8,649	7,806	8,468	27,350
Eligibility from screening					
Ineligible for preenrollment	2,200	7,661	6,567	7,798	24,226
Eligible for preenrollment	227	988	1,239	670	3,124
Preenrollment interview					
Interviews attempted	227	913	1,143	670	2,953
Moved or could not be located	18	177	149	57	401
Refused interview	22	44	88	57	211
Completed interview	187	692	906	556	2,341
Eligibility from preenrollment					
Ineligible for enrollment	50	246	358	174	828
Eligible for enrollment	137	446	548	382	1,513
Enrollment					
Attempts	137	446	413	320	1,316
Moved or could not be located	2	21	7	0	30
No longer eligible	0	3	5	0	8
Refused enrollment	9	40	11	2	62
Enrolled	126	382	390	318	1,216

Source: Kershaw and Fair, *New Jersey Income-Maintenance Experiment*, p. 31.

a response rate of 62 percent of the occupied housing units. In fact, if we combine the refusals and the noncontacts encountered at the different stages, it would appear that less than half of the eligible families were eventually enrolled in the study. This number amounted to 725 families in the various experimental groups and 491 in the control group.[10]

The very high interaction between site and ethnic background is evident from Table 4.3, which shows that most of the whites in the experiment were in Scranton, most of the blacks in Paterson–Passaic and Jersey City, and most of the Spanish-speaking in Paterson–Passaic.

Table 4.3. *Ethnic composition of sample, by city and by experimental treatment*

Group	Trenton	Paterson–Passaic	Jersey City	Scranton	All cities
Black					
Treatment	53	109	118	2	282
Control	52	84	81	1	218
Total	105	193	199	3	500
White					
Treatment	14	30	25	162	231
Control	11	18	27	153	209
Total	25	48	52	315	440
Spanish-speaking					
Treatment	20	137	55	0	212
Control	9	112	84	0	205
Total	29	249	139	0	417
All ethnic groups					
Treatment	87	276	198	164	725
Control	72	214	192	154	632
Total	159	490	390	318	1,357[a]

[a]Includes the original 1,216 families and 141 additional control families in Trenton, Paterson, and Passaic.
Source: Kershaw and Fair, *New Jersey Income-Maintenance Experiment*, p. 36.

Approximately 20 percent of the families dropped out of the experiment during the three-year period, more of the control families (25 percent) than of the experimental families (16 percent). Attrition tended to decline with the generosity of the guarantee level and to increase as the tax rate rose. Thus, only 6 percent of the families dropped out who were guaranteed income at 125 percent of the poverty line as compared to 22 percent of the families guaranteed only 50 percent of the poverty income level. Though numerous reasons were given for dropping out and various attempts were made to induce the families to remain,[11] the incentives offered by the plan itself may well have been the paramount reason. As a result, the number of participating families after three years was down to 1,084.

Findings

Not all the families who had remained in the experiment could be used for the analysis, partly because of missing data and also because of the desire to focus on families that had not experienced any marital disruptions. As a result, the basis of analysis for labor supply response was continuous husband–wife families for whom the necessary data were available, or approximately 690 families.

The results obtained by the experimenters from the analysis of these data suggest that the labor supply response to the experimental treatment was very small. For the key group, "the employment rate for male family heads in the experimental group was only 1.5% less than that for the controls. For the number of hours worked per week, the difference amounted to just over 2%. For earnings per week, the experimentals actually were higher by 6.5%."[12] Major differences were observed by ethnic groups, however. After allowance for a variety of other factors, including distance of a family's normal income from the break-even point of their plan, a statistically significant reduction of about seven hours per week was obtained for Spanish-speaking heads whose income was well below the break-even point. For white family heads, however, the reduction was only about two hours, and a positive labor supply response was obtained for blacks. As is evident from Table 4.4, labor force participation seems clearly to decline only for Spanish-speaking heads.

On the other hand, the labor supply of the wives is unequivocally negative and substantial for all ethnic groups, the average decline being 23 percent in hours worked per week and 24 percent in labor market participation. Because these people worked an average of only a little over four hours per week, the aggregate impact of this decline is much less than it would seem from these percentages and may be more than offset from a social point of view by the increased care they would presumably give to their children (which averaged four in these families).

Moreover, as is also evident from Table 4.4, the nature of the response varies once more by ethnic background. The only appre-

Table 4.4. *Selected labor supply response results of husbands, wives, and families, middle two years, New Jersey Experiment*

Item	White	Black	Spanish-speaking
Husbands			
Labor force participation	−0.40	0.100	−0.900
Earnings per week (dollars)	−0.08	8.290[a]	4.480
Hours per week	−2.07	0.930	−0.980
Employment (percentage)	−2.50	1.100	−4.000
Wives			
Labor force participation rate	−0.094[c]	0.002	0.005
Hours per week	−1.940[a]	0.510	−0.800
Family			
Earnings per week (dollars)	−14.10[c]	12.10[b]	4.40
Hours per week	−7.50[c]	0.16	−1.65

[a]Significant at 0.10 level.
[b]Significant at 0.05 level.
[c]Significant at 0.01 level.
Source: Watts and Rees, *The New Jersey Income-Maintenance Experiment*, 2: 61, 135, 195–6.

ciable negative response is on the part of the white wives, who reduced both their labor force participation and the number of hours worked per week, the latter by almost half on a percentage basis. On the other hand, there was no discernible effect of the experiment on the labor force participation or the hours worked per week of the black wives or the Spanish-speaking wives.

In a similar manner, the overall effect of the experimental treatment on the earnings of the family as a whole, on hours worked, on earnings per week, or on hours worked per week was apparent only for white families, as shown once more in Table 4.4. The effect on earnings and hours worked of black and Spanish-speaking families seemed as likely to be positive as negative, the signs of the coefficients varying with the type of model being used.[13]

In addition, little evidence was found that the labor supply response was much affected by the planned variations in the tax rate or the guarantee level, though the sample sizes were quite small. Rather, the principal effect was found to depend on the distance that the family's normal income was below the break-even point for the plan; if the family income was well below that of the break-even point, the disincentive to work became pronounced.[14]

On the other hand, a reanalysis of these data by John F. Cogan finds that the percentage of families taking part in this experiment varies substantially in relation to the tax rate and the guarantee level, once a distinction is made between families in the program who did not receive benefits and families in the program who did receive benefits. He finds that when the tax rate was held constant at 50 percent, the percentage of families participating in the program fluctuated from 10 percent if income was guaranteed at 50 percent of the poverty line to 84 percent if income was guaranteed at 125 percent of the poverty line. Similarly, for those offered guaranteed income at 75 percent of the poverty line, the relative frequency of participation varied from 86 percent if the tax rate was 30 percent to only 8 percent if the tax rate was 70 percent. The reduction in the hours worked per week for those taking part in the program is found to vary substantially by week but tends to average out at about 14 percent.[15]

No effects of the experimental program on the participants with regard to such other aspects as health, fertility, marital dissolution, and school attendance seem to have been detected.

Evaluative comments

If one thing is clear, it is that this first of the social experiments was a learning experience for everybody involved. With no previous experience to draw upon, the experimenters had to devise a study design and a set of data collection procedures virtually from scratch. They had to make decisions for a wide variety of issues, ranging from the number and type of experimental treatments and sample size allocations between experimental treatments and a control group to where to conduct the experiment, how frequently to interview, and what questions to ask.

The evidence is that they seem to have done a much better job in setting up the conceptual framework than in implementing it. Though some may question the resulting lack of representativeness, the decision to concentrate the experiment in a very few localities and among particular population groups seems, by hindsight, to have been a wise one. Setting up such a study on a national basis and involving the welfare laws of anywhere from 15 to 25 states, plus the field problems that would have arisen, would have very likely made this experiment unmanageable. As it was, the study was seriously affected by the liberalization of the welfare laws in New Jersey, which made unemployed fathers of dependent children eligible for welfare aid in the later years of the experiment, something that had been true all along in Pennsylvania, the site of another portion of this experiment.

The Conlisk–Watts model for sample size allocation in experiments of this type was a major innovation, although in practice it needs modification. In addition, the econometric estimation methods used to gauge labor supply response were very much attuned to the design of the experiment and the type of data to be obtained.

Still, some very puzzling results have emerged from the experiment. That differences in labor response should be so pronounced by ethnic groups is somewhat surprising. Even more surprising is the fact that all the estimates made so far suggest that the labor response of the largest of these groups in the sample, the blacks, is positive. That a negative income tax program should lead a large group of people to increase the hours they devote to their jobs is hard to believe, and the experimenters have no explanation other than to suggest that the labor market activities of the control group may have been atypical. One might attribute the cause to the change in the welfare laws during the course of the experiment, noted earlier, a change that would have affected particularly the members of the control group. It is not clear, however, why this change would have differential effects on the various ethnic groups.

It is more likely that the answer lies in the implementation of the study, in the data collection and field operations. Indeed, all of the survey work was originally intended to be subcontracted. An unhappy initial experience with a subcontractor, however, led Mathematica to set up its own field organization and to undertake the work itself. To set up a completely new survey organization for collecting data from a type of population that would be very difficult even for the most experienced of survey organizations is a learning experience that can produce numerous biases and errors. At least one major error was made in allowing participants to believe that they were supposed to report take-home pay rather than gross earnings, an error that had a longer impact on the members of the control group. Because procedures were evidently not standardized until after the experiment was well under way, there is the possibility that other, less noticeable errors may have been made as well.

An additional explanation is that some sort of self-selection mechanism was operative in the inclusion of the participating families, so that those who were most highly motivated participated in the study. If so, the experimentals would be looking at the negative income tax plan as an opportunity to increase their earning power for the future rather than as a "cushion" on which to relax for a while. The limited term of the experiment could have contributed to this feeling.

There is the further possibility that the results are explainable largely in terms of the economic conditions prevailing at the time. With the rate of unemployment increasing in those areas during the later years of the experiment, experimental families as well as control families may have felt that they had to make an effort to hold onto jobs, at least the job of the main wage earner, rather than rely on an income maintenance payment that would be ending very shortly, especially as the families remaining in the experiment in the second and third year were undoubtedly the more stable ones. The largest number that dropped out were those that moved without leaving any forwarding address.

A frustrating aspect of the analysis has been the very small number of observations available after adjustments are made for such restrictions as panel mortality, absence of data, and heterogeneity due to ethnic background. As a result, the initial sample size of 1,357 families, small as it was, was reduced so substantially for the analytical work that it is very difficult to discern any but substantial differences. Thus, the base for most of the analyses of the labor supply response of the white heads of households is little more than 300 families, of whom only 181 were in one of the experimental treatment plans. The corresponding sample sizes for black families are 234 and 151, respectively, and those for Spanish-speaking families are only 149 and 93, respectively. In view of the considerable amount of noise in behavior data pertaining to individual families, it is surprising that any effects were detected at all.

Whatever the plausibility of these and other explanations and whatever the shortcomings of the New Jersey Experiment, it provided a great deal of information on the labor market response of intact families with a male wage earner between the ages of 21 and 58, albeit for one particular section of the country. Whether the labor market response of these family heads is as moderate as is indicated by the experimenters remains to be tested by further analysis of these data and by the results of the later experiments, to be covered in Chapter 5.

Appendix: On the estimation of response effects

This appendix describes in relatively simple terms how response effects have been and are being measured in the social experiments. The focus is on the income maintenance experiments, as they are the furthest along; three of them (New Jersey, Rural, and Gary) have been completed. The methods used to measure labor supply response in two of these experiments, Seattle–Denver and New Jersey, are described here as they provide an interesting contrast.[16]

In each case, the main focus is on measuring the effect of the experimental treatments (support level and rate at which benefits are reduced by additional income) on the hours of work.

1. Seattle–Denver supply response

We start with an individual's utility function dependent on the amount of leisure (L) and of goods (G):

$$U = U(L, G) \tag{1.1}$$

This is subject to a budget constraint in which total income (Y) is equal to the net wage rate (w) multiplied by the total time available $(T = L + H)$ plus nonwage income (Y_n):

$$Y = wT + Y_n \tag{1.2a}$$

which is also equal to expenditures on goods plus those on leisure,[17] namely,

$$Y = \P G + wL, \ L < T \tag{1.2b}$$

where $\P$ is the price of consumption goods.

These equations lead to a leisure demand function of the general form:

$$L = L(w, \P, Y) \tag{1.3}$$

Differentiating this equation and making relevant substitutions leads to a Slutsky-type demand function:

$$dL = \left.\frac{\partial L}{\partial w}\right|_u dw + \left.\frac{\partial L}{\partial_Y}\right|_w [(T - L)dw + dY_n] \tag{1.4}$$

where the first differential on the right represents the compensated substitution effect and the second differential represents the income effect. Note that the expression in brackets is the total differential of disposable income holding constant the initial labor supply, $T - L$, or hours of work, H_p.

For estimation purposes, Equation 1.4 is put into discrete form, and dL is replaced by its complement dH $(L + H = T)$, because the variable of interest (and which is best measured) is hours of work. The result is, then:

$$\alpha \Delta H = \Delta w + \beta \Delta Y_d \bigg|_{H_p} \tag{1.5}$$

or,

$$H_e = H_p + \alpha \Delta w + \beta \Delta Y_d \bigg|_{H_p} \tag{1.6}$$

where $\Delta H = H_e - H_p$, with H_e denoting hours of work after the experimental treatments have been applied.

A basic assumption of this model is that the labor supply response of different individuals depends not only on the experimental treatment but also on the initial equilibrium position of different individuals as well as on their budget constraints. In Equation 1.6, this initial equilibrium position is represented by H_p. Estimation of net wage rate change for Equation 1.6 was complicated by the fact that a declining tax rate was a feature of this experiment, so that the experimental tax rate, t_e, depends on the labor supply response of the individual. This was dealt with by assuming that the budget constraint for each individual was linear at the preexperimental point but including a dummy variable, *DECLINE*, for those on the declining tax program.[18]

Accordingly, the change in the net wage (Δw) was estimated as the product of a predicted wage rate and the change between the linearized preexperimental and experimental tax rates. This predicted wage rate for all individuals is estimated on the basis of a regression, for workers only, of wages on such personal characteristics as education, experience, and race, separately for female heads, husbands, and wives.[19]

Equation 1.6 was supplemented by a number of other variables. These included experimental variables, such as whether the family was in the three-year program or the five-year program (*YRS*2), and a set of three variables reflecting whether the family was receiving any manpower assistance (**M**).[20] In addition, various explanatory variables that might influence response were included, namely, whether the family was above the break-even level (*FABOVE*), the break-even level of family earnings (*BREAK*), the amount by which family earnings exceed the break-even level (*EARNABOV*). Finally, also included was a set of control variables (**C**),[21] as well as the variables used in the original assignment (**A**) of the families to experimental treatments.

The final function[22] used for estimation of the labor response effect was:

$$H_e = b_0 + b_1 H_p + b_2' \mathbf{A} + b_3' \mathbf{C} + b_y' \mathbf{M} + b_5 Y_d|_{H^p} + b_6 \Delta w$$
$$+ b_7 FABOVE + b_8 BREAK + b_9 EARNABOVE$$
$$+ b_{10} YRS3 + b_{11} DECLINE + \mu \qquad (1.7)$$

Because the dependent variable was truncated, the parameters were estimated by the Tobit model, with separate estimates for two different time periods, the sixth and eighth experimental quarters. The results yielded positive substitution elasticities ranging from about .1 for husbands to nearly .4 for wives and negative income elasticities (relative to hours worked) ranging from .3 for husbands to about .6 for wives.

2. New Jersey Experiment

This approach is based on an additive response function of the form:

$$B = F(\mathbf{Z}) + R(\mathbf{T}, \mathbf{TZ}) + u \qquad (2.1)$$

where $\mathbf{Z}$ is a vector of variables considered relevant to the explanation of the response behavior, B, and $\mathbf{T}$ is a vector of the treatment variables, in this case, combinations of the support level and the tax rate. Two separate functions are postulated, because the first function on the right "explains" the response effect (say, hours of work) in the absence of any experimental treatment, whereas the second represents the effects of the treatment. The second function allows for both direct effects of the treatment and interaction effects between the $\mathbf{T}$ and $\mathbf{Z}$ vectors; u is the error term.

The methodology proceeds to develop different specifications for each function, doing so separately for the married male head of the household, the female spouse, young adults between the ages of 16 and 18, and the family as a whole.

The response function, R, is based on a "spline series" that provides for all eight experimental treatment combinations of the guarantee level (g) and the tax rate (t). This series is:

$$S(k) = \sum_{i=1}^{k} a_i s_i(x, g, t), \quad k = 1, 2, \ldots, 8 \qquad (2.2)$$

where a_i are the unknown coefficients to be estimated and $s_i\,(x, g, t)$ is the set of variables that, in combination with each other, represent the eight experimental treatments used.

Thus, s_1 is defined as:

$$s_1 = x = \begin{cases} 1 \text{ if family is in the experimental group} \\ 0 \text{ if family is in the control group} \end{cases}$$

Hence, $S(1)$ simply measures the average differential between the experimental and the control groups.

The variable s_2 is meant to allow for the different guarantee rates and is defined as:

$$s_2 = s_1(g - .75)$$

In other words, .75 is taken as the "base" for the measurement of guarantee rates. s_2 will be 0 either if the family is in the control group (in which case s_1 is 0) or if the family is at the guarantee level of 75 percent of the basic poverty schedule.

Variation in the tax rate is allowed for by means of s_3, defined as:

$$s_3 = s_1(t - .50)$$

In this case, the 50 percent tax rate is selected as the "base," s_1 indicating once more that s_3 is applicable only if a family is in an experimental group.

s_2 combined with s_3 allow for variations in both the guarantee level and the tax rate. Thus, the formula for S_3 is:

$$S_3 = a_1 s_1 + a_2 s_1(g - .75) + a_3 s_1(t - .50) \tag{2.3a}$$

The value of S_3, for example, for a family at the 100 percent guarantee level and the 70 percent tax rate would be:

$$S_3 = a_1 + .25a_2 + .20a_3 \tag{2.3b}$$

In a similar manner, by adding appropriately defined variables, s_4, . . . ,s_8, allowances are made for additive, nonlinear effects of g and t, as well as for interaction effects between g and t. The interactions between these response variables and the vector of other relevant variables, $\mathbf{Z}$, is carried out in straightforward fashion by combining components of $\mathbf{Z}$ with the $S(k)$. If, for example, education (E) is hypothesized to interact with the treatment variables, this component would be represented as $ES(k)$.

The estimation of $F(\mathbf{Z})$, the function that explains B in the absence of any experimental treatment, involves the specification of a labor supply function in terms of whatever variables are considered relevant. Such a function can be represented as follows:

$$B = f(W, Y_n, \mathbf{D}) \tag{2.4}$$

where W is the wage of the individual, Y_n is nonwage income, and $\mathbf{D}$ is a vector of demographic variables.

The estimation of the wage is a key aspect of this approach. It is assumed to be the sum of three distinct components, namely:

$$W = W^* + \tilde{W} + e \tag{2.5}$$

W^* is the "normal" component representing the wage that an individual with similar personal characteristics would be expected to earn under "normal" circumstances; $\tilde{W}$ is the experimental component, namely, the effect on wages of the experimental treatment; e is a random disturbance.

The normal component W^*, is estimated as a function of seven explanatory variables – age (x_1), years of education completed (x_2), industry of employment (x_3), occupation (x_4), site (x_5), employment status of the spouse (x_6), and time in the experiment in quarters (x_7). The general functional form is:

$$W^* = f_1(x_1, x_2) + f_2(x_3, x_4) + f_3(x_5) + f_4(x_6) + f_5(x_7) \tag{2.6}$$

The separate functions indicate the extent to which interactions are allowed for in the final specification. Thus, in this case, interactions are introduced for age and education and for industry of employment and occupation.

The function itself is arithmetic (with W measured in logarithms), with the variables either of the spline form $(x_1, x_2, \text{ and } x_7)$ or in dummy form (the others).

The experimental component, $\tilde{W}$, is a function of the tax rate (x_8), the guarantee level (x_9) and the quarter for which data are collected (x_{10}). The general functional form is:

$$\tilde{W} = f_6(x_8, x_9) + (f_7(x_{10})$$ (2.7)

which allows for interaction between the tax and guarantee level, by the spline method outlined previously.

The function represented by the combination of Equations 2.6 and 2.7 was estimated separately for each of the three ethnic groups – whites, blacks, and Spanish-Americans – using generalized least squares. Most of the demographic variables were significant either singly or in combination with each other.[23]

A similar estimate was made of normal family income, $\hat{Y}$. These variables were then combined to reflect the influence of financial factors using the following function form:

$$\hat{S}_c = c_1\,\hat{Y}/L + c_2\hat{W} + c_3/\hat{W} + c_4\hat{Y}/\hat{W}$$ (2.8)

The income variable in the first term of this function is normalized by dividing it by the poverty level, L, for that family's size. The remaining terms allow for a nonlinear wage rate effect and for interaction between wages and income. This function form was apparently selected heuristically and is reported to have, "along with linear terms and preenrollment hours and weeks employed in base year, provided a substantial reduction in the variance of the experimental response."[24]

This function was combined with dummy variables to represent the eight plans classified into three categories, namely, low, medium, and high.[25] Regressions were carried out separately for the three ethnic groups mentioned previously as well as for four different combinations of the 12 quarters covered by the experiment.

An alternative approach was to allow for the asymmetrical nature of the experimental treatments, which suggests that response to the treatments will vanish at some point above the break-even level, that is, at the point where net benefits stop because income has exceeded the level at which any benefits are paid. To reflect this phenomenon, a variable, Θ is defined to equal the value 2, if the individual is at the break-even point, and increases progressively as the individual is further below the break-even point. In other words:

$$\Theta_{it} = \frac{M_{it} + 20\hat{W}_{it} - \hat{Y}_{it}}{10\hat{W}_{it}} \tag{2.9}$$

where M_{it} is the break-even level for the ith household at time t; $\hat{W}$ and $\hat{Y}$ are the same as before.

As can be seen from this equation, Θ is scaled in terms of tens of hours, which is felt to be more meaningful than to use a scale in dollar terms.

Using this variable, a six-parameter response function is postulated, namely:

$$X = (\alpha_{11} + \alpha_{12}S_2 + \alpha_{13}S_3)\Theta + (\alpha_{21} + \alpha_{22}S_2 + \alpha_{23}S_3)\Theta^2 \tag{2.10}$$

In this equation, S_2 and S_3 are the linear spline terms in g and t discussed earlier. This equation is homogeneous in Θ, so that the response will be zero when Θ is zero, but it also allows for nonlinear responses in terms of Θ.

Equation 2.10 was combined into an estimation function consisting of S_c (Equation 2.8), preexperimental values of hours per week and weeks per year, and a number of demographic variables, to estimate labor force participation and employment. As before, this was done using, alternately, averages of four or eight quarterly observations, with separate estimates for each of the three ethnic groups.

Taken together, the variables explained from 40 to 50 percent of the variation in labor force participation and somewhat more of employment. Once more, however, no significant response effect was apparent for whites or blacks, but strongly negative effects appeared for the Spanish-Americans.[26]

Similar methods were employed to estimate the response effects in terms of hours worked. Two alternate approaches were used, one based on hours worked without regard to employment status, and the other on hours worked only for those who were employed. This time both approaches provided some evidence for a negative response effect both by the whites and by the Spanish-Americans, though the response effects for the blacks was still positive but not statistically significant. The use in the latter case of a variance component regression model with splines to measure the variation in response due to time and key parameters did not alter these findings.

Evaluative comments

In many ways, the above examples reveal both the strengths and the weaknesses of the measurement approach in these experiments. Although these are by no means the only techniques that could be employed, they do serve to bring out that the basis for any approach is invariably either a model from utility theory, as in the case of the Seattle–Denver approach, or a well-formulated set of hypotheses about the expected nature of the response effects, as in the case of the New Jersey Experiment. The transformation of this theory or set of hypotheses into testable form tends to necessitate an increasing number of arbitrary judgments in refining the basic ideas to the stage of estimating parameters.[27]

A key set of judgments arises in deciding what variables to add to control for various aspects of the experiment, such as the nonrandom assignment of families to experimental treatments, and to control for extraneous influences. Such variables are usually not part of the theoretical or a priori reasoning but are added afterward, as illustrated by these two examples.

Another type of judgment involves the specification of the form of the function and the sort of interactions, if any, that should be allowed for. The results of past studies frequently serve as a basis for these decisions, but the fact remains that some of the key decisions are still made on an ad hoc basis, such as the choice of the form of the function in both of the examples presented here. Still, these decisions are extremely important, because the number of sample members allocated to a particular treatment seems to be highly sensitive to the specification of the response function.

A third set of judgments relates to the time period to cover in the estimation. In the New Jersey Experiment, which covered a period of three years, the data were merged into successive groups of four quarters and of eight quarters and the function parameters estimated separately in each case. In an experiment of that sort, one would expect the middle four quarters (the second year) to yield the most reliable estimates of "permanent" effects, but given the many different views of people's possible reactions to a three-year time horizon it seemed prudent to estimate the parameters for combinations of quarters covering the entire three years. On the other hand, in the Seattle–Denver example, the estimates, though preliminary, were carried out separately for two different quarters, each in the second year of the experiment. Theoretically, there is no reason why these response effects could not be estimated within the framework of a generalized cross-section–time-series regression model with separate parameters for every quarter, though the statistical estimation problems could be messy.

Still a fourth set of judgments revolves around the choice of data to use for the estimation. In the Seattle–Denver example, the analysis of the response effects for the husbands was based on 1,738 observations for the sixth quarter and 1,645 observations for the eighth quarter, representing less than half of the families initially enrolled. To what extent these response effects also apply to the families with similar characteristics that dropped out of the experiment or for whom insufficient information was available is a moot point.

In the New Jersey example, the estimates of the labor supply response effects of the employed male heads of households were based on only 345 observations for *all* three ethnic groups, of an original sample of over 1,300. Might it be that the very fact that the estimates are based on what was clearly the most stable part of the sample jeopardizes their generality? We do not know.

The Conlisk–Watts model has also been criticized because of some of its technical assumptions. The principal ones are the following:

1 The nature of the objective function is such that the entire focus of the optimization process is on the total variances, not on the probability of finding significant differences between treatments. In other words, the allocation acts to maximize the probability of finding significant differences between the treatments as a group and the control group, but at the expense of obtaining any significant differences between treatments.

2 Not unrelated to the preceding point is the fact that in most instances the objective function focuses on the variances of the de-

pendent variables, rather than on the sum of the variances of the treatment set. As a result, the optimization process may yield a solution that assigns very few observations to the individual treatments, especially to the more expensive treatments, so that hardly any information is obtained on the effect of those treatments on the response of the sample members.

3 The optimization procedure is such that one of the key variables that may affect response, family income, also enters into the solution to the number of families that are to be assigned to a particular treatment. This is because the cost of each treatment has been computed as a function of both the amount of the subsidy that would be provided under that treatment and the "normal" income of the family. Hence, the level of normal income will affect the probability of assignment of a particular family to an experimental treatment, and the treatment variable is then not orthogonal to the characteristics of the sample member.

4 One other question concerns the relevance of the particular cost figures used in the budget constraints. In the New Jersey Experiment, and possibly in the Rural Experiment, the cost figures used related only to the experimental costs, so that the ratio of the cost of a treatment observation to a control observation was approximately four to one. If, however, one takes into account interviewing, data reduction, and data-processing costs, this ratio falls to something like two to one. Hence, the model as used originally may have very much overestimated the cost of a treatment observation and underestimated the number of observations that should be assigned to the treatment groups.

Despite these and other questions that may be raised about these procedures, the remarkable fact is that all of the estimates fall within a fairly narrow range, even though the specific economic models and estimation procedures differ from one experiment to another. Thus, by and large they tend to confirm that, as shown in Table 4.4, the effects on labor force participation of an income maintenance plan are relatively small for the main wage earner (whether male or female) but may be substantial for wives and secondary members of the family initially in the labor force. Moreover, all effects are likely to be larger in terms of hours worked than in terms of participation in the labor force, and they also tend to be correlated inversely with the preexperimental level of income of the family. The response functions obtained from these analyses are especially useful in that they can be applied to estimate effects of experimental plans that were not tried (provided that they are within the range of the experimental treatments) or, alternatively, to derive various levels of optimization given certain policy objectives.

5

The other negative income tax experiments

Background

As is evident from the preceding chapter, the scope of the New Jersey Experiment was highly restricted. Families that were not intact, that did not have a main wage earner between the ages of 21 and 58 or had a self-employed main wage earner, that had incomes above 150 percent of the poverty line, and that did not live in an urban area were automatically excluded.[1] As a result, no information could be obtained from this experiment on aged families, on families with only one adult, and on two-wage-earner families (whose income invariably exceeded 150 percent of the poverty line). Moreover, the effect of the three-year time horizon could not be investigated, something that could have seriously distorted the labor supply response of the participants.

To deal with these limitations and provide a broader basis for policy analysis, the Office of Economic Opportunity (OEO) and the Department of Health, Education, and Welfare (HEW), which took over these activities when OEO was abolished, sponsored three additional experiments with the same general objective. The first of these (the Rural Experiment) was a more or less straightforward repetition of the New Jersey Experiment but this time centered in two rural areas – a very poor black rural county in North Carolina and a (supposedly) corresponding poor white farming area in Iowa. In addition, in response to the widespread criticism that the eligibility requirements of the New Jersey Experiment left out a substantial part of the welfare population, this experiment admitted families of any type and with either male or female heads (though the overwhelming majority actually had male heads), and the family did not have to be intact.

A second experiment was launched in Gary, Indiana, with the focus on a key segment of the welfare population ignored so far, namely, black families with only one adult, most often a female, and with at least one dependent (usually, but not necessarily, a child). For this reason, the eligibility requirements for the Gary sample called for only black families, with a requirement that 60 percent of them be headed by a female. In addition, the preponderance of female-headed households with small children present led to the incorporation of a treatment variable involving day care, something that could be incorporated in a national negative income tax program. In fact, such families were eligible for the AFDC plan in Gary, which provided a substantial guarantee and reimbursement of day care costs, though with a tax rate of 67 percent.

The third of the three additional experiments was the most ambitious. Comprising nearly five thousand families initially, it was set up in Denver and Seattle to explore a number of additional ramifications of a negative income tax plan, including the effects of higher support levels, of a declining tax rate, of counseling and training subsidies, and of lengthening the time horizon for participation to as long as 20 years.

Some general characteristics of all four of these income maintenance experiments are presented in Table 5.1, which can serve as a frame of reference for much of the later discussion.

Treatment variables

In all of the experiments, the key treatment variables were, as in the New Jersey Experiment, the guarantee level, g, and the tax rate, t. The Rural Experiment used the same tax rates as the New Jersey Experiment and the same three support levels; the highest support level was omitted because of the smaller sample size and the focus on labor response to lower levels of support. The same general approach was also used in the Gary Experiment, where the focus

Table 5.1. *Background information on income maintenance experiments*

Item	N.J.–Penn.	Rural N.C.–Iowa	Denver	Seattle	Gary
Eligibility					
Race	All	Black, white		All	Black
Age of head	18–58	18–58		18–58	18–58
Sex of head	Male	Both		Both	Both
Type of family	Intact	Any		Two or more	One dependent
Consumer unit	Household	Family		Family	Household
Income relative to poverty line	Under 150%	Under 150%			
Site(s)	Trenton, Patterson–Passaic, Jersey City, N.J., Scranton, Pa.	Two rural areas, one in N. Carolina, one in Iowa	City of Denver	City of Seattle	City of Gary
Treatment variables					
Support levels (ratio to poverty level)	0.5, 0.75, 1.00, 1.25	0.5, 0.75, 1.00	1.00, 1.26, 1.48[a]		0.75, 1.00[a]
Tax rates	0.3, 0.5, 0.7	0.3, 0.5, 0.7	0.5, 0.7, $0.7 - 0.0254y$, $0.8 - 0.025y$		0.4, 0.6
Counseling (c) & training (t) subsidies	None	None	c, $c + 0.5t$, $c + t$		None

Day care subsidies	None	None	None	None	35%, 60%, 80%, 100%
Time horizon (years)	3	3	3, 5, 20	3, 5	3
Experimental combinations	8	5	84	84	4[b]
Sample size					
Initial	1,216	809	2,758	2,042	1,799
Final	983	729			
Period of study	1967–74	1968–76	1971–91	1970–91	1971–77
Period of field work	1968–72	1970–2		1970–76	1971–74
Sponsor(s)	OEO, HEW	Ford Fdn, OEO, HEW		HEW	HEW, Indiana
Principal contractor(s)	IRP, Mathematica	IRP		SRI	MPR

[a] Rough approximations of ratios of dollar support levels.
[b] Excludes four experimental child care subsidy rates applied to selected families

again was on labor response at lower levels of support and at relatively low tax rates; to obtain sharper measures of response, only four combinations of support levels and tax rates were used in that experiment.

On the other hand, the Denver–Seattle Experiment probed somewhat in the other direction, using three support levels, one the poverty level itself and the others approximately 25 percent and 50 percent above the poverty level. These were combined with four tax rate schedules. Two of these tax rates were the same as in the New Jersey Experiment and in the Rural Experiment, namely, 0.5 and 0.7. In addition, however, two declining tax rates were introduced whereby the rate at which benefits were reduced with increasing income was compensated by approximately 2.5 percent of each additional dollar of income. If, therefore, the tax rate is set at 0.7, this type of adjustment serves to reduce it to 0.675. These declining rates were introduced at two levels, at a tax rate of 0.7, to see how it compared with the corresponding tax rate without any such decline, and at a higher tax rate, 0.8, to see how the effects at that rate would compare with that of the two rates at 0.7.

Several other variables were tested in the Gary and Denver–Seattle experiments. In the Gary Experiment, with the heavy proportion of single mothers, day care subsidies were offered. All the families in the experiment, whether in the treatment or in the control group, were allocated to four different child care subsidy rates, namely, 100, 80, 60, and 35 percent, as well as no subsidy. In fact, nearly 60 percent of the families were in the "no subsidy" group. Of the families offered a subsidy, a condition for receiving it in 80 percent of the cases was that the mother be employed or meet some other work requirement, such as attending school.

In the Denver–Seattle Experiment, all families were offered job counseling; approximately a third of the families were offered a 50 percent training subsidy, and another third were offered a full training subsidy. In this experiment the time horizon was varied, also. A random half of the families in Seattle and 40 percent of the families in Denver were enrolled for three years and an equal number for five years. One-fifth of the Denver families were enrolled for 20 years, with the idea of making an exhaustive study of the effect of the time horizon on their labor supply and other types of response.

One additional aspect of the Denver–Seattle Experiment was an attempt to ascertain whether bias was being introduced into the data or into people's behavior by the requirement of monthly income reports from the families in the experimental treatments. To measure possible effects on the data caused by this reporting requirement, half of the families in the control group in Denver were also asked to file such monthly reports.

Sample design

The sample design differs somewhat for the three experiments, and it therefore seems best to discuss each of them separately.

In the Gary Experiment a sample of 1,800 households was projected, approximately 1,000 of which were under one of the four income maintenance plans and somewhat less than 800 in the control group. For both groups, 60 percent were to be families with the husband absent. Sample allocation was based on a modification of the Conlisk-Watts model. Unlike the New Jersey Experiment, nearly a third of the families in the experiment had incomes above 150 percent of the poverty line, particularly in the case of the families with the husband present. The actual sample design by experimental plan and treatment group is shown in Table 5.2.

The final initial sample contained about 1,780 families. As with the New Jersey Experiment, the number that had to be contacted to recruit this many families was far higher. In fact, over 5,000 families were interviewed initially, and approximately 2,400 of this number were administered a more detailed screening interview to ascertain eligibility on the basis of income level, family composition (intact households versus those with female heads), and residence inside or outside Model Cities neighborhoods.[2]

The families eligible for the experiment were stratified into 16 cells on the basis of poverty level (income), family type, and residence and were then allocated randomly to the four experimental treatments and to the control group. The allocation was accomplished by a variant of the Conlisk–Watts model but with a disproportionate number

Table 5.2. *Overall sample design of the Gary Experiment*

Treatment group	Guarantee level	Tax rate	Husband present	Husband absent	Total sample
			Type of family		
Experimental	Poverty level	40%	81	122	20
		60%	76	122	19
	0.75 poverty level	40%	136	177	31
		60%	110	204	31
	All	All	403	625	1,02
Control	—	—	326	445	77
Total	—	—	729	1,070	1,79

Source: Kenneth C. Kehrer et al., *The Gary Income Maintenance Experiment Design, Administration, and Data Files* (Mathematica Policy Research, Augu 1975), p. 34.

of very-low-income families in the less generous treatment plans in order to minimize the cost of the experiment. This allocation was supplemented with additional subsamples from families with income above the break-even level. A number of control families were added who were to be interviewed less often than the regular control group in order to investigate the presence of any Hawthorne effect due to the frequent interviews.

Of the families that were enrolled, nearly three hundred dropped out of the study before it was over. This attrition rate was much higher for families in the control group than for those in the experimental groups, as might be expected, the figures being 23 percent and 12 percent, respectively. Attrition also was clearly and inversely related to the generosity of the treatment, varying from 3 percent for those on the $4,300-40 percent tax rate plan to nearly 20 percent on the $3,300-60 percent tax rate.

Equally noteworthy is the number of families for whom sufficient information was obtained to serve as the basis for analysis of labor supply response. A comparison of these two sets of figures (Table 5.3) shows that this base represented only about 54 percent of the families that were enrolled originally. Moreover, there are substantial

Table 5.3. *Comparison of number of families in original sample and number in analysis sample, Gary Experiment*

Group	Initial sample	Analysis sample	Analysis sample as % of initial
Husband present			
Experimental	403	207	51
Control	326	129	40
Subtotal	729	336	46
Husband absent			
Experimental	625	371	59
Control	445	257	58
Subtotal	1,070	628	59
Total	1,799	964	54

Source: Kehrer et al., *Gary Income Maintenance Experiment*, pp. 34, 49, 66.

differences between the experimental and the control groups and between families with and without a husband present. Families with the husband present were especially likely to drop out, particularly if the family was in the control group. For that category, only 40 percent of the initial families provided the information needed for analysis. Families headed by a female were more cooperative, with more of them providing information and with little difference in the attrition rate between the experimental and the control groups. Even there, however, over 40 percent had to be dropped in the analysis of labor supply response.

The sample for the Rural Experiment was the smallest of all, only 800 families scattered over one county in North Carolina (Duplin County) and two counties in Iowa (Pocahontas and Calhoun counties). These two areas were selected to represent the widespread poverty conditions present in the South, on the one hand, and the scattered poverty in the prosperous Midwest, on the other hand. Not only was the sample smaller to begin with, but it was weakened further for analytical purposes by including both farm and nonfarm households and also, apparently at the insistence of OEO, by including female heads and aged heads. The result was an initial sample of 587 rural, two-parent working families, only about half of which were farm families.

Sample selection was carried out by application of the Conlisk–Watts model, using three categories of family heads (males 58 or under, females 58 or under, and older heads) stratified by five treatment combinations and the control group and further stratified by three income levels and the two locations.[3]

The result of this sample selection process was that more than half of the participants were in the control group. Thus, of the 587 families in the sample headed by a male under 58 years of age, 54 percent were assigned to the control group. The remaining 269 families were assigned to five treatment combinations, the largest number to the middle treatment combination (having a guarantee level of 75 percent and a tax rate of 50 percent).

In the field operations, as with the other experiments, a far higher number of families had to be contacted before the required number of eligible families could be enrolled. Thus, to enroll 512 eligible families (with incomes less than 150 percent of the 1968–9 poverty level for the particular family size) in North Carolina required that nearly 4,000 families be contacted; in Iowa, 8,300 dwelling units had to be contacted before 335 eligible families were enrolled. Even then, later interviews indicated that many of the original income estimates were faulty, so much so that 38 percent of the Iowa families and 20 percent of the North Carolina families had incomes above the prescribed maximum of 150 percent of poverty.

On the other hand, the Rural Experiment was quite successful at retaining families in the program. Of the 809 families enrolled, only 83 had dropped out by the time the experiment had ended three years later.

In the Denver–Seattle Experiment, there were 84 experimental cells, that is, combinations of support levels, tax rates, time in the experiment, and training subsidies.[4] In addition, four stratification variables were used in the sample design – location, race, structure of the family, and time in the experiment. Two locations were chosen,

Denver as an example of a fairly tight labor market and Seattle as an example of a soft labor market, though one is similar to the other in terms of demographic characteristics and sociocultural background of the population. In both cities, blacks were singled out as a separate stratum as were Mexican-Americans in Denver. Family structure had only two classifications – whether or not the family contained a couple (married or otherwise). Eligibility was restricted to families with heads between the ages of 18 and 58. The time of the experiment was an important stratifying variable because of its effect on costs, and this was allowed for by allocating a predetermined proportion of the budget for the three-year group and for the five-year group.

The result of this stratification process was a set of 20 strata. Within these strata, families were allocated to experimental treatments by a nonlinear programming model that sought to allocate families with the objective of maximizing the amount of information obtained for the given budget. In this assignment process, allowance was made for differing income levels, partly to have families at different incomes included in the experiment and partly because this is a key element in determining the benefits that families are likely to receive and hence the cost of the experiment.[5] This allocation, with some further adjustments, resulted in 1,012 black families in each of the two cities, 1,156 white families in each city, and 866 Mexican-American families in Denver, for a total of 5,202. Of this number, about 80 percent were in some treatment group, and the other fifth were in the control group. About half of those in the treatment groups, however, were covered only by the manpower program.

As with the other experiments, the selection of the sample and sample allocation process was much more difficult than had been anticipated. Original estimates of the number of housing units in each city that would have to be listed and contacted turned out to be too low, and supplementary listing and screening procedures had to be instituted.[6] Even then, insufficient eligible families were obtained for particular cells, such as black, two-parent, higher-income families, and other cells were overenrolled, such as Chicano, one-parent, low-income families. In addition, not all the families assigned to the experiment could be enrolled, partly because of refusals and partly because of noncontacts and moves out of the area. As a result, only 2,042 families were enrolled in Seattle, 2,758 families in Denver.

These families represented about 5 percent of the total housing units contacted at the start of the process. The extent to which families were eliminated or dropped out at different stages is shown in Table 5.4. As is evident from this table, the experience in the two cities was very different, largely because in Seattle about 37 percent of the families were screened out as ineligible in the field, a procedure that was not followed in Denver. In that city, the main screening work was done in the office before families were selected for the lengthy preexperimental interviews that sought to establish conclusively the eligibility of the families for the experiment.

The ultimate result seems to have been fairly similar in the two cities, at least in terms of completion rates. As in the other experiments, the final sample represents a very small proportion of the total number of housing units originally contacted, only 5 percent. Although many of those families would not have been eligible anyway, the fact remains that, of the initial families, about one-fourth in Seattle and 15 percent in Denver were refusals, and still more families

Table 5.4. *Summary of sample selection process in Seattle–Denver Experiment*

Stage	Seattle	Denver	Total
Housing units listed	36,024	57,827	93,851
Completed screening interviews	10,126	39,668	49,794
Selected for preexperimental interview	6,981	7,350	14,331
Completed preexperimental interview	4,815	4,683	9,498
Assigned to treatment	2,542	3,361	5,903
Enrolled	2,042	2,758	4,800

Source: Mararka and Spiegelman, *Sample Selection in Seattle and Denver Experiments*, p. 56.

either refused or could not be located at the preexperimental and final assignment stages.

Administration and implementation

The administrative arrangements for the Gary Experiment were very similar to those for the New Jersey Experiment. Families in both the experimental and control groups were required to file monthly reports on income and changes in household composition for which they were paid $10, except for families receiving treatment payments of $10 or more.

The payment formula included an allowance for a six-month carry-over of income in excess of the break-even level. The amount of this carry-over was recalculated every month, and one-sixth multiplied by the tax rate was subtracted from the payment to be made to the family in the following month.

More comprehensive information about the families in this experiment was obtained by means of eight regular interviews during the experimental period (one every four months) and a final interview after the experiment was over. These interviews sought detailed information on labor force participation, school attendance, health, and other aspects of family life and included a set of questions on social-psychological attitudes. Attempts were made to interview every family member over the age of 15, and payments for the interviews were geared to this basis. The payment varied during the experiment but in the final stage was $10 for the interview with the key family member (the one who filed income reports) and $2.50 for each other member interviewed.

The administration of the Gary Experiment followed the same general pattern as that of the New Jersey Experiment. A separate Northwest Council for Families (NCF) was set up to handle the transfer payments; it was assisted by Urban Developmental Services, which looked after the day care and social service arrangements. The monthly report forms were submitted and processed by NCF. The more intensive interviews were carried out by another separate agency, Calumet Research Associates, operating independently of NCF and staffed with indigenous interviewers.[7]

Of special interest from an administrative point of view are the studies undertaken to ascertain the extent of understanding by the Gary families of the income maintenance plan. These studies indicated that the families seemed very knowledgeable about the rules regarding eligibility but did not seem to be very well aware of the mechanics of the income maintenance plan or of such key aspects as the implicit tax rate and the support level.[8] In view of this widespread ignorance, a question can be raised as to whether the behavior of the participants was guided by a clear understanding of the particular plan in which they were enrolled.

Reporting arrangements for the Rural Experiment were similar to those of the New Jersey and Gary experiments. Families in the experimental treatments were required to file monthly income reports and were paid biweekly on the basis of these reports. Control families were requested to file a monthly report on their current address, for which they were paid. In addition, all families were interviewed every quarter to obtain labor force and other information about each individual in the family.

In the treatment of income, however, the guidelines used in the Rural Experiment were different from those of New Jersey or Gary. A major difference was the handling of self-employment income, particularly farm income. Such forms of income involve special characteristics of their own, including the use of property for earning income. For this reason, the definition of income was modified to include the imputed rental value for homeowners as well as rent-free housing in the case of farmers not owning their property. In addition, in the case of farmers and others with assets, 10 percent of net capital wealth (with some deductions) was added to income, on the premise that ownership of such wealth contributes to the production of income.[9] Further, to correct for tax advantages, accelerated depreciation and the investment tax credit were not allowed for farmers and other self-employed. In addition, to deal with the uneven flow of farm income during the year, a one-month accounting period was used but with a 12-month carry-over that allowed income above (below) the break-even level to be carried forward and added to (subtracted from) income received in any of 12 subsequent months in the future in which the family's income was below (above) the break-even level.

Income was to be reported on a cash basis. Applied to farmers, this approach led to numerous difficulties because it became apparent to everyone concerned that by suitable manipulation of the sale of their products the farmers in the experiment could reap substantial gains. That they did so, especially the more knowledgeable group of Iowa farmers, is all too evident from the analytical results.[10]

Indeed, from an operational point of view, by all indications the administration of this experiment seems to have been a highly frustrating experience. On the one hand, one group in the experiment seemed so aware and knowledgeable of the rules that it is not clear who was experimenting on whom, and on the other hand, another group in the experiment, the rural families in North Carolina, failed to understand some of the basic rules even after special instruction.[11] Perhaps for this reason and perhaps because of the nature of the income report, self-employment (including farm) income and farm assets seem to have been substantially underreported, though the data on wages and salary earnings seem to have been reported fairly accurately.

Findings

In general, the labor response of the families in these other experiments has been roughly similar to that found in the New Jersey Experiment. The evidence is that a negative income tax has a negative effect on the labor market response of the participants, the effect being relatively moderate on the main wage earner of the household and more substantial on secondary earners. In the case of the main wage earner (invariably husbands), hours worked as well as employment status are hardly affected at all in the Rural Experiment but decline noticeably in the Gary and Denver–Seattle experiments. In view of questions that can be raised about the reliability of the data obtained in the Rural Experiment, the results from the other two experiments warrant greater attention.

In the Gary Experiment, significant reductions were found in the employment status and hours worked not only of husbands but also of female heads and wives. The reduction in the case of the husbands was fairly moderate, about 5 percent in employment status and 6.5 percent in hours worked, with a roughly equal effect for female heads. The larger effect for female heads may reflect the fact that employment conditions in Gary during the period of that experiment seem to have been worse than employment conditions during the New Jersey Experiment; because jobs were not easily available, especially part-time jobs, an income guarantee was especially likely to induce female-headed households to reduce their labor market participation. On the other hand, there was virtually no effect on the labor market participation or the hours worked of wives.[12]

Further analysis suggests that the effect of the negative income tax on employment varies with the position of the participants (in this case, the husbands). Those above the break-even point for receiving benefits tend to have a reduced probability of being employed full-time in response to increases in the guarantee effect, which is not true of those below the break-even point. On the other hand, the latter group had a reduced probability of being employed in response to increases in the tax rate, which was not true of those above the break-even point. On balance, however, the effect seems to be reduced overall employment because of the rather substantial apparent effect of the guarantee on those above the break-even point.[13]

Reductions in labor supply were especially apparent in the Denver–Seattle Experiment. A longitudinal analysis, allowing for adjustments of the participants to the treatment variables over time, finds that the long-run effects of these treatments would be to reduce the hours of work of husbands by 9 percent, that of wives by 20 percent, and that of female heads of families by 25 percent.[14] Interestingly enough, estimates of the speed of adjustment to these treatments range from 2.5 years for the husbands to nearly 5 years for the female heads. As might be expected, more substantial reductions in working time took place in families with young children, though rather surprisingly the reduction was apparent not only for wives and female heads but also for husbands.

As in the New Jersey Experiment, significant differences in the labor response were found by ethnic group. Unlike that situation, however, the reduction in hours worked by the black and Spanish-American household members was appreciably greater than that for the white households. Moreover, the reduction in hours worked by husbands in Denver was more than twice as large as in Seattle (even after adjustment for the different ethnic composition of the population in the two cities), which may have reflected the looser labor market situation in Denver.

Especially interesting from an experimental and a policy point of view is the fact that the response of all three groups (husbands, wives, and female heads) was appreciably larger for those in the five-year program than for those in the three-year program. This clearly implies that a three-year experiment may not be long enough to yield unbiased estimates of the long-run effect of a negative income tax program and that possibly the effects of such a program may be even larger than are indicated from the data for the five-year groups.

Also noteworthy is the fact that participation in the labor force was especially sensitive to the support level and to the tax rate, the rate of participation increasing with the former and decreasing with the latter.[15]

Results for other aspects of the life style of the participants were mixed. In the Rural Experiment, no significant effects were detected for health, fertility, and marital dissolution. School performance, however, of the children of the participants improved in North Carolina (where there was the greatest room for improvement) but not in Iowa. In the Gary Experiment, experimental families were more likely to reduce medical debt and to increase expenditures on clothing, medicine, and automobile repairs; they were more likely to purchase homes if they did move; they used social services less frequently; and the male teenagers in these families were more likely to continue their high school education rather than go to work.[16] Also, less than 5 percent of the eligible families made use of the day care subsidy, though there was some tendency for the rate of utilization to increase with the size of the subsidy and to be larger for the group for which there was no work requirement.

In the Denver–Seattle Experiment, reimbursement of half of all training costs induced a greater than 40 percent increase in schooling among male heads and an even stronger response by the wives of the male heads and by female single-headed households.[17] Another apparent effect was higher mobility.[18] Still another effect was the tendency for families receiving income maintenance payments to leave subsidized housing, a tendency especially noticeable among families with female heads.[19] Evidently the increase in the level of income leads these families to seek other types of housing.

Especially interesting, and somewhat puzzling, are the findings of these experiments with respect to marital stability. Though the other income maintenance experiments find little significant effect of participation in such a plan on marital dissolution, fairly strong effects are found in the Denver–Seattle Experiment, where the rate of marital dissolution increased among the experimental families for all three ethnic groups, though particularly for black families and for white families. The effect was more substantial, however, for families in the less generous plans than in the more generous plans and also tended to be larger when the wife was not working than when she was.

After further work, the researchers suggest that this strange pattern may represent the averaging of two diverse effects. On the one hand, there seems to be an income effect, meaning that the increased income made possible by the plan acts to stabilize the marriage by reducing economic pressures. On the other hand, there seems to be a countervailing independence effect, meaning that the increased income makes the members of the couple (particularly the wife) less dependent on the marriage and better able to manage economically on their own.[20] Moreover, the independence effect tends to dominate at low support levels and the income effect at high support levels, which is why the effect of the treatments is greater at low support levels.[21]

A not inconsequential factor also may be that, as the researchers point out, participation in a negative income tax program tends to remove the stigma of receiving welfare and hence also serves to make the members of the couple (again, especially the wife) less dependent if they are not satisfied with the marriage. Still, these findings remain highly controversial.

Evaluative comments

Having had the benefit of the experience of the New Jersey Experiment, the three later negative income tax experiments included a number of tests to explore different sources of bias on labor supply response and to investigate whether this response might be altered by other types of variables, such as day care and special training programs. It was for this reason that such experiments were incorporated as varying the time horizon and varying the tax rates.

These experiments have provided much additional information about the factors influencing labor supply response. In addition, the broadened coverage of these experiments served to extend their applicability to more segments of the low-income population, demonstrating that the same general pattern of results held for these other groups, with the notable exception of farmers.

The benefits of the New Jersey experience notwithstanding, these experiments are still subject to much the same set of limitations as that experiment. As with the New Jersey Experiment, the participants in each case constituted a small fraction of the housing units selected initially, with further reduction of sample size as a result of mortality. Moreover, the dispersion of the sample among families of different types meant that the sample size for the analysis was at times so small as to raise serious doubts as to whether really meaningful results could be obtained; this was especially true for the Rural Experiment.

It is in the Rural Experiment that the most serious questions arise with regard to the reliability of the data obtained from the participants. As noted earlier, the labor supply response of the farmers was contrary to most expectations and was, if anything, in line with what would be expected if they were seeking to maximize their returns from the experimental treatments. Ironically, this is the one group that seems to have understood all the rules of the experiment, and, perhaps not unrelatedly, there was ample evidence that the financial data reported by this group were greatly distorted.

For the very opposite reason, a question can be raised about the meaningfulness of the labor supply responses of the wage-earning households in the Rural and other experiments, because the understanding of those participants of the rules relating to the income guarantee, the tax rates, and the break-even level was apparently quite poor. Hence, the labor supply results obtained in these experiments may represent not only understatement of the average response but also understatement of the elasticity of the response with respect to these other variables. This is especially so because if this income maintenance program were put on a continuing national basis the rules relating to it would receive wide publicity in the media, and understanding of these rules would undoubtedly be much more widespread than in the case of these experiments.

One problem of social experiments that was further highlighted in the present instance is the sensitivity of the results to the method by which the experiment is administered. Observation of the operation of these experiments suggests that fully important as the tax rate and the guarantee level may be such parameters as the accounting system, the nature of the carry-over provision to allow for fluctuations in income, and the frequency of payment of benefits. To judge by the experience of the Rural Experiment, these factors are especially critical in dealing with the self-employed. Indeed, in the case of farmers and others who may have appreciable gross assets but low income, one may well question the significance of the income data (even if accurately reported) as a measure of economic well-being. For these groups, a very different concept of poverty may be needed. Even for wage-earning families, however, for whom income is a more meaningful measure of welfare, it is entirely possible that the labor supply response to a negative income tax could vary substantially as the method of administration is altered.

Although no experiments of this type were undertaken in connection with the NIT studies, economists have started to look into the application of the techniques of social experimentation to measuring the effect of these administrative operations. An interesting such experiment was carried out in Denver County, Colorado, in 1976 for the Department of Health, Education, and Welfare by Mathematica Policy Research and the Colorado Department of Social Services.

The focus of this experiment was the effect of a monthly reporting system as a substitute for the usual procedure of having families report their financial position and current needs every six months (every three months for families where the head was unemployed). This monthly reporting system also incorporated retrospective reporting of income for the past month and a highly automated administrative support system. The experiment was applied to a random sample of about 1,200 AFDC recipients (roughly 10 percent of the total case load in the area), with a control group of the same size treated in the usual manner. The results indicated the monthly reporting system to be much more responsive to the needs of the welfare recipients but with a possible increase in administrative costs of as high as 10 percent.[22] This monthly reporting system has since been implemented for the entire county, though without any further experimental aspects.

6

Labor force experiments

This chapter covers two labor force–related programs. They are billed as demonstration projects, but the use of control groups justifies their being classified as social experiments under the definition used in this volume. In the sense that each seeks to ascertain how well a particular social program might work, they are indeed demonstration projects. In the sense that they provide for the use of control groups and comparison of experimental groups with control groups, however, they can also be classified under the rubric of an experiment.

The two programs are covered together in this chapter because both focus on upgrading the quality of the labor force, both are under the direction of the same organization, and, partly for the preceding reasons, both have characteristics very much in common. In one case, the Supported Work Program, the focus is on an attempt to keep in the labor force people who are otherwise hard to employ; in the other case, the Youth Entitlement Program, an attempt is being made to see whether disadvantaged youth can be induced to stay in school if they are provided with guaranteed employment. Each of these programs is described separately, but because of their common characteristics they are evaluated jointly in the final section of this chapter.

Supported Work Program
Background

The objective of the Supported Work Program was to ascertain whether people who traditionally are hard to employ can be trained both technically and psychologically for regular employment. Launched in 1974, the program was carried out by the specially formed Manpower Demonstration Research Corporation, set up with the assistance of five federal agencies and the Ford Foundation.[1]

The basic idea was to help these people become accustomed to holding down a regular job by putting them in a work environment in which they have continual support getting used to job routines and work ethics.

> The concept on which Supported Work is based is simple: some people, because of the workings of the economy and the labor market, because of inadequate motivation or training, or because of the reluctance or discrimination of employers, have never been able to make a successful connection with the world of work. They haven't the habit of work, the discipline, however rudimentary, to get to work on time and remain there all day, or the education or skills or confidence to claim employment in a competitive society. Supported work offers such people two things: a job and the opportunity to make good in it, and a chance to gain permanent employment.[2]

The focus of the program was on four groups that have had very high unemployment rates – AFDC women, out-of-school youth, former drug addicts, and recent ex-offenders. (Alcoholics were also included in one of these projects, and people who were mentally ill in another.) The program began operation in early 1975 with 13 different projects and was extended by the end of the second year, July 31, 1977, to 15 different cities and rural areas. The field aspects of the program lasted from March 1975 through December 1978.

The manner in which the Supported Work Program was set up and its operations are examined in the following sections with focus on the design of the program, on the training of the workers and selection of the project, on the selection of the participants in the program, on the evaluative aspects, and on the results.

Design

As noted previously, the basic objective of the program was to provide an atmosphere within which the participants were placed in a work environment and given support as they adjusted to the routine of a regular job. This "supported work" environment was provided by means of three special characteristics of the job, namely, peer support, graduated stress, and close supervision. These ideas were implemented in a number of ways. Peer support was provided by having the participants work as part of a small team of between four and seven people, one of the group being the supervisor or crew chief. This group concept was reinforced by arranging for periodic meetings of the team, sometimes social meetings, and by attempting to provide a team spirit in getting the work done. Some of the programs provided incentives in the form of bonuses or a free lunch for the team that did the best job in a particular period.

To acclimate the participants to the demands and the routines of a regular job, a flexible approach was taken toward work rules and job requirements. Much greater tolerance was shown toward errors and mistakes when a participant was new in the program than when the individual had been in it for several months. Work rules were tightened gradually, so that work effectiveness and punctuality could increase over time. Bonuses were offered by some programs for good productivity or for regular attendance. The participants were allowed time off (without pay) for personal problems. When participants had to be disciplined, this was done in less serious ways than firing, if possible. Attempts were made simply to suspend them in the hope that they would straighten out.[3]

The third concept of supported work, close supervision, was carried out by using supervisors with experience in dealing with that type of participant, in addition to those with the necessary technical and teaching skills. Where possible, supervisors and participants had similar racial and social backgrounds. In some programs, however, the participants worked for outside agencies, in which cases the supervisor might not have had the desired background. In those instances, attempts were made to have the program supervisor keep in touch with the participants through orientation sessions and other types of meetings.

A key aspect of the Supported Work Program was that all participants had to be terminated at the end of 12 or 18 months, depending on the particular project, whether or not they had found a job or some other type of gainful activity. The choice of the termination date was left up to the individual projects, eight of which chose a 12-month termination, six an 18-month termination, and one a combination of the two.

How were such supported work programs formed? The projects were set up at each site individually with the aid of the Manpower Demonstration Research Corporation (MDRC) and the sponsoring organizations. Each project was incorporated as a separate enterprise with the requirement that funds provided for the operation of the enterprise equal at least one-fourth of the total in the first year and one-half in the second year. The nature of the sponsoring agencies of these projects, their locations, and the type of people covered in the program are indicated in Table 6.1. The type of work undertaken varied considerably with the local conditions and with the type of people in the particular program. AFDC recipients (entirely women) were more likely to be engaged in clerical and general service-type activities (frequently building maintenance operations), whereas the other target groups (mostly men) were more likely to be engaged in construction and manufacturing-type activities.

All of the programs were relatively small operations, varying in size from 100 to 300 participants. Most of the programs engaged in a variety of different activities, as shown in Table 6.2. Service activities were generally the principal source of employment, this sector accounting for over half of all project work and for the primary source at 10 of the 15 sites. The two sectors of services and construction combined accounted for over four-fifths of the total project days and were the dominant sources of employment at every site.

Where did the business come from for these programs? The bulk

Table 6.1. *MDRC Supported Work Demonstration sites*

Location	Sponsoring agency	Target group(s)
Atlanta	Atlanta Urban League	AFDC, youth
Chicago	Options, Inc.[a]	ex-addicts, ex-offenders, alcoholics
Detroit	Supported Work Corporation[a]	ex-addicts, ex-offenders
Hartford	Maverick Corporation[a]	AFDC, ex-offenders, youth
Jersey City	Community Help Corporation[a]	ex-addicts, ex-offenders, youth, alcoholics
Massachusetts	Transitional Employment Enterprises[a]	AFDC, ex-offenders, youth, alcoholics
Newark	Newark Service Corporation[a]	AFDC, ex-offenders
New York City	Wildcat Service Corporation[a]	AFDC, youth
Oakland (Alameda County)	Peralta Service Corporation[a]	AFDC, ex-addicts, ex-offenders
Philadelphia	Impact Services Corporation[a]	ex-addicts, ex-offenders, youth
St. Louis	St. Louis Housing Authority	AFDC
San Francisco	San Francisco Phoenix Corporation[a]	ex-offenders
Washington State	Pivot	ex-offenders
West Virginia (5 counties in northwest area of state)	Human Resource Development Foundation	AFDC, ex-offenders, youth

Table 6.1. *(cont.)*

Location	Sponsoring agency	Target group(s)
Wisconsin (Fond du Lac & Winnebago counties)	Advocap, Inc.	AFDC, youth, mentally disabled

[a]Nonprofit agency established specifically for this project.
Source: MDRC, *Second Annual Report*, p. x.

of it, nearly half, came from public agencies, such as cities and school districts, though the actual percentage of such business varied, in the second year of the program, from as low as 13 percent in San Francisco to over 90 percent in New York City. Another fourth of the business came from private nonprofit agencies such as YMCAs, and YWCAs, and community centers, much of this work involving clerical activities or building maintenance work. A variety of activities was also carried out for private individuals and private firms, including operating gasoline stations, working in production plants, working in hotels, operating cafeterias, and doing subcontract work relating to packaging and assembly operations.

Even so, these projects did not become self-sustaining operations. Funds from MDRC did decline as a proportion of total costs of the local programs, from 59 percent in the initial year to 42 percent in the final (fourth) year. Income from the sale of goods and services rose from 13 percent in the first year to only 17 percent in the fourth year, with funds from the Comprehensive Employment and Training Act (CETA) and other local sources accounting for the principal increase.[4] By the fourth year, further offsets to costs from the sale of goods and services did not seem likely. The projects could not easily expand in the same line of work without getting into serious competition with established organizations (and with union rules); nor was it easy to diversify further, because to do so would have taken more highly skilled personnel than was available to them.

Table 6.2. *Percentage distribution of project days in major industries, 1975–1978*

Site	Agriculture, land-scaping	Construction	Manufacturing	Transportation, communication	Retail & wholesale trade	Services	Total	Total projects days
Atlanta		14.7	7.9		0.7	76.7	100.0	45,099
Chicago	0.2	35.4	10.3	13.8		40.3	100.0	79,178
Detroit	4.7	62.9	0.9		0.1	31.3	99.9	17,990
Hartford	2.7	25.8	20.4	4.2	3.4	43.5	100.0	91,706
Jersey City		38.7	5.1	12.3	12.0	31.9	100.0	111,447
Massachusetts		57.8	17.4		1.3	23.4	99.9	49,140
New York	0.3	2.3		0.1	0.9	96.3	99.9	80,888
Newark	1.3	7.3	8.3	0.2	3.4	79.6	100.1	87,827
Oakland	21.1	37.7	3.8	6.7	11.9	18.8	100.0	61,843
Philadelphia	15.6	59.9	0.7		1.4	22.4	100.0	47,261
St. Louis		6.3		2.9	21.4	69.4	100.0	28,684
San Francisco	6.1	37.7		6.1	5.1	45.1	100.1	21,978
Washington State	1.0	18.9	33.1			46.9	99.9	34,147
West Virginia	5.2	16.4	2.5	6.2		69.4	99.7	54,440
Wisconsin	0.6	40.7	0.9	1.4	1.1	55.2	99.9	49,529
All sites	3.5	28.3	7.8	4.5	4.2	51.7	100.0	861,157

Source: Adapted from Manpower Demonstration Research Corporation, *Summary and Findings of the National Supported Work Demonstration* (Cambridge, Mass.: Ballinger, 1980), Table 2.3, p. 25.

Participants

Approximately 10,000 people passed through the Supported Work Program in its four years. About 38 percent of this number were ex-offenders, 20 percent women previously on AFDC, 12 percent ex-addicts, and 23 percent youth dropouts from school. Data compiled for the first two years show that most of these participants were quite young (under 30 years of age), mostly male (except for the AFDC component, which was all female), heavily black, not married, and that they frequently had one or more dependents (which is true of the AFDC group by definition) and had not graduated from high school, as shown in Table 6.3.

For admission into the program participants had to meet various criteria, which, however, do not seem to have been imposed overly strictly.[5] Thus, AFDC women were required to have been receiving welfare payments for the past three years and to be currently unemployed, with the youngest child six years of age or more. Ex-addicts were required to have worked no more than three months in a regular job in the past six months, to have been in some drug treatment program in the past six months, and to be 18 years of age or more. Ex-offenders were required to be currently unemployed, to be 18 years of age or more, and to have been incarcerated in the past six months. Youth participants were required to be between the ages of 17 and 20, to be unemployed, to have a delinquency record, and either not to have completed high school or not to have been in school in the past six months.

Though these criteria may have been followed as general guidelines, they were not used in every individual case, apparently partly because of the enthusiasm of the referral agencies for placing participants in the program. In fact, this is how most participants came into the program. Thus, members of the AFDC group were referred primarily by the local welfare agencies, ex-offenders by criminal justice agencies, ex-addicts by drug addiction services, and youth and others by county and local agencies.[6]

These various criteria and referral procedures were meant to assure that the population considered for supported work was essentially

Table 6.3. *Percentage distribution of demographic characteristics of employees in supported work programs through June 1977, by target group*

	Percentage distribution and average by target group					
Characteristic	AFDC	Ex-offenders	Ex-addicts	Youth	Other[a]	All groups
Age at enrollment						
17 through 20 yrs.	1.5	13.6	4.3	92.7	7.7	23.5
21 through 30 yrs.	39.5	66.3	68.6	7.3	50.1	50.1
31 through 40 yrs.	39.8	14.4	20.2	0.0	19.2	17.8
41 through 50 yrs.	16.3	4.6	6.3	0.0	12.8	6.8
51 yrs. and older	3.0	1.2	0.6	0.0	10.1	1.8
Total	100.0	100.0	100.0	100.0	100.0	100.0
Average age at enrollment	33.4	26.7	28.4	18.7	32.0	27.2
Sex						
Male	0.0	91.9	82.8	85.1	77.5	71.3
Female	100.0	8.1	17.2	14.9	22.5	28.7
Total	100.0	100.0	100.0	100.0	100.0	100.0
Race						
White	15.2	28.6	16.1	37.5	83.8	29.6
Black	78.9	63.2	75.7	54.4	13.6	63.0
Other	5.9	8.2	8.3	8.1	2.7	7.4
Total	100.0	100.0	100.0	100.0	100.0	100.0
Spanish-American heritage						
Yes	15.2	10.3	11.7	18.7	2.9	12.4
No	84.8	89.7	88.3	81.3	97.1	87.6
Total	100.0	100.0	100.0	100.0	100.0	100.0

Marital status						
Currently married	22.1	22.6	37.9	6.3	21.2	21.8
Currently not married	77.9	77.4	62.1	93.7	78.8	78.2
Total	100.0	100.0	100.0	100.0	100.0	100.0
Average number of dependents	2.7	1.0	1.8	0.5	0.6	1.3
Housing						
Living in public housing	42.3	20.6	13.9	24.7	5.1	23.4
Not living in public housing	57.7	79.4	86.1	75.3	94.9	76.6
Total	100.0	100.0	100.0	100.0	100.0	100.0
Highest educational degree received						
None	58.8	51.8	52.3	96.5	42.3	60.4
High school	33.5	35.8	38.4	2.1	42.6	30.3
GED	6.6	10.9	8.4	1.4	9.4	8.0
Trade/vocational	0.9	0.3	0.3	0.0	2.7	0.5
College	0.3	1.1	0.6	0.0	3.0	0.8
Postgraduate	0.0	0.1	0.0	0.0	0.0	0.0
Total	100.0	100.0	100.0	100.0	100.0	100.0
Average highest grade completed	7.9	8.7	8.4	7.7	9.4	8.4
Base	1,007	2,235	831	966	377	5,417

[a] The "other" target group includes ex-alcoholics (Jersey City and Massachusetts) and mentally disabled (Wisconsin) employees and a small number of people who were employed prior to the supported work demonstration.

Source: MDRC, *Second Annual Report,* p. 7.

really difficult to employ in the sense that they were not skilled, did not have work experience, and were poorly educated. Comparison of participants in the Supported Work Program with those in firms funded by CETA and by the Work Incentive Program indicated that in terms of earnings and employment history these people were at least as fully qualified as those in the other programs.[7]

Performance evaluation

The effectiveness of the Supported Work Program was evaluated in a number of ways. The success of the program for the participants was evaluated partly by studying the participants themselves, partly by comparing their postprogram experiences with those of participants in similar programs, and partly by comparing their experience with that of a control group. In addition, a benefit–cost analysis was undertaken of the entire Supported Work Program, as well as a "detailed process analysis" to examine the relative effectiveness of the different components of the programs and to study each program to ascertain how local actions may have influenced the program's success or failure.

Though not all of these evaluations have been completed at this writing, certain initial findings are clear. Judging by experience data, a little over 30 percent of the participants left the program on a positive note, that is, as a rule, for a new job but sometimes to return to school, as shown in Table 6.4. This was most frequently true of the AFDC women (36 percent) and least frequently of the ex-addicts (25 percent). About 45 percent of the participants were either fired or let go for some other reason, something that was characteristic of only 18 percent of the AFDC group but of over half of the other three groups. On the other hand, nearly a fourth of the group left because they had exhausted their time of service and had to leave even though they did not have a job or for some other "neutral" reason; this was true of about 45 percent of the AFDC women. Clearly, the restriction of the length of service to 12 or 18 months was a major factor in causing members of this group to leave.

Interestingly enough, of those who left the Supported Work Program for a job, more than half had found the jobs themselves. This

Table 6.4. *Participation and distribution of participants by types of departures, Supported Work Program, by target group*

Item	AFDC	Ex-addicts	Ex-offenders	Youth	Other[a]	Total
Attendance rate (%)	89.8	83.9	80.3	75.8	85.6	83.0
Average length of participation (months)	9.5	6.8	5.2	6.8	7.6	6.7
Distribution of departures by type (%) [b]						
Firings	10.9	37.3	32.5	37.2	26.0	29.7
Other negative terminations	7.5	14.6	20.0	16.1	7.6	15.4
Mandatory graduation	24.8	10.7	4.1	5.3	7.7	9.3
Other neutral terminations	20.8	12.3	12.2	12.6	18.6	14.0
Terminations to school	1.5	1.9	2.3	3.0	6.2	2.5
Terminations to a job	34.6	23.1	28.9	25.8	33.9	28.9
Total	100.1	99.9	100.0	100.0	100.0	99.8

[a]The "other" target group is composed primarily of ex-alcoholics (Jersey City and Massachusetts) and mentally disabled employees (Wisconsin).
[b]"Other negative" departures include incarcerations, reinstitutionalizations, and resignations because of dissatisfaction with the supported work job. "Mandatory graduations" are departures that occur when supported workers reach the maximum allowable length of stay in the program without having found postprogram employment. "Other neutral" departures include such things as death and resignations for reasons of personal or family health problems. Percentage distributions may not add exactly to 100 because of rounding.
Source: MDRC, *Summary and Findings*, p. 36.

was much less likely to be true of AFDC women, nearly three-quarters of whom were placed through arrangements made by the Supported Work Program or an outside agency. In many respects, the AFDC women and the ex-offenders seemed to take to the program in very different ways. The former were likely to be more reliable and more stable and to stay in the program for a relatively long time (about 10 months on the average) but not to be very innovative in finding jobs. The latter showed much more initiative but were also more independent, were more likely to get into trouble, stayed in the program for a much shorter time (about five months on the average), but were also most likely to find jobs for themselves.[8]

The job placement experience of those in the Supported Work Program did not seem much different from that of those in the various CETA programs, in each instance somewhere between 25 and 30 percent of the participants leaving for regular employment.[9] Comparisons are difficult, however, because the programs have somewhat different objectives, and the Supported Work Program seems to have focused on a more disadvantaged population.

A key aspect of the evaluation of the effectiveness of the Supported Work Program is whether the participants did significantly better than a control group. To this end, Mathematica Policy Research and the Institute for Research on Poverty of the University of Wisconsin were involved in the selection and monitoring of a control group against which to compare the performance of the participants of the program. This was accomplished by assigning eligible people alternately to the experiment group or the control group at 10 of the sites between April 1975 and July 1977. In total, 6,616 people were studied either as participants or as controls, subdivided by the four groups in the sample – AFDC women, ex-addicts, ex-offenders, and youths. The research program called for these people to be interviewed every nine months, with all members to be interviewed 18 months after the start of the program, some to be interviewed nine months later, and a smaller fraction to be interviewed nine months after that.

Because of the staggered times in which participants were selected for the research program and the limitations on resources, not all those in this evaluation were interviewed for the entire 36-month period. In fact, none of the AFDC subjects was given a 36-month interview because of the delayed start of the program with this group; also, only 774 interviews were made with the other three groups after 36 months, representing a response rate between 60 percent and 77 percent.[10] The base for analysis of the results on a longitudinal basis is even smaller, because continuous interviews over 36 months were obtained for less than 600 of the subjects in the three groups, including both participants and controls. Though much more data are available if the longitudinal analysis is restricted to four interviews (27 months), the validity of the comparisons drops sharply because these time intervals include the 12 to 18 months in which the participants could remain in the Supported Work Program, so that data for only a very short period of time are available to assess what happens to the participants after they leave the program.

With these reservations in mind, the preliminary results indicate that the Supported Work Program produced increases for the AFDC women in the rate of labor force participation, hours worked, and total earnings relative to those not in the program; a moderate increase for the ex-addict participants; and no noticeable effect in these employment indicators for the ex-offenders or the youth.[11] In addition, the program seems to have led to some reduction in the criminal activities of the ex-addicts, though not in their drug use, and seems to have had no effect in these respects for the ex-offenders or the youths in the program. A cost–benefit analysis based on these findings, extrapolating the benefits essentially unchanged for the AFDC women but declining at a rate of 50 percent every five years for the other three groups, indicates that such a program offers clear social benefits for the AFDC women and possibly for ex-addicts.[12] These estimates include allowances for reduced welfare costs as well as the saving to society in the possible reduction of criminal activities and drug treatment costs relating to the participants.

Though favorable results for even one group would seem encouraging, the validity of the findings remains to be established as a result of the skimpy and highly restricted nature of the research design.

Most disquieting is the fact that the one group for which clearly positive results are obtained, the AFDC women, is the one group for which interviews were obtained only over a 27-month period. Because members of this group tended to remain longest in the program and because they could remain up to 18 months, this means that for some unknown proportion of these women postprogram experience information is available for not much more than nine months. From the data available so far, it is not at all clear that the employment situation for this group had stabilized in this short time.[13]

Similar reservations apply to the analysis carried out for the other two groups. Extrapolation based on such short experience seems quite hazardous. Moreover, these results do not take into account possible differences that could have substantial effects.

The total cost of the Supported Work Program during its five years of existence was $82.4 million. The bulk of this amount, $66 million, was spent for the operating cost of the local programs. If we deduct revenues of these local programs, this works out to an average subsidy of $5,740 per participant. This subsidy varies from $4,455 per ex-offender to $8,139 per AFDC participant, primarily because the latter stayed in the program much longer than the former (9.5 months versus 5.2 months). The overall public subsidy per participant per year was actually about $13,000 for the first year of the program and then declined to $10,281 in the third and fourth years.[14]

Youth Entitlement Program
Background

In contrast to the Supported Work Program, the Youth Entitlement program sought to ascertain whether the guarantee of a job would induce disadvantaged youth to at least complete their high school education. The program was mandated by Congress, approved by President Carter in August 1977, launched in the first half of 1978, and ended in September 1980. Like the Supported Work Program, this program was managed by the Manpower Development Research Corporation. The selection of youths and arrangements for work were the responsibility of CETA sponsors in 17 locations.

Basic design

The operational success of this program depended to a large extent on the ability to provide disadvantaged youth with employment while at the same time verifying that they continued their education toward a high school diploma. The responsibility for carrying out this task was placed on selected agencies involved in the CETA program. In September 1977, the U.S. Department of Labor invited applications for the management of such a program from over 450 CETA sponsors. This led to the submission of 153 proposals, of which 17 were selected to receive Youth Entitlement Program grants. Seven of these programs, covering entire cities, were denoted as Tier I sites and received grants ranging from $8.5 million to $23 million to enroll between 3,000 and 8,000 teenagers each. The 10 smaller grants, Tier II sites, covered less populated areas or smaller portions of large cities and received between $750,000 and $1.25 million each to enroll between 200 and 1,000 teenagers.

It was the duty of the prime sponsor to recruit the teenagers for the program, establish their eligibility, arrange for the necessary jobs, maintain contact with the schools to verify continuously the eligibility of the participants, and otherwise manage the program in their area. To this end, the grants to the prime sponsors included not only the usual funds for program management but, in addition, authorization to subsidize up to the full cost of wages and fringe benefits for the youths. It was felt that in this way participation of private employers in the program would be encouraged, so that the private sector could be more heavily involved.

To be eligible for participation in the program, a youth had to:

1 be a resident of the designated entitlement area
2 be between 16 and 19 years of age
3 be a member of a family either receiving cash welfare assistance or having income at or below the poverty level
4 be enrolled in high school or a General Education Development (GED) program.[15]

A youth who was otherwise eligible but not in school could enroll in school and thereby establish eligibility. To remain in the program, the youth had to perform satisfactorily both in school and at work.

Recruitment

The procedure used by the different prime sponsors to recruit youth varied somewhat by site but especially by the type of efforts directed toward those in school and those out of school. By its very nature, the in-school recruitment effort could be better focused and generally involved the cooperation of the school systems, especially their guidance and employment services. Attempts to reach those out of school were based on media campaigns of various types as well as referrals from agencies that deal with such youths, such as neighborhood action groups, private youth service agencies, and local recreational and community centers. In fact, however, three-fifths of the youths enrolled in this program were recruited through the schools, as is shown in Table 6.5. As much as a fifth of the out-of-school participants were recruited through the school system. Friends, however, were the most important recruitment source for those out of school, accounting for more than a third of the total, and were followed by the school systems, the community organizations, and a variety of other sources.

Altogether, nearly 60,000 had been enrolled by August 31, 1979. Approximately 90 percent of these enrollees were at the larger, Tier I sites, and the remainder were at the Tier II sites. Further, approximately 90 percent of the enrollees were already in high school (or in an equivalent high school degree program), and only a small percentage were school dropouts. Not surprisingly, marked differences are evident in the characteristics of the enrollees who were in school and those who were out of school, as is evident from Table 6.6. Those in school were more likely to be 16 or 17 years of age, female, black, and further along in their education. Those out of school were more likely to be 17 or 18 years of age and somewhat more frequently male, less likely to be black (especially in the smaller areas, the Tier IIs), and likely to have further to go until they finished their studies. Those out of school were also more likely to be enrolled in a GED program than in a regular high school curriculum. In both groups, about half of the enrollees were members of families receiving cash

Table 6.5. Enrollees in the Youth Entitlement Demonstration through August 1979, by educational status in semester prior to enrollment

Prior educational status	Number of youths enrolled	Percentage distribution[a]						
		School	Friends/ relatives	Community organization	Government manpower agencies[b]	Newspaper, radio, TV	Other	Total
Tier I								
In school[c]	47,759	64.4	15.8	9.5	3.0	2.0	5.3	100.1
Out of school	5,275	18.3	38.7	15.7	5.6	9.4	12.3	100.0
Total	53,034	59.8	18.1	10.1	3.3	2.7	6.0	100.0
Tier II								
In school	5,456	68.4	17.3	5.3	2.0	1.1	5.9	100.0
Out of school	238	36.9	25.8	9.4	5.6	6.4	15.9	100.0
Total	5,694	67.1	17.7	5.4	2.1	1.4	6.3	100.0
Total demonstration								
In school	53,215	64.8	16.0	9.0	2.9	1.9	5.3	100.0
Out of school	5,513	19.1	38.1	15.4	5.6	9.3	12.5	100.0
Total	58,728	60.5	18.1	9.6	3.2	2.6	6.0	100.0

[a]"Percentage distribution" is based on those youths whose enrollment forms indicated a recruitment source. This accounts for approximately 99 percent of all enrollments in the demonstration.
[b]Includes the prime sponsor agencies, Employment Security, and other manpower agencies.
[c]"In school" includes youths who were in either a high school degree program or an equivalency degree program in the semester prior to enrollment.
Source: MDRC, *The Youth Entitlement Demonstration: Second Interim Report on Program Implementation* (New York, March 1980), p. 64.

Table 6.6. Enrollees at the time of enrollment in the Youth Entitlement
Demonstration, through August 1979, as a percentage of total by prior status

Characteristics at time of enrollment	Tier I		Tier II		Total	
	In school[a]	Out of school	In school[a]	Out of school	In school[a]	Out of school
Age						
16	56.9	24.2	55.1	26.1	56.7	24.3
17	27.7	26.4	28.5	28.3	27.7	26.5
18	11.9	29.2	12.9	26.6	12.1	29.1
19	3.5	20.1	3.5	19.0	3.5	20.0
Sex						
Male	48.9	50.7	46.5	46.2	48.7	50.5
Female	51.1	49.3	53.5	53.8	51.3	49.5
Ethnicity						
White (non-Hispanic)	17.2	18.6	17.2	52.3	17.2	20.0
Black (non-Hispanic)	74.5	70.1	64.2	20.3	73.4	68.0
Amer. Indian/Alaskan native	0.6	1.4	0.6	1.3	0.6	1.4
Asian/Pacific Islander	1.9	0.4	1.5	0.4	1.9	0.4
Hispanic	5.8	9.5	16.5	25.7	6.9	10.2

Highest grade completed						
0–7	1.9	10.3	0.8	3.0	1.8	10.0
8	9.4	19.5	6.8	16.9	9.2	19.4
9	30.1	30.4	29.5	28.3	30.1	30.3
10	35.3	26.6	38.2	33.7	35.5	26.9
11	23.3	13.2	24.7	18.1	23.4	13.4
Current educational status						
In high school	94.5	30.2	95.1	36.6	94.6	30.5
In GED program	5.4	67.8	4.8	54.9	5.3	66.5
Special waiver	0.1	2.7	0.1	8.5	0.1	3.0
Total number	47,759	5,275	5,456	238	53,215	5,513

a"In school" includes youths who were in either a high school degree program or an equivalency degree program in the semester prior to enrollment.

Source: MDRC, *Youth Entitlement Demonstration: Second Report*, p. 72.

welfare payments, and over a third had participated in a CETA employment program.

The distinction between in-school enrollees and those who were out of school is also of prime importance in examining the extent to which this program was able to attract all eligible youth in the areas covered. Study of this question at four sites to the end of December 1978 indicates that approximately 46 percent of eligible in-school youth were enrolled but only 13 percent of those who were not in school.[16] Clearly, it was much more difficult to attract into the program youths who were no longer in school, partly perhaps because they were older and partly because they possibly had more inherent disinclination to attend school.

Enrollees tended to stay in the program for more than 12 months on the average, the time of participation tending to vary inversely with the age of the participant. As of the end of August 1979, about 30,000 had left the program. Of this number, nearly a third departed because they had graduated from high school. About an equal proportion left for various negative reasons, such as unsatisfactory performance either on the job or in school.[17]

Job creation

Despite efforts to involve the private sector, and despite the fact that wage subsidies up to 100 percent could be offered, approximately 85 percent of the jobs obtained for the participants were with public institutions or with nonprofit organizations, as is shown in Table 6.7. Over one-fifth of the participants were employed in the school systems and a third in other types of public agencies.

The types of jobs held by the participants were heavily of a clerical and service nature (clerks, teachers' aides, janitors, and day care workers). Though an appreciable number of jobs were classified as "professional," they were in fact more in the nature of technical support positions, such as a program aide or a recreation leader. The relatively few jobs in the private sector were mainly with retailing, wholesaling, and service firms. Even so, there seemed to be no problem in finding jobs for enrollees in most of the sites. The principal problem seemed to be having assignments for the enrollees after jobs were found, though that process seemed to be improving over time.[18]

Research and evaluation

The research and evaluation component involves four aspects:

A study of the participation rates of eligibles and of the program's impact on their school and labor market behavior; a study of the cost of operating Entitlement and projections of what these costs would be under various options for continuation, should that be desired; an analysis of the program's implementation in order to determine whether and how well the program accomplishes what it was designed to achieve in operation and the factors that affect those results; and a number of special studies concerning particular aspects of the demonstration.[19]

A major basis for assessing the impact of the program on the participants was to be several waves of interviews with a random sample of eligible youths and their parents at four sites and at four matched nonentitlement sites.[20] As of this writing, however, results from those interviews do not seem to have been published. The cost analysis and the implementation analysis are still in the early stages, too. These do not involve any experimental aspects; rather, the intent is to observe and to study carefully the operations at the different sites, to collect information on the costs incurred and on the methods of operations, and then, it is hoped, to generalize from these data as to the cost effectiveness of different ways of dealing with the participants and as to the likely costs and benefits of such a program on a national scale.

A very preliminary analysis of the effect of the program on the participants showed some indication of higher return-to-school rates of dropout youths in the demonstration sites in the fall of 1978 than in the control sites, plus indications of positive effects based on anecdotal reports from school administrators.[21]

A somewhat later evaluation finds that

Table 6.7. *Distribution of work time in the Youth Entitlement Demonstration, through August 1979, by site and work sponsor*

Site	Total hours recorded (000)[a]	Percentage distribution of job hours, by type of work sponsor[b]					Percentage of job hours at above- min. wage	Percent- age of all hours as training
		Public education inst.	Other public agencies	Private sector	Non- profit org.[c]	Total		
Tier I								
Baltimore	6,508	17.6	44.4	11.9	26.0	99.9	0.0	0.1
Boston	4,087	7.7	36.8	17.4	38.1	100.0	0.0	0.0
Cincinnati	1,849	19.3	11.4	12.9	56.4	100.0	0.0	1.5
Denver	1,735	9.3	31.4	27.9	31.4	100.0	0.0	0.0
Detroit	2,790	28.2	14.7	36.3	20.8	100.0	0.0	1.3
King–Snohomish	1,747	31.3	32.1	3.8	32.7	99.9	2.5	0.4
Mississippi	5,093	42.0	36.6	10.0	11.4	100.0	0.0	0.5
Total Tier I	23,809	22.8	33.6	15.9	27.6	99.9	0.4	0.4
Tier II								
Alachua County	184	52.3	41.8	5.1	0.8	100.0	0.0	2.4
Albuquerque	274	54.5	40.7	0.0	4.8	100.0	0.0	0.0
Berkeley	542	34.0	27.3	1.8	36.8	99.9	0.0	0.1
Dayton	40	12.3	17.8	7.1	62.8	100.0	4.7	0.0
Hillsborough	115	0.4	4.1	64.3	31.2	100.0	57.3	1.2

Monterey	127	16.4	14.1	64.8	4.7	100.0	0.0	2.8
New York	343	1.1	26.5	34.4	37.9	99.9	0.0	0.0
Philadelphia	152	1.3	8.4	62.4	27.9	100.0	0.0	4.8
Steuben County	109	53.4	41.5	0.0	5.1	100.0	0.5	0.0
Syracuse	527	13.1	24.4	25.6	36.9	100.0	2.9	3.5
Total Tier II	2,413	24.6	26.7	21.6	27.1	100.0		1.5
Total demonstration	26,222	23.0	33.0	16.4	27.5	99.9	0.6	0.5

[a]Total hours includes both job hours and training hours.
[b]A work sponsor is an organization/company/agency where youths are placed (employed) while in the entitlement demonstration.
[c]Nonprofit organizations include private and parochial schools.
Source: MDRC, *Youth Entitlement Demonstration: Second Report*, p. 129.

Entitlement has large absolute and proportionate effects on the level of employment for use in the target population. Entitlement led to a large 90 percent increase in the employment rate of disadvantaged youths in the demonstration sites, going from 25.4 percent without the program to an estimated 48.3 percent during the fall of 1978. Its effects were particularly strong for youths who did not have jobs before joining the program.[22]

Particularly noticeable was a sharp increase in the rate of return to school for youths who had been out of school; the net effect of the program is estimated to have increased school enrollment by between 4 and 6 percent of the target youth population. The principal effect of the program in this early period, however, seems to have been to increase the employment rates of the participating youths.

Evaluative comments

From an analytical point of view, both of these programs have similar advantages and disadvantages. In each case, the approach to the problem was quite innovative, and there was some allowance for data collection and for monitoring the projects at the individual sites. Still, there are questions as to whether the design in each case was adequate to achieve the objectives of the program. In each instance, the basic problem seems to be the usual one of compromise of principles with reality. Not only did most of the projects cover very different activities but they operated independently of each other.

As a result, it is not clear to what extent MDRC had achieved standardization of procedures in the face of local pressures and local circumstances. The implementation of the same concept, such as graduated work habit requirements, seems to vary among projects, so that it is difficult to estimate whether a particular effect is due to this variable itself or to local circumstances. Similarly, in the case of the Youth Entitlement Program, such key aspects as satisfactory performance of the youth were left to the discretion of the local groups, so it will be difficult to compare performance at different sites. The designers of these programs clearly opted for diversity in terms of activity and implementation at the expense of experimental control.

The requirement for participants to leave the Supported Work Program within 12 or 18 months, whether or not they have a permanent job elsewhere, seems unduly restrictive. It is not unlikely that all of this period (certainly at least 12 months) was needed to accustom many participants to the normal demands of the labor market. Too early a termination can be a clear invitation to regress to previous habits. This could be a problem especially for the AFDC women, who tended to stay in the program longer than the other participants and seemed to have more difficulty in finding other employment.

As noted earlier, comparison with controls of participants in the Supported Work Program show that only the AFDC group did clearly better in terms of earnings, economic well-being, (reduced) welfare dependence, and (reduced) remission to their former condition. It remains to be seen whether these results will hold up when multivariate methods are applied to these data. Perhaps the key shortcoming, however, is the fact that the participants were not followed for very long after they had left the program. Under those circumstances, to extrapolate results for the first few months or the first year seems questionable.

Perhaps even more questionable is the lack of any plan to follow the participants in the Youth Entitlement Program after its termination. Apparently the intent is solely to ascertain whether these youth complete their high school education while the program remains in operation. This objective seems rather shortsighted, however, in view of the widespread tendency among older youth, as well as other people, to drop out of school for a while and then return at a later time. It would seem highly desirable to investigate whether the same phenomenon is prevalent among youth who participate in this program. This could easily be accomplished by arranging for follow-up interviews with the youths who have not completed their high-school education, say, two or three years after the termination of the program.[23]

In terms of generalizing the results of either of these programs to a national scale, the emphasis on the convenience selection of the sites makes it highly questionable whether reliable estimates of this type can be obtained. In each of these projects, a major determinant in the selection of the sites and of the individual project was the interest and perceived capability of the local groups. The intent was to select those groups that are more involved and would be most likely to carry out the program successfully. At these sites, also, the sponsors were clearly aiming to attract the most promising participants in the program, with emphasis very likely on those who would be most likely to benefit from it. From this point of view, the concentration of the individual projects in areas of high unemployment would be a biasing factor because a larger pool of candidates would then be available and it would thus be easier to select more promising individuals.

As a result, the sites selected are hardly likely to be representative of the type of administrative and management operations that would be encountered in a national program, nor are the participants likely to be representative of those who would be attracted if such programs were operated on a national scale. This is especially so because the publicity attendant on a national program would undoubtedly attract marginal participants, and management of these projects when planned on a national scale would be likely at a lower level. On the other hand, one may argue that the experience gained with the operation of these projects at this experimental stage might yield sufficient information to help a national program to avoid problems that would otherwise arise.

7

The Health Insurance Study

Background
In recent years an animated debate has taken place in the United States about ways to provide more Americans with assured health services. In part, this debate has been fortified by the experience with socialized medicine in the United Kingdom and in the Scandinavian countries. Although there is broad recognition of the need to improve health insurance in the United States, there is little agreement on the specific program to be instituted.

Much of the disagreement about alternative plans centers around their effects and costs. Thus, there is little wonder that efforts to learn more about the various aspects of alternative plans are called for, and with this in mind the Health Insurance Study (HIS) was initiated. HIS was designed to estimate how the quantity of medical care demanded changes as the price paid by insured patients is reduced, either in a fee-for-service system or in a prepaid group practice.[1] It was also designed to detect changes in the use of particular services, quality of care, patient satisfaction, and health status.

From a policy point of view, HIS has a very pragmatic objective. Its purpose is to provide reliable information to decision makers who are considering the development of national health insurance legislation.

The specific questions to be answered by the experiment are, as follows:

1   How is the demand for medical care service affected by such cost-sharing arrangements as different deductibles and coinsurance rates? Are poor households affected more than rich households and, if so, how much more? How much does it cost to cover such medical services as dental or mental health services, and prescription drugs?[2]

2   If more medical services are fully paid for by insurance, what are the direct consequences for health status, quality of medical care and patient satisfaction?

3   Does a prepaid group practice have an advantage over a fee-for-service system insofar as health status of the population is concerned? When families join a prepaid group practice, does utilization differ from that by a similar group which continues to receive care under a fee-for-service plan?

4   What change in the pattern of ambulatory (non-hospital) care delivery takes place as the degree of stress on the primary care delivery system changes? What adjustments are made in time spent with patients, hours physicians work, the manner paramedical personnel are employed, etc., when demand for physician services is high relative to supply?[3]

This demand experiment focuses on the price the consumer pays for health services for a variety of reasons. Foremost is the fact that government health insurance programs change the price paid by consumers and thus influence the demand for health services. Moreover, price is a common denominator for measuring the effects of variations in insurance policies.

The demand analysis must keep in mind the key policy questions. How much will a national health insurance program with coinsurance and deductibles stimulate changes in the volume and type of health care demanded? Thus, information is sought as to whether the effect of price varies with income and total expenditures on health services, whether different income groups respond differentially to price changes, and whether families with major illnesses respond differently than do those with minor illnesses.

The substitution effect related to price is also examined. Does relatively generous coverage of in-patient services shift patients from the office to the hospital? Do generous health insurance programs reduce the demand for preventive services? Finally, will participants supplement their insurance by buying additional health insurance (in part depending on the tax treatment of such insurance)?

No less important than estimation of the demand response is the estimation of the benefits that are likely to be associated with various health insurance programs, benefits measured in terms of changes in health status. There exists, moreover, the difficult issue of determining whether reduced prices for health services induce participants to seek, and providers to supply, what may be defined as "unnecessary care."

HIS is also designed to shed light on administrative aspects of a health insurance program. In this connection, the fact that a total of 2,750 families at only six sites constitutes the entire sample somewhat reduces the experiment's ability to produce definitive answers. Nevertheless, although HIS does not offer information about how a national plan by a large private or public organization would be administered, highly pertinent data can be obtained. Information is sought about what problems of claims processing are to be expected, what the volume of claims is likely to be, what information can be obtained from claims forms to permit ongoing evaluation of the insurance plan, and so forth.

Treatment variables

The major treatment variables relate to levels of coinsurance for different types of medical care and to expenditure limits, that is, the maximum percentage of income spent for medical care. Altogether, 11 treatment plans were devised, plus three control groups, as shown in Table 7.1. The experimental plans can be divided into five general types:

Table 7.1. *Descriptions of plans in Health Insurance Study*

Code	Plan type	Description
05	2	Pays 75 percent for covered services until maximum spent, then pays 100 percent; maximum is 5 percent of income
06	2	Pays 75 percent for covered services until maximum spent, then pays 100 percent; maximum is 10 percent of income
07	2	Pays 75 percent for covered services until maximum spent, then pays 100 percent; maximum is 15 percent of income
08	3	Pays 50 percent for covered services until maximum spent, then pays 100 percent; maximum is 5 percent of income
09	3	Pays 50 percent for covered services until maximum spent, then pays 100 percent; maximum is 10 percent of income
10	3	Pays 50 percent for covered services until maximum spent, then pays 100 percent; maximum is 15 percent of income
11	1	Pays 100 percent for all covered services
12	1	Pays 100 percent for covered out-patient services; pays 80 percent for covered in-patient services until maximum spent, then pays 100 percent
13		Pays 100 percent for covered in-patient services; pays 5 percent for covered out-patient services until fixed-dollar individual deductible met ($150 per person/$450 family maximum)
14	4	Pays 5 percent for covered services until maximum spent, then pays 100 percent; maximum is 5 percent of income
15	4	Pays 5 percent for covered services until maximum spent, then pays 100 percent; maximum is 10 percent of income
16	4	Pays 5 percent for covered services until maximum spent, then pays 100 percent; maximum is 15 percent of income
17		Pays 50 percent of covered dental and out-patient psychiatric services and 75 percent of all other covered services until maximum spent, then pays 100 percent; maximum is 5 percent of income
18		Pays 50 percent of covered dental and out-patient psychiatric services and 75 percent of all other covered services until maximum spent, then pays 100 percent; maximum is 10 percent of income

Table 7.1. *(cont.)*

Code	Plan type	Description
19		Pays 50 percent of covered dental and out-patient psychiatric services and 75 percent of all other covered services until maximum spent, then pays 100 percent; maximum is 15 percent of income
30		Group Health Cooperative experimental facilities
97		Charleston preenrollment group
98		Group Health Cooperative control families

Source: Rand Corporation, *Annual Report of the Health Insurance Study, July 1, 1976–June 30, 1977* (Santa Monica, AR-1804-HEW, July bv 1978), pp. 49–50.

1 care free to the family
2 25 percent coinsurance
3 50 percent coinsurance
4 95 percent coinsurance
5 95 percent coinsurance to $150 per individual per year, with no coinsurance above that amount

All five of these types (codes 05 to 19 in Table 7.1) involved the usual form of medical arrangement in which people paid for medical services as they were performed – the fee-for-service (FFS) arrangement.

A further distinguishing feature is that plans in the second, third, and fourth classes have a ceiling on annual out-of-pocket expenditures that is either 5, 10, or 15 percent of family income, except that the maximum out-of-pocket expenditure per year regardless of plan is $1,000. Plans in the other two classes are supplied at no cost to the family.

In addition, in Seattle a sample of 450 families was selected at random from families that were not members of group health cooperatives, and this group was enrolled in a prepaid group practice, the Group Health Cooperative of Puget Sound. Another sample of approximately 300 families, already members of the Group Health Cooperative, was also enrolled, to test whether those who have self-selected a prepaid group practice are systematically different from those who have not.

Essentially, control groups in this experiment were of two types, the usual control group receiving no treatment and selected by random assignment from the total sample of eligible families, and another random segment offered membership in the Group Health Cooperative of Puget Sound. These and other controls were included for a number of reasons. First, a control group was needed to provide a basis for measuring any Hawthorne effects due to the families in the experiment being under continual observation. A special attempt was made to ascertain whether the frequency with which information was sought might affect health care behavior. This was accomplished by having a random part of one of the control groups fill out health reports on a continuing basis, while the other part was not requested to do so. The focus here was on ascertaining whether the process of filling out health forms on a continuous basis affected utilization of medical services in terms of requests for screening examinations and incentive to file claims.

A second objective was to obtain some measure of transitory demand, in the sense that the availability of these benefits at reduced rates might have the same effect as "taking advantage of a sale." This type of demand was felt to be most important for benefits relating to vision, hearing, dentistry, psychiatry, and surgery selected at the initiative of the patient (for example, removal of a wart).

A third objective of the control groups was to ascertain the effect of specific exclusions in existing policies, such as psychiatric services and various forms of preventive services. A fourth objective was to measure the effects of covering in-patient services but not out-patient services.

Fifth, use was to be made of the control groups to obtain information about the degree to which health care providers might take advantage of the more generous plans to increase their charges.

In addition to payments received for participating in an interview and returning forms, participants in the treatment groups were paid enough to ensure that they would not incur financial losses by participating in the experiment. This was necessary for both scientific and ethical reasons, and the money was independent of the family's utilization of medical care. Families who kept their prior insurance in force were reimbursed for premiums to ensure that they would not become uninsurable at the end of the experiment and that they could readily withdraw from the experiment if they so chose. Moreover, experimentals were assured an amount equal to the most they could lose by participating in the experiment. In turn, families were asked to assign the benefits of their existing policies to the experiment.

The impact of these different plans on the cost of health care is to be studied in three respects, namely, the effect of the plan on the annual expenditures for medical services by individuals, on the expenditures for a specific service, and on the cost of a particular health episode or incident. Three different models are being used to estimate these effects.

The first is an analysis of covariance model, which estimates the mean annual cost of each plan, reflecting demographic characteristics of individuals assigned to different plans:

$$Y_i = \sum_k \partial_k \mathbf{D}_{ik} + \sum_{ij} \beta_j \mathbf{Z}_{ij} + \varepsilon_i$$

where Y_i = annual expenditure on medical services of the ith person; $\mathbf{D}_{ik}$ = a set of dummy variables with the value of 1 if the person is enrolled in the kth plan and 0 if not; $\mathbf{Z}_{ij}$ = the vector of demographic characteristics of the ith person, for example, age, income, and so on.[4] This model expresses annual expenditures by an insured for medical services as a linear function of the particular plan in which the insured is enrolled and a number of demographic characteristics of the insured.

Second is a traditional demand model based on economic theory:

$$Y_i = \alpha + \sum \beta_j \mathbf{Z}_{ij} + \partial_1 P_{i1} + \partial_2 P_{i2} + \varepsilon_i$$

where Y_i = expenditure for a specific service rather than total expenditures; P_{i1} = price facing the ith individual for in-patient services; P_{i2} = price for out-patient services.[5] In this model, expenditure for a particular service by the insured is the dependent variable. It is expressed as a linear function of the price for in-patient services, the price for out-patient services, and a number of demographic characteristics of the insured. P_{i1} and P_{i2} are functions of the insurance plan. With the aid of ∂_1 and ∂_2, own-price and cross-price elasticities of demand for the service can be estimated.

The third model focuses on health expenditures per episode in the experiment. A consumer is viewed as incurring an illness episode and then deciding whether to seek care. Should he do so, his physician decides how much care is needed, taking into consideration the probability that the consumer will exceed the expenditure limit at some time during the accounting period. Expenditures thus must be classified by episode and data collected on this basis.

The data needs for implementing these models are substantial. To this end, data collected during the study include information on demographic and socioeconomic variables; use of medical, dental, and mental health services; types of health care service providers patronized by patient; patient satisfaction; and health status. Prior to actual enrollment, as well as at periodic intervals thereafter, demographic and socioeconomic characteristics have been collected. Data on use of services come from claims submitted – chiefly by the health care provider – for reimbursement of services rendered.

In order to estimate the effect of treatment variables, it is essential to define health status and quality of care in a manner that lends itself to quantitative measurement. In the experiment's framework, a number of exogenous variables, for example, genetics and environment, are seen to impinge on health status and its major dimensions. According to the definition of health proposed by the World Health Organization in 1948, three dimensions are identified for measurement: physical, mental, and social health. Physiological health was singled out as a fourth dimension.[6]

Physical health is operationally defined in terms of functions – performance of or capacity to perform a variety of activities by an individual in good health. Operational definitions of mental health constructs in the HIS focus chiefly on psychological states rather than a combination of physiological and somatic states, and both unfavorable and favorable aspects of these constructs are included.[7] Social health is operationally defined in terms of interpersonal interactions (for example, visits with friends) and activities indicative of social participation (for example, membership in clubs).

Health status data have been sought by a variety of methods. They include a base-line interview completed in the respondent's home approximately four months prior to enrollment in the experiment, a self-administered questionnaire on medical history, biweekly health reports from the head of the household, an annual self-administered health questionnaire, a self-administered exit medical history questionnaire, and a multiphasic (general medical) screening examination given to a randomly selected sample of families on enrollment and to all families on exit from the study.[8] Through these means, it is hoped that adequate data will be obtained on preexisting disease conditions, on health habits, and on how the quality of care affects health status. Data are also being obtained on the utilization of health care, including the quantity of services received, the timeliness with which they are provided, and the appropriateness of the services for the condition in question.[9]

Basic design

The sample design of HIS was assisted by a number of non-experimental econometric studies seeking to estimate the relationship between the demand for medical care services, on the one hand, and out-of-pocket payments by patients, on the other. Most of the studies defined medical care services as services by physicians, hospitals, or dentists and included drugs. In a summary of these empirical studies, J. P. Newhouse concluded that the demand for medical care services increases as out-of-pocket payments for them decline, but the magnitude of this response is "somewhat uncertain."[10] Some of these studies indicate, however, that demand for many health care services appears to increase by 50 to 100 percent as full coverage replaces no coverage. On the other hand, no exact information is available on how response varies with income, for example, whether the responsiveness of poor patients is greater than that of rich patients.

Armed with this empirical information, HIS enrolled a sample of 7,915 people in 2,823 families at six sites across the country, some for three and others for five years. The sites were chosen to represent the four census regions of the country and an urban–rural mix and to ensure that the amount of stress on the ambulatory medical care system would vary.[11] Eligibility of families in the experiment was restricted to those with annual incomes under $25,000, individuals under 65 years age, and those who did not have access to the military medical care system. This is the group that would be most affected by a national insurance program, because such a program would not affect those covered by the military medical system and would most likely leave the Medicare system intact.[12]

Site selection has two dimensions: determination of the optimal number of sites and selection of the sites. The optimal number of sites was determined from an extension of the Conlisk–Watts model.[13] This number was chosen to minimize the sum of between-site and within-site variances (the measure of expected total sample error), subject to a budget constraint and a cost function of the form,

$$C_s = C_f + \sum_{i=1}^{n} c_i$$

where C_s = total cost per site; C_f = fixed cost per site; c_i = expected cost of an additional observation in any site.

The selection of the sites was not random. Because of the small number of sites, a strictly random selection could have resulted in poor estimates of national parameters. Moreover, because cooperation of state and local officials as well as local providers is necessary for a successful experiment, random selection was out of the question. Instead, sites were chosen purposively, the desirability of a potential site being assessed with the aid of the finite selection model.[14] It sought to take into account the fact that utilization of health care in an area would be expected to be influenced by the capacity of the health care system and by the cost of medical care. For this purpose, the capacity utilization of the local ambulatory care systems was ascertained by making a telephone survey of physicians about workloads, scheduling of patients, and waiting times for appointments; and medical care price indexes were computed for each site. Further, the availability of a health maintenance organization

and various other types of medical organizations was a prerequisite
for a site to be considered for this experiment.

Administration and implementation

In 1971 the Office of Economic Opportunity called for proposals for a health insurance experiment. By May 1972 the Rand
Corporation and Mathematica had been selected to do the work, and
by November 1973 enrollment of a pilot sample had started in Dayton, Ohio. On the basis of the pilot sample, it became clear that
families would be willing to enroll in the experiment, and confidence
was gained that such an experiment could administer the necessary
insurance services. Based on these results, enrollment of the regular
sample started in Dayton in November 1974. In 1975 Seattle, Washington; Fitchburg and Franklin County, Massachusetts; and Charleston and Georgetown County, South Carolina, were selected as additional sites, with enrollment carried out in 1976.

In view of the enormous administrative effort of such an experiment, much of the work was subcontracted. The survey work was
contracted to the National Opinion Research Center, administrative
services to Glen Slaughter and Associates, and medical screening
examinations to American Health Profiles. To deal with the participants, site offices were opened in Dayton, Ohio; Seattle, Washington;
Fitchburg, Massachusetts; and Charleston, South Carolina.

About 60 percent of the fee-for-service (FFS) families – codes 05
to 19 in Table 7.1 – and of the Group Health Cooperative (GHC)
families – codes 30 and 98 in Table 7.1 – originally selected for
enrollment or selected during the enrollment field period were eventually enrolled. Losses due to nonrefusal – ineligible, moved out of
the area, vacant dwelling unit, and so forth – constituted about 21
percent. A further 19 percent refused the enrollment interview or
refused the actual offer of enrollment. Approximately 50 percent of
the preenrollment group (PEG) families selected were eventually enrolled, and 30 percent refused; 20 percent were lost for nonrefusal
reasons.

Of the families that were contacted, about 25 percent of the FFS
and GHC families refused to participate in the experiment, as did

more than one-third of the preenrollment group. As shown in Table 7.2, most of these families refused after the enrollment offer was made to them; this was especially so among the GHC families.

As of October 1978 it was estimated that the total cost of the experiment, to 1981, would amount to $63 million. Of this, $14.7 million was to be paid to families either as claims payments or as worst-case payments. The Rand Corporation would receive $19.9 million for administering the program, and $28.5 million would go to subcontractors to carry out the field work.

The field work on the Health Insurance Study has stretched over a number of years in addition to covering six different locations. The field work was further extended by virtue of the fact that some of the families (70 percent) were enrolled in the experiment for three years and others were enrolled for five years. Altogether, approximately 8,000 individuals in 2,750 families have been involved in this experiment.

The initial field work, essentially an experimental phase, was carried out in Dayton with the enrollment of 390 experimental families in the fall of 1974. The field work in that area was completed in 1977 for the families enrolled for three years and in 1979 for the families enrolled for five years. Families in other sites were enrolled mostly during 1976 and early 1977. Those enrolled for three years had completed their participation by 1979, but those in the experiment for five years would not be finished until 1981.

In addition, 425 families were enrolled at the two South Carolina sites in the last quarter of 1978 and early 1979. These families constitute a preenrollment group (PEG) to be included in the experiment for a period of three years. This PEG sample included participating PEG families, some who had enrolled in 1976 but later dropped out and also some who refused to enroll in 1976. Of 559 eligible families who were contacted, 425 were successfully enrolled.[15] Refusal rates were lower than in earlier years – 11 percent refused before the enrollment offer and 12 percent after the offer was made, for a total refusal rate of 23 percent.

In the data collection process, the same phenomenon has appeared as in other social experiments – some people will not accept a free

Table 7.2. *Refusal and response rates for families contacted, 1976 (by percent)*

Item	Dayton, Ohio	Seattle, Wash.			Fitchburg, Mass.	Franklin County, Mass.	Charleston S.C.		Geogetown County S.C.		Total		
		FFS	GHC/C	GHC/C			FFS	PEG	FFS	PEG	FFS	GHC	PEG
Refused before enrollment offer	1	10	9	7	15	13	12	13	11	13	10	8	13
Refused after enrollment offer	7	14	18	15	17	15	17	21	23	27	14	17	24
Refusal rate	8	24	27	22	32	28	29	34	34	40	24	25	37
Response rate	92	76	73	78	68	72	71	66	66	60	76	75	63
Total	100	100	100	100	100	100	100	100	100	100	100	100	100

Source: Rand Corporation *Annual Report of the Health Insurance Study, 1976–77*, p. 57.

good, even for their own benefit. Refusal rates were low in some areas but very high in others. Thus, whereas Dayton had an 8 percent refusal rate, the refusal rate of the Georgetown County preenrollment group amounted to 40 percent. Completion of reports has been erratic, also. Thus, 99 percent of the annual income reports were returned from Dayton, whereas the corresponding percentage for South Carolina was only 77 percent.[16]

Participation by physicians has been somewhat lower, as might be expected. In the case of a physician capacity utilization survey, completion rates varied from 83 percent for Charleston–Georgetown pediatricians to 43 percent for Fitchburg–Franklin general practitioners.[17]

Attrition and termination do not seem to have been as high as in other social experiments. Thus, as of June 28, 1977, about one year after the main field work had begun, 7,912 individuals in 2,888 families were enrolled. Only 79 families – 425 individuals – had left the study by that time, either voluntarily (attrition) or due to failure to perform all the study obligations (termination).

Findings

Much of the data are still being collected or processed, so the results from this experiment may not appear until well into the 1980s. Preliminary examination of the experimental data has focused more on the major analytical problems than on the effect of the different experimental plans. In particular, these results have highlighted the following problems or characteristics of the data.[18] One finding is that medical expenditures among family members within a family tend to be positively correlated, with correlation coefficients of about .2 or .3. This means that the variance of family expenditures is likely to be much more than the sum of the variances of the medical expenditures of the individual members of the family. This also means that there is a larger probability of family medical expenditures exceeding a particular limit than if no such intrafamily correlation existed.

Second, although the frequency distribution of family medical expenditures tends to follow a lognormal distribution in the case of zero coinsurance plans (the insurance plan pays all the cost), with nonzero coinsurance plans there is a higher than expected concentration of very large expenditures. To some extent, the reason is undoubtedly that all of the nonzero coinsurance plans had ceilings on family out-of-pocket expenditures, so that beyond a certain expenditure level the coinsurance plan was in effect transformed into a zero insurance plan.

Because such a phenomenon is also likely to be characteristic of a national insurance plan, and because a substantial part of all medical expenditures occurred in the right-hand tail of the distribution, it appears that the accuracy of estimating the cost of a national insurance plan will depend to a large extent on ability to explain, and anticipate, this end of the distribution.[19]

Third, it was found that a large proportion of families spent nothing on medical care during a particular year. Hence, the problem of estimating the effect of a national insurance plan would seem to involve two different stages: first, estimating what proportion (and type) of families will incur any medical expenditures during a year; and second, estimating the amount for families that are predicted to incur such expenditures.

Taken together, these and other preliminary findings indicate that estimating the cost of national health insurance from these data will not be easy. A coinsurance feature is clearly a complicating factor, but it cannot be ignored because it very likely will be a feature of a national plan. Many other variables also will affect the demand for medical services, and it remains to be seen how well they can be combined into efficient estimates of the cost of alternative plans, especially given the relatively small sample sizes.

Evaluative comments

This experiment seems to have been designed and implemented much more carefully, and successfully, than earlier social experiments, from which it undoubtedly benefited. The design seems quite efficient, and the field work has been quite good, given the resources. The limitations of the experiment are inherent to a large extent in the fact that it is an experiment. Thus, a major limitation of the study design is that it singles out the demand side without regard to the possible effect of demand shifts on supply. Increased demand for a particular service, for example – say, for regular medical check-ups – may be stifled if the health care industry does not have adequate facilities. To the extent that supply is a constraint (actual or perceived), demand response will be affected; and to the extent that demand is not influenced by the current supply situation, generality of the results will be further restricted.

A limited experiment with 2,800 families at six locations is very different from a national health insurance program in at least five important dimensions. First, there is great uncertainty about how supply would respond to a national program as compared with a limited local program.[20] Shortages in supplies or medical equipment in a particular area may be much more easily remedied than shortages on a national scale. Second, there is a cost dimension. The less the quantity of services supplied responds to changes in demand, the more prices will be held up as consumers compete for limited services, and the higher price of services would result in a smaller increase in demand.

A third dimension relates to changes in the quality of care; hospitals may increase the sophistication of services at a time when an entire market is more fully covered by insurance, which may be beneficial but would not be detected in a local experiment. A fourth dimension relates to redistribution among health care providers, such as a possible shift from the need for dentists to fill cavities to a need for dental hygienists to clean teeth and for other preventive measures as a result of the free nature of the latter under an HMO plan. The implications of a national financing plan for redistribution of demand among providers make the supply system's response to alternative plans a crucial issue, and this too may not be apparent in a local experiment.

A fifth consideration is the extent to which the payment guarantees may influence the participants in the treatment groups to more freely incur medical expenditures than they otherwise might. Because many of the plans provide ceilings for the annual out-of-pocket expenditures that a family might incur, a family in a situation where expenditures of this magnitude may be a possibility could well be less hesitant to incur the additional expenditures, as the marginal cost of these expenditures to them becomes zero. The possibility of such bias becomes more likely given the early results mentioned previously of the "fat tail" at the upper extreme of the family medical expenditure distribution.

Finally, and perhaps most important, there is the issue of technology and innovation. To the extent that there are major changes in demand over many years, new methods to produce and deliver health care services will tend to develop. Not only will manufacturers of drugs and equipment be inclined to seek new technologies, but the financial community is then more likely to provide the necessary funding.

Those in charge of the experiment are not unaware of these limitations and have accordingly been quite modest in their claims. Thus, Newhouse has stated, "the experiment is not a 'pilot' national health insurance plan. Nor is it a 'field trial' of any proposed legislation. Rather, it is designed to estimate how various insurance plans affect the demand for medical care and the health status of individuals."[21] In other words, the principal results to be expected relate to the response effects on the part of individuals engendered by the different insurance plans. Such information could serve as one input to guide policy makers in choosing what sort of national health insurance, if any, should be adopted. The other ramifications of a national health insurance program would have to be obtained by other means, however.

In fact, even the validity of the demand effects may be somewhat in doubt, partly because of the limited geographical scope of the experiment and partly because of its limited duration. The lifetime of the experiment is three to five years, about the same as many of the income maintenance experiments but substantially shorter than that of the 15-year lifetime of the housing allowance experiment or the 20-year lifetime of a portion of the Denver–Seattle Income Maintenance Experiment.

8

Electricity peak-load pricing experiments

Background

Electricity is a highly perishable commodity; yet the demand for electricity varies by the hour, by the day, and by the season of the year. Thus, temporal demand and supply of electricity tend to be mismatched. This is inefficient and costly. With energy prices at an extremely high level, there is, therefore, great interest in seeking to reduce the overall social costs of energy and the need for new generating capacity. One method advocated for this purpose is load management through peak-load pricing, that is, charging higher rates during hours, days, and seasons of highest demand. Higher rates at peak periods, it is argued, encourage the conservation of energy at times when the greatest fuel and capital resources are required to produce it. Lower off-peak rates are alleged to help shift energy usage to periods when excess capacity is available and average fuel costs are lower.[1]

The objective of the electricity rate experiments is to ascertain how much electricity consumption can be reduced in certain peak periods by charging higher unit prices, thereby achieving savings through lower requirements for generating capacity and hence through the use of more cost-effective generating equipment. These experiments are referred to frequently as demonstration projects, in the sense that they seek to explore the feasbility of peak-load pricing and the problems involved in its implementation. From our point of view, however,

142

they are experiments because all of them utilized control groups and seek to measure the effect of one or more peak-load pricing structures against control groups.

With these objectives in mind, in 1966 the Electricity Council of the United Kingdom initiated a five-year electricity pricing experiment.[2] In each of six Area Boards, about 1,500 households were included in experiments that applied different electricity rates during the summer and winter, respectively, and during the day.

In the United States, in January 1975, the agency that is now the Department of Energy solicited proposals from utilities for electric rate experiments. Of 35 responses, 10 were accepted. In response to a second request in January 1976, 41 proposals were submitted, of which 6 were funded. Thus, electricity pricing experiments designed to elucidate load management alternatives are of recent vintage.

Treatment variables

In order to affect electricity demand, users can be offered rates that vary during the day as well as during different seasons, namely, summer and winter. Treatment can take the form of at least seven different pricing plans. The 16 experiments carried out in the United States use different combinations of the following seven plans, unfortunately, though, not according to an overall design.

> declining block rates, with lower prices per kilowatt hour for greater quantities of usages
> time-of-use rates, in which the prices are higher (lower) according to whether the electricity is consumed during peak (off-peak) periods
> flat rates, with a uniform price per kilowatt hour for all customers and levels of usage
> "lifeline" rates, in which residential customers with specified minimum levels of usage receive reduced rates
> inverted rates, in which the price per kilowatt hour is higher for greater quantities of usage
> three-part rates, in which there is a charge for the peak demand registered at any time during the month and/or a customer charge, in addition to a charge for the number of kilowatt hours used
> time-of-use/lifeline rates, in which rates above specified minimum usage level are higher (lower) if the electricity is consumed during peak (off-peak) periods

As shown in Table 8.1, the experimental plan tested most frequently involved time-of-use rates with declining block rates as a control.

Some analytical problems

The estimation of consumer response to time-of-day pricing raises some unique problems of theoretical and empirical analysis.[3] These problems stem from the fact that consumption of electricity is more or less continuous, so that it is a question not only of the effect of the price for all the time periods that price is varied but also of the definition of the time intervals to which particular prices apply. Moreover, the demand for electricity is a derived demand that can be influenced particularly by the life style of the members of the household and by the type of electrical appliances owned by that household.

For these reasons, one must distinguish between short-run and long-run effects of time-of-day pricing. In the short run, say, one to two years, life styles are fixed, as is the stock of appliances. Hence, any adjustment of the household to time-of-day electricity rates is not likely to be very great because such adjustment would take place primarily in the time of use of the present stock of appliances rather than in any change in that stock or, for that matter, in life style. In the long run, however, a household faced with a time-of-day pricing schedule may well adjust its stock of appliances and its life style, perhaps by purchasing appliances with automatic timers so that, say, washing machines will go on automatically during the night when electricity rates would be lowest.

One would therefore expect the long-run effects of time-of-day pricing to be more substantial than in the short run, but there is no telling by how much. Because all of the experiments so far deal with periods of only one to two years and the households in these experiments were well aware of this fact, only short-run effects can be anticipated.

From a theoretical point of view, one would ideally estimate response to time-of-day pricing within the framework of a complete set of demand equations, with expenditures for electricity as one component of the consumer budget. In practice, this is not possible,

Table 8.1. *Treatment plans tested in various electricity pricing experiments and type of model*

Location	Declining block[a]	Time of use	Flat	Life-line	In-verted	Three-part	Life-line	Time of use	Demand model	Analysis of variance model
Arizona	x	x						x	x	
Arkansas	x	x								x
California	x	x								x
Connecticut	x	x								x
Edmond, Okla.	x	x								x
Los Angeles	x	x	x	x				x	x	
Michigan	x									x
New Jersey	x	x	x							x
North Carolina	x	x				x				x
Ohio	x	x								x
Puerto Rico	x	x		x	x					x
Rhode Island	x	x				x	x			x
Vermont[b]	x	x			x	x				
Washington	x				x					x
Wisconsin	x	x	x			x		x	x	x

[a]Used as a control for comparison with other rates.
[b]Interruptible and contract rates are also included.

because complete consumption data for the sample households are not available. It is also questionable to use a complete set of demand equations for a component that is such a small proportion of the consumer budget. Such an approach is not needed in any event if one makes use of the concept of separability. In the present instance, this implies that the household makes a decision initially about the share of its expenditures that goes for electricity and the share that goes for all other commodities. Second, the household is assumed to allocate its electricity expenditures over time solely on the basis of the rates for electricity and of various other characteristics (weather, stock of appliances, life style) that do not involve prices of other consumption goods. On this basis, therefore, one can postulate response equations for electricity that do not involve other components of consumer expenditures.

Although economic theory has played a major role in the specification of the response functions in many of these analyses, some of the basic tenets of the theory are of questionable validity. Thus, the idea of homogeneity, that a proportionate increase in all prices will leave unchanged the budget shares that are allocated to different expenditures, receives little support from these studies (as well as from studies dealing with other items of expenditure). The somewhat weaker principle of homothetic separability also seems to be invalid, in the sense that if overall expenditure on electricity increases by x percent, expenditures on electricity in each period having different rates will not each increase by x percent.

Still another principle of doubtful validity is the Slutsky condition of symmetry of the cross-price elasticities. This means that an increase in the peak rates would have the same effect on off-peak electricity consumption as would an increase in the off-peak rate on consumption during the peak period. Indeed, in the case of differential electricity rates by time of day, such an assumption hardly makes sense. Thus, higher peak rates may well increase off-peak use of electricity, but higher off-peak rates are likely to have much less, if any, effect on peak consumption.[4]

A basic problem with the theoretical approach to consumer demand analysis is that so much emphasis has been placed on the study of price and other substitution effects and so little on the effect of non-price variables, and they can have substantial influence on time-of-day response. This means the effect not only of other socioeconomic variables but also of variables such as weather. One can attempt to take such variables into account in the same way that price variables are taken into account in the neoclassical demand functions and subject to the same sorts of restrictions; and a number of ways of doing so have been developed.[5]

Some interesting innovations have been made in recent years to deal with this problem. One approach has been to estimate the effects of the parameters in these response functions in two stages. In the first stage, a more or less standard demand function is estimated following the postulates of neoclassical demand theory. In the second stage, the parameters of this demand function are expressed as a function of weather and sociodemographic variables.[6] In still another variant of the two-stage approach, electricity consumption has first been estimated as a function only of the different time-of-day periods, the latter expressed as a set of dummy variables. In the second stage, the coefficients of these variables are expressed as a function of the electricity rates and other variables, such as the socioeconomic characteristics of the houshold.[7] This approach permits considerable flexibility in the estimates of response to time-of-day pricing, because the various influencing variables may enter in different ways into each equation and the cross-price elasticities are not limited to be equal to each other.

One aspect of the analysis of response to time-of-day pricing that is simplified by economic theory is the question of whether to use compensated price elasticities as a basis for policy decisions.[8] In the present instance, the choice becomes inconsequential because the difference between the two elasticities involves a term that contains the fraction of the total consumer budget spent for electricity. As this fraction is very small, as a rule about 1 percent, the two different types of elasticities are in practice virtually the same.

From a statistical point of view, a basic analytical question concerns the time period to be used as the observation for measuring electricity consumption. Should it be the period during which the price is the same, or should it be very small intervals of time? Theoretically, the use of short intervals of time would seem best, especially for estimating the shape of the load curve, but in practice there are difficult estimation problems. One can also argue that use of electricity in a small interval of time, such as during a 15-minute period, is highly unstable and contains a great many exogenous influences that cannot be explained by present models.[9] In terms of estimating generating capacity, such estimates are nevertheless highly desirable, and this need can be at least partially fulfilled by plotting load curves by 15-minute intervals without attempting any estimation of the influencing factors responsible for the variations in loads. For measuring consumer response, broader time aggregation is clearly preferable, both to make the estimation process more manageable and to better isolate the pricing effects, and this is the procedure that seems to have been followed in virtually all of the analyses of these experiments so far.

Basic design

Rather than try to describe some common elements in the 16 experiments in the United States as well as those in the United Kingdom, we shall present, respectively, the basic design of perhaps one of the most sophisticated experiments that seeks to estimate a household demand function, and a rather simple experiment that seeks only to carry out an analysis of variance. The first is the Los Angeles Peak-Load Pricing Experiment for Electricity, and the second is the Connecticut Peak-Load Pricing Experiment.

The objective of the Los Angeles Experiment was to construct a *demand function* to analyze load responses of residential customers to peak-load pricing.[10] The experiment was designed to study three major questions:

1 Is seasonal pricing more efficient than existing tariffs?
2 Are the efficiency gains from time-of-day pricing sufficient to cover the additional metering and billing costs?
3 What is the effect of the level and structure of electricity prices on residential patterns of electricity used?

To ensure that the data base be more robust, the experiment was designed so that demand curves rather than analysis of variance models (*ANOVA*) could be estimated. The latter would be appropriate if the goal were to measure the magnitude of the difference between two particular tariffs. If, however, estimates are sought on a range of tariff alternatives, including combinations of rates not tested, a method leading to derivation of demand functions is more suitable.

It was assumed that the functional form of the household response would be quite complex, and price and policy options were selected to cover likely contingencies in the supply of electricity. An effort was made to provide for tests for the existence and magnitude of experimental biases.

The choice of experimental tariffs was determined by the "allocation model" of Conlisk and Watts.[11] It incorporated a separate cost for each treatment, a functional form modeling the behavioral response, and the policy objective to be examined – for example, the response to a tariff of six cents per kilowatt hour in the summer and three cents per kilowatt hour in the winter. For a predetermined experimental budget, the allocation model determined the number of households to be assigned to each experimental tariff in order to minimize the variance of the specific parameter combinations corresponding to the policy questions. Thus:

> The Allocation Model was used to select the test set of experimental tariffs (combinations of peak/off-peak rates and length of peak – called design points in the experimental literature) and to determine the optimal number of households for each design point subject to an overall budget constraint. The basic procedure was to: (1) specify the types of analytic equations to be estimated; (2) assign weights to the different parameters of this set of equations to reflect the relative importance for policy analysis of the parameters to be estimated; (3) to identify the cost per observation on each of the different design points; and (4) then to select the set of observations that would give the maximum weighted statistical significance within the overall budget constraints available for the experiment.[12]

The design points were chosen to cover a wide range of peak/off-

peak rate combinations in order to yield results that could give estimates of price response under many different pricing situations. Price
variations were built into the design on two bases – by time of day
and by the season. With the production costs of electricity ranging at
that time between one cent and four cents per kilowatt hour, it was
felt that to cover future possibilities the range of rates could be anywhere from one to 13 cents per kilowatt hour. Off-peak rates were
set, therefore, between one cent and three cents per kilowatt hour and
peak rates between four cents and 13 cents per kilowatt hour. Variation was also allowed in the definition of the peak pricing period. As
a result, 47 different pricing and peak-period combinations were devised and were entered into the allocation model. Using that model,
17 of these combinations were selected, as shown in Table 8.2. In
practice, 34 different time-of-day plans were adopted, because to
gauge differences in peak pricing weekdays and on weekends half of
the sample members in the experimental groups were asked to pay
the peak price on weekdays and the other half to pay the peak price
for the entire week.

For the seasonal rate experiment, the year was divided into a summer period, June to September, and a winter period consisting of the
remaining eight months. Once more, to allow estimates of response
effects over a wide range of prices, 13 different combinations of
seasonal rates were set up, and also four sets of flat rates, with prices
ranging from two cents per kilowatt hour to eight cents per kilowatt
hour. Using the allocation model, four of these combinations were
selected for use in the experiment, in addition to one group at a flat
rate of two cents per kilowatt hour, another group at a flat rate of five
cents per kilowatt hour, and a control group, as shown in Table 8.3.

In both types of experiments, the basic approach was to select the
treatment plans with extreme values of peak/off-peak prices as well
as a few with intermediate values to detect curvature in the response
surface. Also, in each case a plan was selected with a rate plan
opposite to the others (such as a peak rate in the winter rather than in
the summer) to increase the precision of the estimates.

To select the sample of test households and assign households to
particular experimental tariffs, use was made of the "finite selection

Table 8.2. *Time-of-day tariffs selected by the allocation model*

Peak period	Peak/off-peak price (¢/kwh)	Number per plan (rounded)
9 a.m.–noon	5/2	80
	9/2	60
	13/2	20
Noon–3 p.m.	9/2	40
	13/2	20
3 p.m.–6 p.m.	5/2	20
	9/2	80
	13/2	80
6 p.m.–9 p.m.	5/2	20
	9/2	60
	13/1	60
3 p.m.–9 p.m.	7/2	40
Noon–9 p.m.	5/1	120
	9/1	20
9 a.m.–9 p.m.	5/1	20
	9/1	80
9 p.m.–9 a.m.	Controls	160
Total		980

Source: Acton et al., *Lessons to Be Learned*, p. 24.

Table 8.3. *Seasonal flat tariffs selected by the allocation model*

Tariff		Number per plan (rounded)
Summer	Winter	
Controls		400
2 (flat)	2 (flat)	350
5 (flat)	5 (flat)	110
5	2	140
8	2	50
2	5	150
2	8	20
Total		1,220

model" of Carl Morris.[13] By means of this model an attempt is made to select households in such a manner that characteristics that may be influencing electricity consumption are orthogonal (unrelated) to the features of the experimental plan. Such variables are, for example, income, appliance ownership, and housing characteristics. Households with these characteristics are selected disproportionately by the finite selection model, so that these factors are not related to the experimental plans. As described by the researchers:

> Our actual field strategy was to select approximately 200 neighborhoods using the 1970 census. These neighborhoods were chosen from throughout the City of Los Angeles to represent the full spectrum of climate, appliance ownership, income, housing, and ethnicity. We then randomly selected 12,000 customers from these 200 neighborhoods using the DWP customer billing file and stratified customers by their level of electricity usage. [Figure 8.1] shows the proportion of all DWP residential customers in each of these strata. In general, statistical precision will be increased by considerably oversampling in the high-consumption D stratum, because households in that category have more electric appliances. We deliberately sample disproportionately from the four strata in accord with policy questions of particular interest.[14]

Whether seasonal or time-of-day pricing was of primary interest, the sampling procedure involved more than proportionate selection among heavy users. This was especially true of time-of-day groups, where heavy oversampling was carried out among households using over 400 kilowatt hours per month, because responses of these households would be critical in assessing the effects of peak rates on capacity utilization of power facilities.

On the basis of these two methods, the following design was derived:

1   980 customers on 17 *time-of-day* tariffs, with peak periods varying from 3 to 12 hours in length; peak prices ranged from 5 cents to 13 cents per kilowatt hour and off-peak prices from 1 cent to 2 cents per kilowatt hour

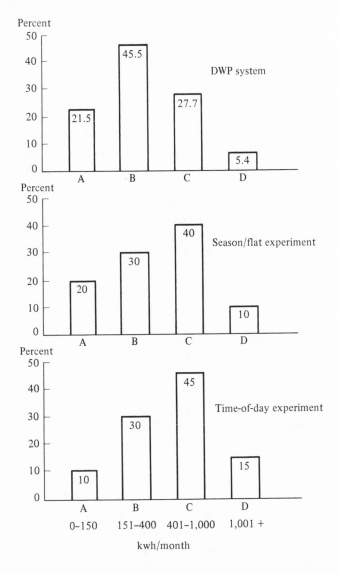

Figure 8.1. Proportion of households in DWP system and on specific experimental tariffs. *After*: Acton et al., *Lessons to be Learned from the Los Angeles Rate Experiment in Electricity*, p. 27.

2   360 customers on 4 *seasonal* tariffs, with peak prices varying from 5 cents to 8 cents per kilowatt hour and with off-peak prices of 2 cents per kilowatt hour

3   460 customers on 2 *flat-rate* tariffs at 2 cents and 5 cents per kilowatt hour

4   400 customers on a *conventional* declining-block tariff, namely, the control group

The design was stratified by four intervals of preexperimental annual energy consumption and three climate zones. Time-of-day tariffs were further differentiated according to whether peak prices apply on weekends. The duration of the experiment was 30 months; it started June 1976.

The various types of decisions entering into the design of this experiment are summarized in Figure 8.2, which shows how these decisions interrelate and where the allocation and sample selection models fit in. It highlights the central role played by these models in this experiment.

Though the expected overall sampling variance of the model is not known, rough estimates of its magnitude can be obtained by using information from the five-year rate experiment carried out by the Electricity Council of London.[15] From that experiment, it can be inferred that the variance under a time-of-day rate experiment might be as large as the average consumption observed in the peak-use period. Calculations by J. P. Acton and his colleagues suggest that the typical standard error of such parameters as the effect of a peak price between noon and 9:00 P.M. is likely to be about 9 percent of the mean level of consumption in the seasonal experiment.[16] The corresponding percentage in the time-of-day experiment tends to be about 6. Thus, should, for example, 200 kilowatt hours be consumed per month during peak-charge hours of noon to 9:00 P.M., a standard error of about 12 kilowatt hours could be expected.

Let us next turn to the design of the Connecticut Experiment, which was designed to provide data to implement an analysis of variance model (*ANOVA*).[17] It began with a pretest sample of 250 customers to obtain information on patterns of electricity use. Interviews were conducted during August and September 1975, with 199 of the original 250 test customers agreeing to participate. Participants

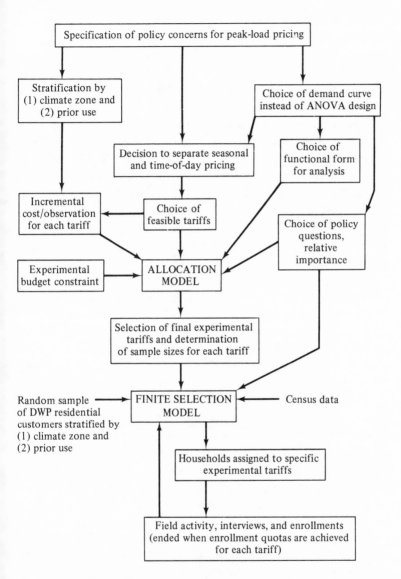

Figure 8.2. Experimental design decisions.

were scattered throughout the state of Connecticut, which is served by Northeast Utilities.

Based on an examination of the load characteristics of Northeast Utilities, peak hours were determined to be 9:00 to 11:00 A.M. and 5:00 to 7:00 P.M. in the winter, and 10:00 to 12:00 A.M. and 1:00 to 3:00 P.M. in the summer. Low hours were during the night, and the balance of the hours was designated as intermediate or "shoulder" hours. Rates were set at 16 cents per kilowatt hour during peak hours on weekdays, 3 cents per kilowatt hour on Saturdays, Sundays, and holidays, 3 cents per kilowatt hour during the shoulder hours and 1 cent per kilowatt hour during the off-peak hours. The rate included a two-dollar monthly customer charge. Customers selected for the pretest were given a payment of approximately 25 percent of their average annual bill, that is, $50 to $150, prior to commencement of the test to offset higher charges they might incur.

Following the pretest, the actual experiment was begun with a sample of 200 other households, the data collection period starting October 16, 1975, and continuing to October 15, 1976; the experimental rates remained in effect at the discretion of the project management team and with the approval of the Public Utilities Commission until December 31, 1976. Recording tape cartridges in the residences of both test customers and control group customers collected data every quarter-hour and were changed on a monthly basis. Matching weather data, including temperature, wind speed, and a measure of solar radiation, were also collected, resulting in an enormous amount of data, approaching 12 million bits of information.

The sample design utilized stratification based on household annual electricity usage in 1973. Five strata were set up on this basis, each stratum constructed so that customers in that stratum accounted for 20 percent of residential energy use. Thus, the lowest stratum, containing 20 percent of the customers in the sample, was designed to represent those 47 percent of customers in the service area using less than 6,300 kilowatt hours per year. High-use customers were oversampled to provide a usable subsample of space-heating customers in an area with low space-heating penetration.

Only customers who paid their own electric bills and who, during the most recent 12 months, had not defaulted were included in the sample. At the very beginning, customers who moved were replaced. In fact, however, all customers remaining in the sample by September 1976 had not moved in over three years.

More than 10 percent of those selected in the sample refused to participate, in spite of substantial financial advantages. Their main reasons appeared to be inability to shift loads, either because of little time-discretionary consumption or because of absence from home during the day and an inability to shift load sufficiently during other hours.

Of the 200 customers selected for participation in the experiment, only 119 provided sufficiently good usage data throughout the experiment to warrant their inclusion in the final analysis. Of those, four additional customers were deleted because of missing socioeconomic data.[18] Counting the refusals, therefore, a final response rate of only about 50 percent was obtained for analysis of the results.

Administration and implementation

Most of the electricity rate experiments have been carried out by the public utilities themselves, though specialized research organizations were usually employed for the design of the sample and analysis of data. In the case of the Los Angeles Experiment, for example, the Rand Corporation participated in the training of employees of the Los Angeles Department of Water and Power.

Findings

Results from the experiments where field work has been concluded have not been too encouraging, in part because of design defects. Thus, in Arkansas, the test of alternative rate structures provided for substantial variations in the time-of-day rates only in the five summer months of May–September 1976; and even then participants were apparently informed of these different summer rates only in May of the same year. Moreover, while the experiment was mandatory, in the sense that participants were not given any choice about rate structures, much of the data were collected by mail and about one-fourth of the metered information was lost for one reason or another.

The Connecticut Experiment tested only one set of prices, so price elasticities for peak power cannot be estimated. Its results permit comparison of customer response to one time-of-day rate schedule with the response of a control group under the usual declining-block rate schedule. Thus, it can only answer the question: Is there response to this particular time-of-day pricing schedule? The findings show that this responsiveness of household demand to peak-period pricing is strongly related to the presence of electric heating and dishwashers, to the number of adults in the houshold, and, to a lesser extent, to the typical annual energy use of all major appliances and the presence of electric water heating.[19]

Test group customers were found to shift a significant portion of their daily energy consumption from peak to off-peak hours. Thus, peak-hour consumption represented 13 percent of the test customers' total use in the year prior to the test but only 10 percent during the test.[20] Because of this shifting consumption, loads coincident with the system peak loads were reduced. As a result, the load factor of the group based upon its load coincident with the system peak was improved from 0.55 in the year prior to the test to 0.60 in the test year.

Laundry, meal preparation, and meal cleanup schedules were the activities most often changed to take advantage of peak-load pricing. These activities were mentioned by one-third to two-thirds of test households. Participants appeared willing and able to change their living patterns to take advantage of test rates, with more than 80 percent adjusting their living patterns.

Pretest and posttest surveys of customers revealed preference for time-of-day pricing over the current declining-block rate pricing. A large majority of test customers expressed a favorable reaction to the test, and 82 percent indicated a willingness to continue participating in the test for another year.

Of the electricity rate experiments in the United States, only those in Arizona, Los Angeles, and Wisconsin utilized substantial price variation to estimate time-of-day electricity demand.* The Arizona Experiment was the first of these to be completed, and its data have led to diametrically opposite conclusions. Scott Atkinson reports substantial response to time-of-day prices, whereas Lester Taylor finds little or no price-induced substitution response, using the same data. The differing results are related to the manner in which the two studies measured these response effects. Atkinson uses a system approach (indirect translog utility functions) to derive demand equations for electricity, whereas Taylor used two alternative sets of single equation specifications to explain levels (or shares) of electricity consumption under the different time-of-day prices.[21]

In commenting on the Atkinson and Taylor estimates, Willard G. Manning, Jr., notes: "The European residential experience suggests that there is only a small adjustment in consumption beyond that implied by the use of storage water and space-heating devices . . . The design of the Arizona experiment should not lead to very precise estimates."[22] The basis for this statement is the fact that the 140 experimental households in Arizona were assigned to 28 different time-of-day rate schedules, five to each schedule. Because of missing information and dropouts, these numbers were further reduced to the point where, for some of these rate schedules, data were available for only two or three households, or a total of 113. Though data could be, and were, pooled over time to yield many more observations as a basis for parameter estimation, these observations are clearly not independent of each other, and the fact remains that some of the regressions were based on data from as few as 20 households.

Results of the five-year experiment in the United Kingdom were more conclusive but not encouraging. In each experiment costs exceeded benefits, if meter equipment purchase costs related to the experiment are added to fuel and meter maintenance costs.[23] A cursory review of the 1966–72 results leads to the conclusion that in

*For a general review of the findings of these experiments with focus on the price elasticity estimates, see Aigner, Dennis J., "The Residential Electricity Time-of-Use Pricing Experiments: What Have We Learned?", National Bureau of Economic Research, Conference on Social Experimentation, March 5–8, 1981.

spite of major price-level changes in the United Kingdom, the cost–benefit ratio had not changed sufficiently to warrant either new experiments or time-of-day pricing. The picture was expected to change only if a major breakthrough in metering equipment should occur and greatly reduce metering cost.[24]

Some early results from the 30-month Los Angeles electricity rate experiment have become available.[25] A key finding was that the price elasticity of demand increased steadily with the total monthly electricity use. Price responsiveness was not uniform, however. It was markedly greater in households with, for example, swimming pools (about five times as great as households without pools). Thus, only a relatively small percentage of residential users exhibited a sufficient degree of price responsiveness to offset what amounts to substantially higher metering costs. On the assumption that meters cost $150 installed and are amortized over 15 years, the study found that average welfare gains exceeded metering costs only in cases where consumption exceeded 1,100 kilowatt hours per month. Only 4 percent of Los Angeles residential users met this requirement, though they accounted for over 17 percent of residential electricity use. Swimming pool owners were estimated to have welfare gains exceed assumed metering costs whenever their monthly electricity consumption exceeded 800 kilowatt hours. Clearly, the particular values depend on metering costs, level and timing of peak charges, and characteristics of the residential population.

The study concluded: "At the foreseeable costs of new meters, time-of-day rates would benefit only a fraction of the residential class. The level of monthly electricity consumption provides a useful guide to selecting the appropriate subclass."[26]

Evaluative comments

Although referred to as demonstration projects, the electricity rate experiments in the United States and in the United Kingdom qualify as social experiments. From a design point of view, their aim is to test particular treatments in a rigorous manner, relative to control groups subject to the usual declining-block rate. From an operational point of view, however, these experiments seem to have serious deficiencies that are bound to raise numerous questions about the validity of the results.

Perhaps the major problem is the lack of coordination of the different experiments. This was apparently the result of a conscious decision by the former Federal Energy Agency to allow each utility to design and conduct the experiment in the manner it considered best. As a result, for the first round of experiments, no guidelines at all were suggested for their execution. For the second round of experiments, some general guidelines were prepared by Westat, Inc., for the Federal Energy Agency, but no attempt seems to have been made to ensure that they were being followed. As a result, control over sample selection was left to each of the 16 utilities, as was the manner in which the study was carried out, the time horizon, the sort of data to be collected, and the analytical methods used.

One consequence of this haphazard approach is that each project defined its universe differently. By and large, certain households were excluded because they were considered "atypical" in a certain subjective way. Thus, excluded were inside meters where no adult was home in the daytime, customers with billing problems, "complainers," and people recently moved. In some instances, participation by sample households was mandatory; in others it was not. As a result, coverage is estimated to be restricted to from 1 percent to 70 percent of the stated target population of residential customers. Further, even where the coverage of the populations is defined similarly in terms of household composition, there may be little comparability. In the Los Angeles rate experiment, for example, a unique requirement was imposed in the sample selection process, namely, that contiguous households should not be included because they might communicate with each other. To the extent that such communication may affect electricity consumption, the results are bound to be biased, because in a national program communication among households is a foregone conclusion. But does such communication take place only, or mainly, among neighbors, particularly in sprawling suburbia?[27]

From an analytical point of view, few of these experiments seem to be based on an explicit model of consumer behavior (the Los Angeles and Arizona experiments are notable exceptions). The tendency seems to be to test particular pricing plans within the context of a simple experimental framework rather than to design a model of the demand for electricity and use that model as a basis for selecting factors to be controlled and for the plan of the experiment.

As a result, these experiments pose serious analytical problems. One such problem is the time horizon, which for many of the experiments is less than one year. In such a short period, there is virtually no likelihood that a household will adjust its stock of electricity-using equipment to a new rate system; indeed, it would be foolish to do so. Another problem is that in many of the experiments particular customer classes are faced with only one pricing structure, thus making it virtually impossible to estimate price elasticities. Still another problem results from the failure to allow for variation in treatment variables that interact with price effects. Thus, though participating families are being exposed to substantial education efforts on peak-load electricity use, efforts that will no doubt affect the response to price, no attempt appears to have been made to vary educational treatments.

On the other hand, a single experimental treatment (set of time-of-day rates) does have the major advantage of maximizing the chances of detecting a main effect if one exists. Considering the almost innumerable forces that affect the behavior of individual households, and considering that the analysis of these data is based on only a few hundred households (less than 150 for some of the Arizona and Connecticut analyses), detection of main effects may be all that can reasonably be expected.

Specific experiments were subject to a variety of biases. Thus, for example, the Connecticut Peak-Load Pricing Experiment selected its sample from customers who paid their own electric bills and who had 12 months of "good bills" preceding the experiment. All customers with bad billing histories were omitted. Moreover, the experiment discriminated against high-mobility groups generally and multifamily-housing-unit customers specifically. Furthermore, as noted earlier, in addition to the 10 percent of customers selected for inclusion in the sample who refused to participate, of the 200 actually participating in the experiment complete data sets were available for less than 140; the rest had to be discarded.

Nor do the Connecticut and some of the other experiments permit determination of load curves by end use. Statistical comparison of households with varying stocks of appliances can make it possible to identify appliance-specific diversified load curves. Most of these experiments, however, had too few households to allow this decomposition of the total load curves to be carried out reliably.[28] Still another source of bias is the possible interaction of incentives with response effects. In the Arizona and some of the other experiments where participation was voluntary, households were guaranteed that their monthly bill under a time-of-day rate schedule would be no more than they would have to pay under the customary schedule. Given such a guarantee, one may well question how seriously some households might seek to take advantage of time-of-day pricing. To be sure, if households are motivated, or under pressure, to save, the time-of-day pricing structure would offer an additional opportunity, as they would be able to keep the savings. If they are not under pressure to save, however, or if their life style with relation to the use of electricity is quite rigid, they could keep consuming electricity to the same extent and in the same pattern as previously (if not more lavishly!), secure in the knowledge that they will not be penalized for such behavior. Under such conditions, one would expect a built-in bias toward support of the null hypothesis.

9

The cash housing allowance experiments

Background

In 1949 Congress called for the realization as soon as feasible of the goal of a "decent home and suitable living environment for every American family."[1] Since that date the federal government has sought to implement this policy with the aid of a variety of programs, among them urban renewal, public housing, and model housing. None of these policies has worked well, and in the early 1970s a new approach was considered, one that called for cash allowances to low-income families toward covering the cost of housing.

In the discussion of this policy, it was brought out that little was known about the likely effectiveness of such a program. Thus, it was not clear how households would make use of housing allowances and what the effect of alternative means of computing housing allowances would be on use patterns. Moreover, there was the question of the extent to which these income transfers to low-income families would enrich landlords rather than increase the supply of housing.

The effectiveness of such a policy has been the focus of the Experimental Housing Allowance Program (EHAP). The basic idea involves providing regular (monthly) cash allowances to lower-income households on the condition that they use the funds to meet housing requirements established by the program.

Financed by the U.S. Department of Housing and Urban Development, the EHAP has sought to measure the effect of such a program

164

both on the demand for housing and on the supply of housing; and also to compare the effectiveness of different means of administering such a program. In line with these objectives, the overall organization of the EHAP was split into four parts – three parts concerned with each of these three broad objectives, and a fourth component combining the results from the three experiments into an integrated analysis of the likely effects of such a program if implemented on a national scale.

The three component experiments may be briefly described as follows:

1 The Demand Experiment: Starting with approximately 1,250 households each in Allegheny County, Pennsylvania (Pittsburgh), and Maricopa County, Arizona (Phoenix), the objective of this three-year field experiment, completed in 1977, was to ascertain how households use housing allowances and what would be the effect on these use patterns of alternative means of computing housing allowances.

2 The Supply Experiment: Covering Brown County, Wisconsin (Green Bay) and Saint Joseph County, Indiana (South Bend), this field experiment covered five years (though 10 years in the field); its aim has been to measure the supply effect of a full-scale housing allowance program on housing markets.

3 The Administrative Agency Experiment: The objective of this three-year field experiment, completed in 1976, was to measure the effectiveness of different means of administering housing allowances by having two of each of four different types of agencies administer such a program, each in a different area. Coverage varied in the eight areas, from about 370 to about 870 households, depending on the area.

An overall view of the specific policy questions that serve as the focus of each of these experiments is provided in Table 9.1. As is evident from this table, many of the policy questions involve data from all three experiments, particularly in analyzing household response. Such data are necessarily collected whether a family receives an allowance as part of the Demand Experiment, the Supply Experiment, or an Administrative Agency Experiment. On the other hand, aggregative effects, such as supply responses in the housing market, and effects of different agency arrangements are distinctive to that particular type of experiment. It was the responsibility of the inte-

Table 9.1. *Relationship of experiments to policy questions*

Question	Demand	Supply	Administrative Agency
1. How much do families receiving housing allowances improve the quality of their housing?	X	X	X
2. Does a housing allowance encourage families to take responsibility in the operation and maintenance of their own housing?			X
3. Whom does a housing allowance benefit, and who bears the cost?	X	X	X
4. How do the locational choices of families receiving housing allowances compare with existing residential patterns?	X		X
5. What is the effect of allowances upon the market for assisted housing?		X	
6. What effect, if any, does a housing allowance program have on housing prices?		X	
7. Would a housing allowance program improve the maintenance and stimulate the rehabilitation of existing dwellings? Would it encourage new construction?		X	
8. What are the total allowance and administrative costs of a housing allowance program?	X	X	X
9. What is the appropriate administrative and management means for operating a housing allowance program?			X
10. To what extent can the objectives of an allowance program be defeated through adverse actions by participants, landlords, market intermediaries, and administrators, and how can these be minimized, controlled, or prevented?	X	X	X

grated analysis (undertaken by the Urban Institute) to bring these separate sets of data together to provide comprehensive answers to these different policy questions.

From an experimental point of view, it is clear that three different types of experiments are encompassed within the framework of this single social experiment although, as we shall see, only one of these is really an experiment in terms of statistical design. The focus of this chapter is, therefore, on an examination of each of these three types of experiments, with some final attention to the integrated analysis being undertaken to synthesize the various results.

The Demand Experiment
Treatment variables

In line with its title, the focus of the Demand Experiment was to ascertain how the demand for housing by low-income families varied with alternative forms and amounts of housing allowances offered to them. As in the income maintenance experiments, the focus is on the response of households to different treatments, in this case the treatment being some type of housing allowance and the response referring to the manner in which families use these allowances. To measure the effect of these treatments, control groups are clearly needed, and as a result this experiment, the only one of the housing experiments to do so, satisfies the traditional requirements of experimental design.

The experimental treatment for housing allowances was a combination of two variables – the payment formula and the earmarking constraint, each composed of two separate parts. The payment formula is based on either computation of a so-called housing gap or a percentage of actual rents. The housing gap (G) calculation is based on the difference between the estimated annual rent required for a family of that particular size in that location (based on an appraisal of local housing conditions), (C), and a percentage of the current income (bY), namely: $G = C - bY$.

Based on the traditional standard that a moderate-income family should be spending about one-quarter of its income for housing, the value of *b* in these experiments was set within a relatively narrow range around 0.25 – 0.15, 0.25, and 0.35.

Basing the payments as a percentage of the rent is the other payment-formula approach, the idea being that this approach gears the payments more directly to the type of housing that the family has and therefore might influence housing choices more directly. In the Demand Experiment, five different rates were used – 0.2, 0.3, 0.4, 0.5, and 0.6.

The purpose of the other treatment variable, the earmarking constraint was to help ensure that the household obtain housing that satisfies minimum quality standards. Indeed, one of the earmarking constraints was exactly that: A household must live in a residence that meets minimum standards as set by the EHAP. If these minimum standards were not met within a specified period of time, the household received no further housing allowance.

The other earmarking constraint, minimum rent, was meant to ascertain whether the same objective could be fulfilled more easily by requiring that households spend minimum amounts of rent for their dwelling unit.

These and various other aspects of the experimental design are summarized in Table 9.2, which also provides comparative information on the corresponding design aspects for the other experiments. In addition to providing information on various other aspects of the Demand Experiment, Table 9.2 helps to bring out more clearly the experimental aspects of the Demand Experiment and the nonexperimental features of the other two experiments.

Sample design

As in the case of the income maintenance experiments, not all combinations of these treatment variables were used, only those that seemed most likely to be considered for implementation on a national basis and with due regard to budgetary constraints. The specific combinations of earmarking and of the two payment formulas used are shown in Table 9.3. As is evident from that table, 17 treatment cells were used in one combination or other, 12 with the housing-gap formula and five with the percentage-of-rent formula; the latter has an automatic earmarking feature. Though the sample sizes were small, the 12 combinations of treatment variables for the housing-gap formula were felt sufficient to enable some estimates to be made of response to the payment formula and the type of earmarking, including whether earmarking itself makes much difference. Similarly, the five variations in the percentage-of-rent payment formula were meant to provide a basis for assessing the influence of variations in that formula on housing choice.[2]

As noted in Table 9.3, there were two control groups in this experiment. One of these groups received information about housing (principally through group sessions, to which participants were invited, dealing with housing and neighborhood choice, landlord–tenant relations, Equal Opportunity information, and legal services), and the other group received no such information; all families in the experimental groups were offered this information.

In the present instance, the budget apparently dictated a maximum sample size of about 1,200 families per site. The allocation formula used, as in most such cases, indicated that optimal results from a cost point of view would be obtained by assigning relatively more families to the control cells than to the treatment cells and fewer families to the cells where higher payouts would be expected (such as $a = 0.6$ for the percentage-of-rent formula, and $C^* = 1.2$ for the housing-gap formula). Constraints were put on the allocation process, however, so that no cell would have an expected number of observations less than 30.

Administration and implementation

As noted in Table 9.2, the sample for the Demand Experiment was selected at each site using area probability methods, with prelisting of dwelling units in predesignated low-income areas (based on Bureau of the Census data), and then making random selections within these areas.[3]

In fact, the process of selecting households was a long and cumbersome one and quite costly in terms of response. It involved the following steps:

Table 9.2. *Key program design elements in the Experimental Housing Allowance Program*

Design element	Demand Experiment	Supply Experiment	Administrative Agency Experiment
Number of sites	2	2	8
Administrative mechanism	Abt Associates, Inc., site office staff	Housing Allowance Office established by Rand Corp.	8 public agencies: 2 each of 4 types
Program control	Tight	Tight	Loose
Scale of program	1,250 households at each site	Open enrollment	400–900 households at each site
Sample design	Area probability	All eligible households	Nonprobability with quotas
Household contact	Individual solicitation	Areawide promotion	Areawide promotions; referrals from social service agencies
Experimental variables	Payment formula; earmarking	None	None
Payment formula	Center of design: housing gap ($G = C^* - bY$); other variations tested	Housing gap ($G = C^* - bY$)	Housing gap ($G = C^* - bY$)
Earmarking constraints	Minimum standards; minimum rent	Minimum standards	Minimum standards

Definition of household unit	Households of 2 or more related individuals; elderly, disabled, or handicapped single persons	Households of two or more related individuals; single persons	Households of two or more related individuals; elderly, disabled, or handicapped single persons
Tenure eligibility	Renters	Homeowners and renters	Renters
Technique for estimating rent and adequate housing (C^*)	Center of design: panel of experts (percentage variations of this estimate also tested)	Rent survey and panel of experts	Panel of experts
Household contribution rate (b)	Center of design: $b = 0.25$; other variations tested	$b = 0.25$	$b = 0.25$
Income definition	Gross income minus federal, state, and social security taxes; less $300 annually per earner for work-related expenses; other specific deductions	Gross income minus $300 exemption per dependent and each secondary wage earner; 5% standard deduction (10% for elderly); other specific deductions	Gross income minus $300 exemption per dependent and each secondary wage earner; 5% standard deduction (10% for elderly); other specific deductions.
Rent definition	Either gross rent or contract rent plus formula-based allowance for utilities paid by household	Either gross rent or contract rent plus formula-based allowance for utilities paid by household	Either gross rent or contract rent plus formula-based allowance for utilities paid by household
Nonmonetary assistance	Housing information and Equal Opportunity support	Housing information and Equal Opportunity support	Housing information and Equal Opportunity support (varied by agency)

Source: Adapted from U.S., Department of Housing and Urban Development, *A Summary Report of the Current Findings from the Experimental Housing Allowance Program* (Office of Policy Development and Research, April 1978), pp. A-5, 6.

Table 9.3. *Treatment cells of Demand Experiment, EHAP*

Formula basis	Parameters		MS	MR = 0.7C*	Specific earmark		None	Total
					MR = 0.9C*	% of rent		
Housing gap	b	C*						
	0.25	1.2	30	30	30			90
		1.0	45	45	45		45	180
		0.8	45	45	45			135
	0.15	1.0	45					45
	0.35	1.0	50					50
Percentage of rent	a							
	0.6					32		32
	0.5					95		95
	0.4					95		95
	0.3					95		95
	0.2					63		63
No payment								
Housing info.	—						170	170
No housing info.	—						170	170
Total			215	120	120	380	385	1,220

Source: Abt Associates, *Second Annual Report of the Demand Experiment, December 4, 1973–December 31, 1974* (Cambridge, Mass., February 1975), p. 20.

1 A short screening interview on a door-to-door basis in census blocks meeting particular requirements (such as annual median income under $12,000 and 90 percent or more renter-occupied units)
2 A longer screening interview dealing with income, household composition, and housing with those households that passed the initial interview
3 A base-line interview to obtain complete information on households classified as eligible
4 An enrollment interview inviting the household to participate
5 With those agreeing to participate, preparation of an initial household report form as a basis for compiling operating data and calculating the first allowance payment

This process took approximately 15 months, beginning in January 1973 and finishing in March 1974. The cost of this process in terms of response is evident from the fact that to enroll approximately 1,200 households at each site required over 37,000 screening interviews in Pittsburgh and over 32,000 screening interviews in Phoenix.[4] In other words, to enroll one eligible household in the program required on the average about 30 completed screening interviews in Pittsburgh and about 26 screening interviews in Phoenix. If we take even the base number of households eligible after screening, only about a third were finally enrolled at each of the two sites. Although some of the families were not eligible, the fact remains that by the usual survey standards the percentage of the eligible population actually included in the study (at least at the beginning) is remarkably low. This is especially so as the total number of attempted screening interviews, a figure that could not be ascertained, is undoubtedly more than the number of screening interviews completed.

Unlike the income maintenance experiments, the principal contractor, Abt Associates, exercised direct control through local offices on the recruitment and handling of individual households, with housing information provided by the Pittsburgh Urban League and the Phoenix Urban League in those cities. Survey work was subcontracted, principally to the National Opinion Research Center.

Despite the individual contact made with the households and the various types of informational assistance offered to them, participation in the program does not seem to have been high. Only about 85 percent of eligible households contacted in the first year agreed to enroll in the program, and only about 43 percent met all the requirements and received assistance payments, which averaged about $70 per month. The experience in Phoenix was slightly better than in Pittsburgh, the relevant percentages being 86 percent enrollees and 44 percent recipients in Phoenix, and 82 percent enrollees and 41 percent recipients in Pittsburgh.[5] The fact that the housing market was tighter in Pittsburgh than in Phoenix may account for these differences, though the experience of the other housing allowance experiments was also that less than half of the eligible households contacted or applying for the program became recipients.

Findings

Perhaps the most important finding of this experiment has already been indicated, namely, the apathy of eligible households toward the program. With less than half of the eligible households participating and only about 20 percent of the households in an area eligible for the program, the macroeffects of a housing assistance program are not likely to be noticeable, particularly as approximately half of the participating households already lived in acceptable housing according to the standards of the program and the pressure for improvements in housing or for different housing units would come at best from 5 percent of the population and even then from only part of the cash allowances paid out.[6]

Reflecting this low rate of participation were the mediocre results of the housing information program offered to the participants. The program consisted of five group sessions offered to eligible households by the National Urban League at each of the sites. At each site, attendance at any of the sessions did not exceed 40 percent and in Phoenix was as low as 19 percent by the last session.[7] Even though special inducements were introduced to stimulate attendance, such as offering reimbursement for private transportation, baby-sitting, and locating the sessions in areas central to participants' residences, attendance did not pick up and, in fact, declined noticeably at both sites for the later sessions.

Why was participation so low? Some low-income working households seem to have been reluctant because of an apparent welfare stigma attached to the program. Older people were much less likely to participate, partly for the foregoing reason and partly because they were satisfied with their present dwelling units and did not care to move simply to satisfy the minimum housing standards of the assistance program. Indeed, households that occupied lower-quality housing were less likely to become participants in the program than other households. Low-income households, which were more likely to occupy substandard housing, were therefore less likely to qualify for the housing payments, as was also true of minority households.

The problem was exacerbated by the tight housing market in Pittsburgh, which apparently discouraged many households from even looking for better housing. Indeed, in Pittsburgh only half the households in the control group searched for better housing, and less than a quarter actually moved, as compared with 63 percent and 47 percent, respectively, in Phoenix. The fact that nearly identical percentages were noted in the two cities for the control group suggests that the state of the housing market may have been a more important consideration in the housing decisions of these households than the assistance payments offered to them.

The housing units that participated in the program and received payments did lead renter households to spend more for housing, and at the same time reduced the burden of housing expenditures on their budgets. About half of the assistance payments were allocated to increase housing expenditures (83 percent in the case of movers); and after adjustment for the increased expenditures that would have occurred in the absence of the assistance payments, it was estimated that approximately 30 percent of the housing payments went for increased housing expenditures (40 percent in the case of movers).

In terms of the standards imposed by the experiment, an appreciable proportion of the households improved the quality of their housing; over 40 percent of the households met these standards after enrolling in the program. Most of the upgrading was made by repairs, however, rather than by a move to a different unit, and the repairs were usually of a very simple nature, with labor supplied by the tenants or their landlords and with cash outlays at a modest level.[8]

Where households did move, the move was usually within the same general area (within the central city rather than from the central city to the suburbs, and within areas dominated by the same ethnic groups), to neighborhoods with lesser concentrations of low-income households and with better services and access to public transportation. There was little evidence, however, that the housing allowances did much to support racial integration.[9]

Price elasticities were estimated by means of a stock-adjustment model with alternative definitions of income.[10] The results yielded low, nonsignificant price elasticities for Pittsburgh and somewhat higher, statistically significant elasticities for Phoenix, ranging from − .3 for the short run to − .6 for the long run. As might be expected, the price elasticity was much higher for movers. The overall rate of adjustment to the housing allowance was estimated to be quite low, suggesting that, in the aggregate, between 20 percent and 25 percent of the gap between the current housing level and the equilibrium level would be closed each year.[11]

Evaluative comments

The results of this experiment provide useful information on the extent and the nature of participation of low-income families in a cash housing allowance program. They highlight the fact that, contrary to expectations, low-income families do not flock to participate in such a program, even when contacted individually, and do not want to change their housing accommodations even when offered a subsidy of as much as $100 per month. In fact, even when payment levels were doubled, the participation rate increased only about 17 percentage points.[12] Moreover, even with housing allowance payments earmarked for better housing, only 40 percent of the payment actually goes for housing (though the figure is about 10 percent if the payment is not constrained).

Although these are very useful results, one may question whether some of them are not biased or are artifacts of the experiment. Thus, the low rate of enrollment, and of later participation, might be lower still if allowance were made for the extreme difficulty of finding eligible households in the first place. To the extent that eligible households refused to participate even in the screening process or could not be contacted at that stage, the estimated rate of participation has to be adjusted downward. In view of the very low proportion of eligible households identified in the screening stage, such an adjustment may be substantial.

There is the further question of the representativeness of the two sites for the purpose of this experiment. They seem fairly typical of large urban areas, one representing a tight housing market and the other a softer housing market. Still, these are only two cities, and it is not clear how well they may reflect the reactions of low-income households in similar cities elsewhere or, for that matter, in other types of urban areas or in rural areas. To some extent, the other two housing experiments help to deal with this limitation.

The Supply Experiment
Objectives

The Housing Allowance Supply Experiment (HASE) is unique among social experiments in its main objective, which was to find out, not how individuals respond to a policy change, but how an entire market responds. Specifically, HASE sought information on housing supply increases and rent and housing price increases in response to heightened housing demand generated by a housing allowance. For this purpose, it was necessary to saturate an area, providing every eligible person with housing allowances. Because of the need for saturation, only a very small number of geographic areas could be studied, and even this was very costly. For this reason, the areas selected for the experiment had to have characteristics that would permit inference to much of the rest of the country, a very difficult matter because HASE had to settle for merely two sites.

Although the major purpose of HASE was to learn how housing supply responds to housing allowances to low-income households, there were a number of additional objectives relating to housing improvements, effects on market intermediaries and indirect suppliers, residential mobility, and neighborhood change.

Basic design

In a strict sense, the Supply Experiment is a demonstration project rather than a social experiment; it has in fact no experimental variables.[13] Eligibility requirements were broader than for the Demand Experiment because it admitted homeowners as well as renters who met the income and household unit restrictions. Payment of housing allowances was based on a fixed formula, namely, the housing-gap formula with the parameter, b, equal to 0.25 and with minimum standards for the housing unit as the earmarking requirement. The basis for estimating the cost of adequate housing included a rent survey as well as a panel of experts. All households were supplied with extensive information about housing and were given Equal Opportunity support as requested.

In an attempt to select two study sites from which inferences could be drawn to the rest of the United States, Brown County, Wisconsin, and Saint Joseph County, Indiana, were chosen from among metropolitan areas with 1970 populations under 250,000, a size limit influenced by the funds available for the study. The emphasis was on contrasts likely to have a major influence on the results of a housing allowance program – tight versus loose housing markets and racial integration versus a segregated minority population.

In the mid-1970s, when the study started, Brown County had about 170,000 inhabitants or about 48,000 households.[14] The housing market has been consistently tight despite considerable new construction, mainly as a result of rapid employment and population growth. About 60 percent of all dwellings were built after 1944, so that the housing stock was in relatively good condition. No seriously blighted neighborhoods existed, even in the urban core. The county's population was racially homogeneous, and its housing market was therefore unsegregated.

Saint Joseph County in 1975 had about 240,000 inhabitants or 76,000 households.[15] The central city, South Bend, had a large surplus of deteriorating housing, and even suburban vacancy rates were rising. The looseness of the housing market was a direct result of a sharp decline in manufacturing employment since the end of World

Table 9.4. *Initial housing conditions at HASE sites*

Area	Habitable units	Average vacancy rate	Annual turnover per 100 units	Average vacancy duration
Regular rental housing[a]				
Brown County	14,700	5.1%	65.6	4.0
St. Joseph County	16,400	10.6	57.4	9.6
Central South Bend	8,000	12.3	59.5	10.7
Rest of county	8,400	8.9	55.3	8.4
Homeowner housing[b]				
Brown County	31,700	0.8	7.4	5.6
St. Joseph County	57,000	2.4	9.9	12.6
Central South Bend	13,600	4.2	8.5	25.7
Rest of county	43,400	1.9	10.2	9.7

Note: Data are for 1973 in Brown County and 1974 in Saint Joseph County.
[a]Excludes mobile-home parks, rooming houses, farmhouses, and federally subsidized dwellings.
[b]Excludes mobile homes.
Source: Rand Corporation, *Fourth Annual Report of the Housing Assistance Supply Experiment* (Santa Monica, May 1978), p. ix.

War II, accompanied by population losses. About 10 percent of the county's population were minorities, mainly blacks. Virtually all the blacks lived in South Bend, constituting about 18 percent of all households there. Shortly before the two studies began, unemployment in Saint Joseph County was about twice as high as that in Brown County, 14 percent in 1974 and 6.5 percent in 1973, respectively.[16]

Statistics on initial housing market conditions in the two locations, as shown in Table 9.4, bear out the much tighter situation in Brown County. In particular, its vacancy rate was much lower than that of Saint Joseph County, as was the average duration of a vacancy.

The eligibility requirements for households in the HASE were broader than in the other two housing allowance experiments. Homeowners were eligible as well as renters, and single persons were eligible as well as households of two or more related individuals. Opening eligibility to homeowners created a substantial increase in the eligibles, because in practice homeowners constituted half of the eligibles in Brown County and 70 percent in Saint Joseph County. By family composition, the eligible households were principally of four types – young couples with children, elderly couples, single parents with children, and elderly single individuals, with the last two types the most numerous.[17]

Administration and implementation

The planning for the Supply Experiment began in April 1972. Program details were worked out, research methods designed, and sites selected during the following two years. As in other social experiments, the research effort was separated from the transfer payments system. The research work was handled by the Rand Corporation, which used various contractors for the survey work. For the transfer payments system, a contract was negotiated by the U.S. Department of Housing and Urban Development, with a local housing authority at each site for the operation of the housing allowance system for a 10-year period. The local authority in turn delegated program operations to a nonprofit corporation established with the assistance of the Rand Corporation, namely, the Housing Allowance Office (HAO). It was the responsibility of the HAO to stimulate applications, screen applicants, evaluate housing of the applicants and later that of the participant households, and disburse funds and monitor the payment system.

Enrollment began in June 1974 in Brown County and in April 1975 in Saint Joseph County. At the end of September 1979, after 63 months of enrollment efforts in the Green Bay area, 53 percent of the eligible households had been enrolled in the program. In Saint Joseph County, after 57 months of operation, about 44 percent of the estimated eligible households had been enrolled.

The status in the two locations as of September 1979 is summarized in Table 9.5. As of that date, about 7.5 percent of the total households in each county were receiving payments. These payments averaged about $86 monthly, augmenting the recipients' gross incomes by about 22 percent.

From an administrative point of view, five major administrative

Table 9.5. *Enrollment data at HASE sites, as of September 1979*

Item	Brown County	St. Joseph County	Total
Applications	17,317	32,611	49,928
Total ever enrolled	9,540	15,256	24,796
Terminations or suspensions	4,365	5,978	10,343
Not authorized for payments	1,486	3,558	5,044
Currently receiving payments	3,689	5,720	9,409
Percentage of total households receiving payments	7.7	7.6	7.6

Note: The date, September 1979, is after 63 months of full operation in Brown County and 57 months in Saint Joseph County.
Source: Adapted from Rand Corporation, *Sixth Annual Report of the Housing Assistance Supply Experiment* (Santa Monica, 1980), p. 16.

functions can be distinguished – outreach, enrollment, error control, housing evaluation, and services to enrollees.[18]

The outreach function, namely, bringing the program to the attention of eligible households, relied heavily on advertising and presentation to community groups. The two HAOs spent an average of $10.58 per eligible household during the first 30 months of program operations. After that, applications per $100 of media advertising fell sharply in Brown County but slowly in Saint Joseph County. It appears that about equal participation rates could have been achieved with lower outreach costs during the second year.

Inquiries concerning enrollment were screened by telephone before formal applications were submitted. As a result of screening and voluntary dropouts, only about 45 percent of all those who inquired were actually interviewed, and only a third of the initial inquiries resulted in enrollment.

A major effort was undertaken to control errors in payments to recipients. It was estimated that such errors occurred in no more than 9 percent of enrollments, with overpayment averaging under five dollars per recipient year in both counties.

Housing evaluation and certification were based on model housing codes developed by national organizations, with consideration given to the peculiarities of the local code. Each enrollee's dwelling was visited by a trained evaluator who examined each of 38 items bearing on the dwelling's habitable space, facilities, and conditions. Average evaluation cost in 1976 was $27, with office procedures related to housing certification adding another six dollars.

Services to enrollees included sessions to discuss different aspects of leases, landlord–tenant relationships, housing discrimination, local housing alternatives, home purchase, HAO housing standards, and home improvement methods. Legal services were offered to those who encountered housing discrimination. Despite substantial efforts to draw people to such sessions, however, only 9 persons in Brown County and 178 in Saint Joseph County ever attended.[19]

Overall administrative costs, when normalized by workload units, were about the same in the two sites. Enrolling an applicant household and qualifying it for payment cost in 1976 about $249 – 24 percent outreach expenses, 49 percent enrollment-processing expenses, and 27 percent housing certification. Annual cost of subsequent services to a recipient was about $133, with 58 percent for semiannual and annual eligibility recertification, 26 percent for housing recertification, and 16 percent for operations in support of monthly allowance payments.[20]

When the expenses of client intake are amortized over a postulated average enrollment duration of three years, total administrative costs per recipient year were estimated to be $216. Of this amount, $146 was for income transfer functions and $70 for administering housing requirements.[21]

The research effort involved a massive amount of data collection. Included were not only interviews every year with the household participants in the HASE but also interviews with landlords and financial intermediaries. Information was also sought from various parts of the construction and housing industry on the state of the housing market and on residential construction as well as costs. In 1977, for example, interviews were completed at both sites with approximately 1,900 landlords, 3,500 renters, and 1,200 homeowners.[22]

Findings

The results of the five years of the Supply Experiment can be summarized in terms of general housing market effects and the direct effect of housing allowances on participants in the program. In addition to supply responsiveness, there is also concern about the effect of such a program on market intermediaries and residential mobility and neighborhood change, in particular, housing integration.

Supply responsiveness

Of particular concern is the extent to which income transfers in the form of housing allowances to low-income households would drive up rents and home prices rather than result in better housing. Thus, it was feared that these income transfers would be dissipated in price inflation. Based on an evaluation of the first two years of the study, the conclusion was reached that "attempts of program participants to secure acceptable housing have had virtually no effect on rents or home prices in either site, but have resulted in a modest improvement in the quality of existing housing."[23]

The results are particularly interesting because they cover the period of rapid enrollment, when rent inflation was most likely to occur. Still, with 20 percent of all households eligible to enroll and only a third of them enrolled, the inflationary pressure generated by the program could not be very large.

Rent increases did occur in both sites during the early years of the experiment, but they were quite moderate for those years. Thus, the average annual increase in contract rent (the amount paid for space only) amounted to about 4.4 percent in Brown County between January 1974 and March 1977, and 3.1 percent in Saint Joseph County between November 1974 and August 1976. Average annual increase in gross rent (which includes heating and other utilities) were 6.7 percent and 5.0 percent, respectively.

As brought out in Table 9.6 for Brown County, approximately 70 percent of the increase in gross rent in 1974 and in 1977 was due to rising fuel and utility bills. The rent that the tenant paid for space

Table 9.6. *Components of gross rent increase for typical dwelling, Brown County, 1974–1977*

Period	Shelter rent	Fuel and utilities	Gross rent
Typical monthly expense			
January 1974	$128.89	$41.11	$170.00
January 1975	131.03	49.70	180.73
January 1976	135.40	61.05	196.45
January 1977	141.44	70.69	212.13
Change in expense			
1974–5	1.7%	20.9%	6.3%
1975–6	3.3	22.8	8.7
1976–7	4.5	15.8	8.0
Annual average	3.2	19.8	7.7

Note: Estimates are for a five-room dwelling meeting HAO standards and renting for $170 (including fuel and utilities) in January 1974. Gross rent inflation was estimated from survey data for the years indicated; inflation in fuel and utility expenses was estimated from consumption norms and local rate schedules. Shelter rent inflation was derived as a residual.
Source: Adapted from James P. Stucker, *Rent Inflation in Brown County, Wisconsin: 1973–78* (Rand Corporation, WN-10073-HUD, forthcoming).

increased by an average of only 3.2 percent annually, a rate that led the researchers to the conclusion that "the allowance program's contribution to rent inflation must have been negligible."[24]

As is noted by the researchers, the annual rent increases in Brown and Saint Joseph counties compare favorably with the average increases in north-central cities with populations of 50,000 to 250,000. The overall average in 1974 was 4.6 percent compared with 3.7 percent in Brown County; in 1975, 5.0 percent versus 4.4 percent; and in 1976, 7.1 percent versus 4.8 percent. The 1975–6 percentage increase in Saint Joseph County of 3.1 compares with an overall average of 5.0 and 7.1 percent in 1975 and 1976, respectively.[25]

There are a number of possible explanations for the muted rent effects of the program.[26] Renter enrollees never accounted for more than 15 percent of all renters in each county. Even in central South Bend, where rental units constituted 37 percent of all dwellings and where about 27 percent of all renters enrolled during the first two program years, rents did not increase more than for comparable dwellings elsewhere in the county.

Rent inflation, however, is only one possible supply response to an increased housing demand resulting from housing allowances. Housing improvement and housing construction are perhaps equally important. Thus, the question is whether the housing allowance program increased the supply of safe and sanitary housing.

The answer is not clear. During the first two program years, 49 percent of the dwellings of enrollees in Brown County and 55 percent in Saint Joseph County failed initial evaluation. Of the two sites taken together, 32 percent of the failed dwellings lacked adequate space or interior privacy, 29 percent lacked adequate kitchen or bathroom facilities, and 83 percent had one or more hazardous conditions.

In fact, however, about 8 of 10 enrollees managed to meet the housing standards established by the program and qualify for payments. Improved housing was obtained mainly by repairing the dwelling in which the applicant resided rather than by moving into a new building. These initial repairs usually were quite small and sought to remedy health and safety hazards, although repairs made to remedy problems uncovered in later inspections were more likely to relate to major structural defects or deterioration of the dwelling.

Because of the nature of the repairs and the extensive use of unpaid, nonprofessional labor, the cost of the repairs was very modest. In fact, most of the repairs were carried out by tenants or by joint efforts of tenants and landlords. Only 12 percent of all initial repairs were carried out by professional contractors. The median cash outlay for repairing dwellings was $10. Three out of four substandard dwellings were repaired for less than $25 in Brown County and for less than $30 in Saint Joseph County.[27] Homeowners who participated in the program typically spent $80–$140 more on annual repair than did unenrolled homeowners in the same income bracket.

As a result of this program, about 4,000 dwellings in Brown County and 6,500 dwellings in Saint Joseph County were repaired through September 1979 at the initiative of households seeking to qualify for payment, about two-thirds of all initially defective dwellings. In the annual evaluation of the dwellings of the participating households, however, about one-fifth in Brown County and a third of those in Saint Joseph County failed to meet the current standards. Of those that were repaired once more, the large majority (approximately 90 percent) did come up to standard. At the same time, about 15 percent of the households in Brown County and 8 percent of those in Saint Joseph County whose dwellings had been rated acceptable moved after qualifying for payments.[28]

Finally, repairs by enrollees appear not to have spilled over in the sense of motivating others not in the program to follow suit, nor is there any evidence that the program stimulated new construction.

Market intermediaries

Although such market intermediaries as real estate brokers, mortgage lenders, home improvement lenders, and contractors could have substantial effect on housing market conditions, the results of the HASE indicate that any actions by these agents as a result of this experiment had little effect on altering the housing situation. As reported by the researchers, "members of those industries have mostly conducted their business as usual."[29] It has been estimated, for instance, that in Saint Joseph County participants and their landlords paid about half a million dollars to home repair contractors during the first year of the program and about a million dollars in the second year. Yet, these numbers are very small relative to the approximately $46 million estimated to have been spent in those two years by all residents in that county for repair of dwelling units.

Residential mobility and neighborhood change

During the first two program years, about one-fifth of all participants moved, many of them renters. Although 40 percent of the participating renters in Saint Joseph County moved during the period, only 33 percent did so in Brown County. Much of the moving took place during the rather brief interval between enrollment and first housing certification – half of the moves in Brown County and 75 percent in Saint Joseph County. Apparently more than half of the precertification movers did so because of inability to arrange for repairs, and the others seem to have been dissatisfied with their preenrollment homes. Moving rates dropped off after certification to a level below that of the general population.

Though the moving behavior of homeowners appeared not to be affected by the program, that of renters was. They appeared to move about 10 times as frequently as homeowners, and renters under 62 years of age moved about three times more often than elderly renters. By the end of the second program year, about one-third of the renters at each site had moved. Apparently, program requirements affected the timing, if not the long-run incidence, of moves by renters, because there were more frequent moves from uncertified dwellings than from certified ones. Of the renters who did move, about 75 percent paid more for their new quarters than for their former ones and were typically paying 35–50 percent more in contract rent than at the time of enrollment.

In spite of the fact that three of four moves crossed neighborhood boundaries, the net effect on neighborhoods was apparently small. Only a handful of neighborhoods in each site gained or lost 10 or more households because of these moves. The largest changes in neighborhoods in either county, however, represented less than 2 percent of the neighborhood's population. In central South Bend, program-related moves culminated in small net shifts of blacks from neighborhoods that were heavily black to those with a more even racial mixture, as well as in a small net outflow of whites from the core of the area to its fringes. Yet, interestingly enough, moves into and out of central South Bend balanced almost exactly for both blacks and whites.

The overall evidence is that moves by program participants have been neither numerous enough nor selective enough to change the social order or disturb the housing market of a particular neighborhood.

Direct housing allowance effect

There is evidence that the housing allowances greatly benefited the enrollees, typically offsetting from one-third to two-thirds of a recipient's housing expenses. In terms of participants purchasing their own homes, however, the Housing Allowance Program contributed very little. Thus, during the first two program years, only 28 renters in Brown County and 82 in Saint Joseph County bought homes.[30] The low property values in Saint Joseph County are the most likely explanation for the higher purchase rate in that area.

Evaluative comments

A review of the results of the first three years cannot overlook the relatively low rates of participation in the program. A variety of factors can be considered responsible. First, the promotional campaigns were not too effective and seem to have been planned in anticipation of a seller's market. Second, when applications did come in large numbers, the agencies were not prepared to process them quickly, which led to disenchantment among the applicants. Third, certain groups in the population were especially reluctant to participate, notably some of the elderly and the homeowners. Although these two categories are not mutually exclusive, distinct reasons seemed to be involved, such as suspicion of the program and its information requirements by the elderly and a feeling by homeowners that the program was meant mainly for renters.

Under the circumstances, it is hardly surprising that the effect of this program on housing prices seems to be negligible. The 7 percent of households that were receiving housing allowance payments at any one time represent a small proportion not only absolutely but also in relation to the 20 percent of all households that were eligible to enroll. It should be noted, however, that these are average participation rates, and there may be many central city areas where a much higher percentage of renters would participate, should there be a national housing allowance program and more effective promotion.

A second important consideration is that assistance averaged $86 per month per participant household in Green Bay and in South Bend, substantial amounts for the families involved but relatively little compared with aggregate housing costs in those areas. Under these conditions, a substantial housing gap remained. Even after deducting their housing allowances from their housing expenses, two-thirds of all renters and a third of all owners were spending in excess of one-fourth of their incomes for housing. Hence, Congress may have to offer more generous allowances in a national program.

Has the program improved housing conditions for the participants? In terms of the proportions of families whose housing meets minimum standards, the answer is clearly yes, as noted earlier. In Green Bay, where experience is longest, nearly 80 percent of these households had improved their dwellings to meet the standards, and the trend in South Bend was similar.[31] Nevertheless, a question remains regarding the significance of such minimum standards when three of every four substandard dwellings could be repaired for less than $25 in Brown County and for less than $30 in Saint Joseph County. More than half the repairs involved fixing windows or handrails, for example. Under these conditions it is little wonder that the program had little effect on home repairs, policies of landlords, rents, home prices, or mortgage lender activities. To what extent such improvements represent real gains in housing quality can be questioned, because only in a very small proportion of these cases was the dwelling improved in any substantial way.

A final problem relates to the extent to which one of the two sites, Brown County, represents an adequate base for generalization to the rest of the country. The county's population contains a large proportion of people of Scandinavian origin, and the residents are known to place considerable emphasis on having quality housing; they have a reputation for maintaining housing in good condition even when incomes are low. Hence, if housing is already in good condition, the provision of a subsidy for obtaining improved housing is not likely to have much effect. To what extent the worse than average conditions in Saint Joseph County serve to offset the tendencies in Brown County is not clear.

Be that as it may, by the summer of 1978 it became sufficiently clear that there was little prospect of this program having any effect on the housing markets, given the low participation rate of eligible households and the high turnover when they were enrolled in the program. In addition, whether it was because of the ability of enrollees to bring their dwellings up to standards at very moderate expenditures or because of much lower income elasticity of housing demand than was anticipated, negligible pressures were exerted by the program on the market either for housing repairs or for improved, different dwelling units. Hence, continuation of the field work on this social experiment was suspended with four waves of interviews; in Saint Joseph County the field work was to be terminated with a fourth annual wave of interviews in 1978 (the fourth wave of interviews in Brown County having taken place the preceding year).[32]

The Administrative Agency Experiment
Objectives
The Administrative Agency Experiment (AAE) of the EHAP was set up primarily to obtain information about the costs of a cash housing allowance program. From an experimental point of view, it was more or less a hybrid between a social experiment and a demonstration project. The experimental aspect was carried out rather loosely, with no statistical control. It consisted of the assignment of the same task, a housing allowance program, to eight public agencies, each in a different city. The agencies were selected by the Department of Housing and Urban Development (HUD), with the overall conduct and coordination of the experiment subcontracted to Abt Associates.

As is evident from Table 9.7, the agencies were of various types and were selected from widely different parts of the country. Some were state housing agencies, some were city or local housing authorities, and some were social service agencies. Some of the agencies were in metropolitan areas, others were in smaller cities, and still others were in rural areas. Housing conditions and vacancy rates also varied rather drastically, from a loose housing market in Tulsa and San Bernardino to a tight housing market in Jacksonville and Peoria.

Treatment variables
To provide as much focus as possible on obtaining cost information, the AAE contained no experimental variables. Each agency was required to enroll a designated number of families in a cash housing allowance program, certify the eligibility of the households, and provide monthly cash assistance payments for two years.

HUD encouraged the agencies to follow their own procedures, presumably to allow each agency to have the flexibility to develop as cost-effective procedures as possible. Eligibility requirements were similar to those of the Demand Experiment, admitting low-income households of two or more related individuals or single-person households where the occupant was elderly (65 years of age or more), disabled, or handicapped. Unlike the Demand Experiment, the payment of housing allowances was based on a fixed formula, namely, the housing-gap formula with the parameter, b, equal to 0.25, and with minimum standards for the housing unit as the earmarking requirement.

Sample design

Although the agencies were free to follow any administrative procedures they felt best, each agency was restricted in the number of households it could enroll to a figure between 400 and 900, as shown in Table 9.8. No sampling plan was followed by these agencies, because the objective was to obtain applications for the housing assistance program by informational and promotional campaigns, not by individual solicitation. Hence, the usual measures of survey performance are not applicable. About all that can be examined is the extent to which applications were received from the eligible population and the degree to which these applications were transformed into active participants in the program.

From the information of this type in Table 9.8, it is clear that the agencies had only moderate success in these respects. Partly perhaps because response was overanticipated and partly because every agency was assigned an enrollment quota, the applications to the program were considerably fewer than the number of eligible households in any of the areas. The proportion of the estimated eligible households that applied varied from 10 percent to 48 percent. The lower limit was encountered in an area with a relatively large number of eligible families (Jacksonville), but even this figure was obtained only after a second round of applications was sought.

Somewhat over one-third of the applications were enrolled, this percentage varying from 30 in Jacksonville to 55 in rural North Da-

Table 9.7. Characteristics of the eight AAE sites

Location of administrative agency	Site characteristics				Demographic characteristics				Housing market		
	Contracting agency	Census region	Population of program area	Geographic character	% Families below poverty	% minority	No. eligible population (household)	Eligible households as % of total households	% Rental	% Lacking plumbing	Rental vacancy rate
Salem, Ore.	Housing Authority of City of Salem	Pacific West	186,658	Metropolitan area	7.9	1.7	5,232	9	37.3	1.5	7.2
Springfield, Mass.	Commonwealth of Massachusetts Dept. of Community Affairs	New England	472,917	Metropolitan area (4 cities and 15 surrounding towns)	6.6	5.0	17,572	13	41.5	2.7	6.2
	State of Illinois Dept. of Local										

City	Agency	Region	Population	Jurisdiction							
Peoria, Ill.	Government Affairs, Office of Housing and Buildings	East-North-Central	196,865	City of Peoria and Fulton County (rural); Woodford County (rural)	5.9	6.3	5,235	10	30.9	3.0	4.5[c]
San Bernardino, Calif.	San Bernardino County Board of Supervisors	Pacific West	547,258	Valley portion of San Bernardino County (10 incorporated cities and towns and an equal number of unincorporated places)	9.8	23.0[a]	13,745	12	36.4	0.9	12.0
Bismarck, N. Dak.	Social Services Board of North Dakota	West-North-Central	104,187	4 rural counties (Burleigh, Morton, Stark, and Stutsman), each with 1 major city	11.8	0.8	2,176	9	31.4	5.9[b]	8.1[d]
Jacksonville, Fla.	Jacksonville, Dept. of Housing and Urban Development	South Atlantic	545,900	Metropolitan area (all of Duval County)	14.0	22.9	17,429	11	32.7	4.4	4.0[c]
	Durham County Dept. of			Durham County (city of Durham as well as rural)							

Table 9.7. (*continued*)

Location of administrative agency	Contracting agency	Site characteristics			Demographic characteristics				Housing market		
		Census region	Population of program area	Geographic character	% Families below poverty	% minority	No. eligible population (household)	Eligible households as % of total households	% Rental	% Lacking plumbing	Rental vacancy rate
Durham, N.C.	Social Services	South Atlantic	132,681	portion of county)	14.0	37.6	5,620	14	53.0	2.9	6.0
Tulsa, Okla.	Tulsa Housing Authority	West-South-Central	342,00	Metropolitan area	9.0	12.5	8,734	7	33.0	1.9	13.6

[a]Includes 16% "Persons of Spanish Language or Surname."
[b]More recently housing studies of Bismarck indicate that the degree of substandardness in the city's housing is considerably lower than census figures for the full program area suggest.
[c]Vacancy rates for Peoria and Jacksonville are adjusted for standardness (locally defined).
[d]Vacancy rate for the city of Bismarck is 6.1%; for the full program area, 8.1%.

Source: Frederick T. Temple et al., *Third Annual Report of the Administrative Agency Experiment Evaluation* (Cambridge, Mass., Abt Associates, 1976). Bismardk population and housing figures revised to include full program area, using U.S. Bureau of the Census, *County and City Data Book, 1972* (Washington, D.C. U.S. Government Printing Office, 1972).

kota. These low rates partly represent ineligibility of households at the initial stages of screening and certification (most often as a result of exceeding the income limits) and also the difficulties of enrolling households and their qualifying for payments in terms of the standards set by the different agencies.

Administration and implementation

As is evident from the preceding section, the implementation of the plans, though not particularly complicated, proved quite difficult. This becomes clear when we consider the various administrative tasks that had to be carried out, namely, outreach, certification, supportive services, and inspection.

The function of the outreach stage (a fancy term for generating applications) was to recruit a sufficient number of household applications for the program to produce the required number of participants. Operating on the mistaken assumption that people would flock to apply for the program once they were aware of it, relatively little promotion work was undertaken at the outset by most of the agencies, with heavy reliance placed on referrals from other social service agencies and local community groups.[33] As a result, many of the agencies did not receive enough applications to fill their quotas for recipients. Moreover, an average of only 17 percent of those eligible to participate applied to the program, a percentage that ranged from 10 percent in San Bernardino and Jacksonville to 48 percent in Salem (Table 9.8).

Furthermore, the applicants generally underrepresented the elderly, male-headed households, white households, and the "working poor" (nonelderly households with no welfare support). In fact, the bulk of the applicants turned out to be households on welfare, which may have imparted a stigma to the program that deterred those without welfare support from applying.

The experiences at Jacksonville, Florida, were particularly frustrating and brought out very clearly the sorts of problems that were being encountered to a greater or lesser degree at all sites. As a result of limited and ineffective publicity, only about 10 percent of the eligible households in that area were enrolled in the program, with

Table 9.8. Enrollment experience of agencies at AAE sites

| | Households | | | Total eligible | Applications as percentage of eligibles | Enrolled as percentage of applications |
	To be enrolled	Actually enrolled	Applying[a]			
Site						
Salem, Ore.	900	870	2,527	5,232	48.3	34.4
Springfield, Mass.	900	861	2,478	17,572	14.1	34.7
Peoria, Ill.	900	835	2,242	5,235	42.8	37.2
San Bernardino County, Calif.	900	776	2,050	19,745	10.4	37.8
Rural North Dakota	400	367	665	2,176	30.6	55.2
Jacksonville, Fla.	900	541[b]	1,806[b]	17,429	10.4	30.0
Durham, N.C.	500	483	1,337	5,620	23.8	36.1
Tulsa, Okla.	900	825	2,283	8,734	26.1	36.1
Total	6,300	5,558	15,388	81,743	18.8	36.1

[a]Refers to households formally screened by the agencies.
[b]After two enrollment periods.
Source: Dickson, *Certification*, pp. 2, 13.

heavy representation from black households and from those on welfare.[34] The publicity seems to have been especially poor in reaching elderly households, and this fact, combined with the reluctance of the working poor to enroll in what seemed to be another welfare assistance program, led to a highly atypical group of enrollees.

It is clear that in their "outreach" stage, the agencies followed the most economical approach they could think of, making as little use as possible of the media and of advertising techniques. In fact, however, the media and general advertising techniques tended to produce higher proportions of the households usually underrepresented, and it was on these techniques that the agencies later placed more emphasis.

The certification stage raised further problems. Households had to be certified for the program in terms of their income and household size. This was carried out in a variety of ways ranging from self-reports by the applicant households to verification by the agencies using outside sources. Not surprisingly, the latter approach was found to be more time-consuming and costly, but it also tended to be more accurate. Using outside verification tended to produce higher estimates of income for about half of the households, with a consequent reduction of their payments or a finding of noneligibility.

Many of the enrollees never became participants because they were unable to meet the relatively strict housing standards imposed by the agency. Ironically, black households were much less likely to qualify than other households, partly because they were already in low-quality units and partly because they were unable to move due to a tight housing market.

Moreover, a considerable proportion of the applicants that would have been otherwise eligible were unable to meet the minimum housing quality requirement. In seven of the eight areas, the proportion meeting these requirements varied between 65 and 86 percent; in Jacksonville, the proportion was only 33 percent, presumably because of a tight housing market.[35] Of the households that became recipients in the program, about one-fifth had dropped out by the end of the first year (nearly half because of ineligibilities or voluntary dropouts), a percentage that varied from 15 in Durham to 29 in Jacksonville.

The eligibility problem was especially serious in Jacksonville, partly because of the tight housing market and partly because of the low level of supportive services provided by the agency.[36] Furthermore, partly because of racial discrimination, minority households in substandard housing were unable to move elsewhere or to upgrade their present housing. Only 22 percent of the black households enrolled in Jacksonville, for example, initially were successful in meeting the housing standards and receiving housing allowances, compared with 53 percent of the white households enrolled in the area and 77 percent of households enrolled at the other seven sites. What made things worse was that Jacksonville was one of the sites where housing quality standards were rigidly enforced, something the agency did not want to alter despite the problems encountered.

The fact that the supportive services provided by the Jacksonville agency were not strong contributed further to the mediocre results obtained in that city. In addition, the agency in Jacksonville did not make much effort to assist enrolled households in finding better housing or (at least initially) to deal with the resistance of the housing industry to the Housing Allowance Program. Moreover, when the agency did finally make an attempt to improve the program's image, there is little evidence that much success was achieved.[37]

Supportive services were of two types: formal services provided through group meetings and meant to inform participants of the various aspects of the program; and responsive services designed to assist individual households as problems arose.[38] Formal services were intended primarily to help enrolled households meet the requirements of the assistance program and become recipients of allowances. These services were offered in all but one site on a mandatory basis, though apparently there was little uniformity among the agencies in the type of services offered.

The discretionary nature of these services apparently also carried over to the data collection procedures, with the result that only one agency, Springfield, maintained careful records of attendance at formal sessions and use of responsive services. The indications from this one set of records are that the formal services were not very effective in increasing the likelihood of enrollees becoming recipients of the program. The responsive service approach, however, which gave individualized attention to enrollees, seemed to have some effect in helping people to become recipients, particularly people who were planning to move, who were black, and who were living in a tight housing market.[39] "Among households that planned to move, 52% of those who received only formal services succeeded in becoming recipients, compared to an 80% success rate among those who received additional services."[40] At two sites where low levels of responsive services were offered in a tight housing market, only one-fourth of the black households planning to move were successful, as compared with nearly two-thirds of the black households who were planning to move in other tight housing markets where more intensive responsive services were provided.

Inspection of the housing facilities of the participants was carried out by experts in some agencies and by regular agency personnel especially trained for this purpose in others. Not surprisingly, the results varied, with the experts being more likely to find a housing unit ineligible in terms of the standards imposed but with other agency personnel making increasingly similar judgments as the amount of their training increased.[41]

The evidence seems to be, however, that the principal determinant of the ability of the participants' housing units to meet the quality standards were the standards themselves rather than the method by which the inspection was carried out.

Findings

The principal findings of this experiment relate to the administrative aspects, particularly to the administrative arrangements and to the costs of a housing allowance program.

In terms of the administrative arrangements, as might be expected, a variety of such procedures were developed by the agencies to handle this program. Appreciable differences were noted in the procedures used by the agencies to acquaint families in their area with the program and to obtain information on and validate the incomes of the applicant households. The housing standards applied to the participants' dwelling units also varied considerably, as well as the amount and nature of supportive services provided to the participating households.[42]

The conclusion of the researchers, however, was that none of these differences seemed to have much effect on such key variables as program participation, enforcement of program requirements, improvements in the participants' housing, or administrative costs. In view of the small number of agencies involved and the lack of any experimental control, such a conclusion would seem hardly surprising.

In terms of administrative costs, the principal result was that the administrative costs were found to vary substantially among the eight areas, as is shown in Table 9.9. Intake costs (generating household interest and helping households to become participants) varied from $151 per enrollee in Peoria to $292 in Tulsa, with a median of $225. Maintaining households in the program varied from $129 per recipient in Salem to $322 in Jacksonville, with a median of $205. Assuming that an average family stays in the program five years, the median estimate of the administrative cost of a cash housing allowance program per household is estimated at $276 with a range of $137 to $551 per household if costs are calculated for agencies with the lowest unit costs and those with the highest unit costs.[43]

For some types of costs, the variation was so substantial that it is hard to attribute much significance to the data. Some extreme examples for particular intake functions are: outreach (per applicant), $1.00–$27.00; services (per enrollee), $6.00–$45.00; housing inspections (per enrollee), $2.00–$26.00. Among maintenance functions, examples include: services (per recipient year), $11.00–$85.00; housing inspections (per recipient year), $1.00–$15.00.[44] Moreover, it is not at all clear that the costs for the same activity from different agencies are comparable, because the quality of the performance or the amount of service delivered varied from one agency to another.

Table 9.9. *Administrative costs at the AAE sites (annual rate per household assisted)*

Site	Intake costs[a]	Maintenance costs	Total administrative costs[b]
Bismarck	$215	$235	$278
Durham	233	231	278
Jacksonville	230	322	368
Peoria	151	171	201
Salem	178	129	165
San Bernardino	246	178	227
Springfield	219	267	311
Tulsa	292	144	202
Median site cost	225	205	250

[a]Costs adjusted by median site costs of working with families that later dropped out of the program without becoming recipients.
[b]Assumes intake costs amortized over five years; thus, "total administrative costs" are one-fifth of "intake costs," plus "maintenance costs."
Source: David B. Carlson and John D. Heinberg, *How Housing Allowances Work: Integrated Findings from the Experimental Housing Allowance Program* (Washington, D.C.: Urban Institute, 1978), p. 41.

Evaluative comments

In view of the absence of any controls on the procedures used by these agencies and the relatively small number of agencies, only the most general type of information seems to have been obtained about operating experiences and administrative costs. Presumably, the fact that there were two public agencies of each type was to provide a base for evaluating differences by type of agency. The huge differences between the individual agency operations and the characteristics of the sites suggest, however, that this variable is of little relevance; and no use seems to have been made of this distinction in the analysis of the data.

The fact that the length of this particular experiment in the field was only two years introduces still another complication, because recent experience indicates that two years is hardly enough time for a program of this type to become established. There is little doubt that hardly any agencies were aware of the sorts of problems they would be getting into, and as a result appreciable portions of time, and costs, were devoted to learning how to deal with the administrative problems of such a program. To what extent costs obtained in such a "shakedown" process are meaningful can be seriously questioned. At best, the results provide information on the types of problems that need to be faced in administering a cash housing allowance program and, possibly, on means of dealing with these problems. One may well ask, however, whether the same information would not already have been available from the Demand Experiment and the Supply Experiment.

Moreover, the experiment does not seem to have yielded much information on the one question in Table 9.1 for which it was meant to serve as the sole source, namely, on the appropriate administration and management means of operating a housing allowance program. The results show the sort of problems involved in administering a housing allowance program and indicate that a variety of social service agencies, if left to their own resources, are not likely to deal very effectively with these problems, at least within the short period of two years. In terms of how a housing allowance program should be administered, however, the principal results seem to relate to pitfalls and types of activities that should not be undertaken, rather than to the best methods of organizing and administering such a program.

Integrated analysis

Bringing together the results of the three cash housing allowance experiments and using the combined data to determine how the housing allowance concept ties into a national housing policy are the tasks of the integrated analysis by the Urban Institute. In addition to bringing together the results from the various experiments,[45] the data have been used as inputs into a "transfer program simulation model" (TRIM) to estimate the cost and implications of operating a cash housing allowance program at a national level.[46] The results obtained to date are in line with the findings summarized in the previous pages. Very briefly, the model projects a participation rate of no more than about 40 percent of all eligible households, or somewhat over 7 million households, with an average subsidy of about $65 per month.[47] The total cost of such a program, including administrative costs, is estimated at about $7.4 billion in 1976 dollars.

Evaluative comments

Whether a subsidy of approximately $1,000 per year per household is the best way of improving housing standards is a question to which the policy makers will no doubt give considerable attention. It would seem, however, that prior consideration should be given to the reliability of the data on which these estimates are based, in view of the methodological difficulties noted previously. Confounding these methodological difficulties is the lack of comparability of the different experiments in various respects. These include differences in the meaning of, and procedures used to check, housing quality; differences in definitions of income; and inclusion of home-owners only in the Supply Experiment.

Overall comments

As originally designed, the plan for the cash housing allowance experiment seemed logical. There were to be three sets of experiments: one to investigate the effect of cash allowances on the demand for housing; one to investigate the effect on the supply of housing; and one to investigate the effect of methods of administration. Unfortunately, the problems that arose vitiate many of the advantages of this design. One problem is that these aspects are not independent and cannot be studied separately from each other. Thus, the demand response to a system of cash housing allowances clearly depends on the tightness of the supply of housing, and the response of the suppliers of housing depends on the extent of demand generated by the housing allowances. Moreover, both sets of responses are not independent of the method of administration, particularly the way the system is communicated to the potential participants, the criteria used to establish acceptable standards for housing, and the rigidity with which the system is administered. One could well argue that much sounder information would have been obtained about the management of these experiments had the funds for the Administrative

Agency Experiment been merged with those of the other two experiments and various management aspects been tested with suitable control.

Second, problems of implementation, as in other social experiments, seriously reduced the validity of the results. The fact that only a small proportion of the eligible households contacted were enrolled in the Demand Experiment and that less than half the eligible households in the sample areas chose to participate in the Supply Experiment raises serious doubts about the generality of the results. The generality of the results from the Supply Experiment is further hampered by the questionable nature of the two areas where the study was carried out. In the case of the Administrative Agency Experiment, the highly variable procedures used by the different agencies combined with the complete absence of any controls make possible only the most general estimates of the cost effectiveness and efficiency of different management methods.

To be sure, it is easy to point out shortcomings of these experiments by hindsight. Indeed, the question has been raised whether these experiments were really necessary in the first place, whether the same results could not have been obtained by conventional methods.[48] Of course, some of the key results might have been fairly clear in terms of response, given the poor implementation of some of these experiments combined with the situation of the housing markets in those areas. Still, the fact remains that a great deal of useful information has been obtained on housing response to different types of cash housing allowances, particularly from the Demand Experiment. We also have a pretty good idea that, short of almost universal participation by low-income families in a cash housing allowance program, there is likely to be little effect on the supply of housing or on the functioning of the housing market. Finally, a great deal of information has been obtained about the pitfalls that are encountered in the administration and management of such experiments.

10

What have we learned?

Although some of the social experiments covered in previous chapters are still underway, sufficient information would now seem to be available to provide some fairly conclusive evidence on the value of this relatively new tool of economic analysis and to place social experimentation in proper perspective. As a basis for doing so, the first part of this chapter seeks to synthesize what has been learned from the social experiments that have been carried out so far. This synthesis is undertaken from two points of view. First, what has been learned about economic behavior? And second, what has been learned about the pitfalls of social experimentation? Based on this synthesis, the concluding part suggests conditions under which social experimentation might be used advantageously for economic decision making.

Economic behavior

Much is being learned about economic behavior from these social experiments. Skeptics may allege that much of this information could have been predicted from economic theory, but usually this is true only of the general direction of effects and not of the magnitudes involved, and even then predictions would differ by the type of theoretical approach that is used.

There is little doubt that much more has been learned about economic behavior from some of these experiments than from others.

Even the best of these experiments could have been improved if hindsight were available. In some of the other experiments, unfortunately, the conditions under which the experiment was carried out – or the failure to consider key aspects of the experiments – seriously affect the validity of the results. If, for example, an experiment seeks to obtain estimates of price elasticities but makes virtually no allowance for price variation, little can be inferred from the results. Fortunately, most of the mistakes made in these experiments were much less consequential. To place this discussion in proper perspective, however, it seems useful to indicate not only what has been learned about economic behavior from these experiments but also what has not been learned, or at least what has not been established, about the topics under investigation. The two experiments not discussed in this section are the Health Insurance Study and the Youth Entitlement Program, because few findings relative to economic behavior are available at this writing.

From a positive point of view, the principal findings about economic behavior to date have emerged from the negative income tax (NIT) experiments and the cash housing allowance experiments. In the former case, the results are fairly conclusive that an NIT program tends to reduce labor supply moderately for principal wage earners but substantially for secondary earners, relative to control families. To be sure, whether a 5–10 percent decrease in the labor supply of low-income families (perhaps a 1–2 percent decrease for all families) is really moderate is a matter of judgment; also, its effect on wage rates could be substantial if the decrease were concentrated in particular types of occupations. Moreover, the extent of this (relative) decrease, especially for principal wage earners, is itself likely to vary with economic conditions, tending to be smaller in a tight labor market than in a soft market. That control families are likely to work more in prosperity than in depression makes this type of variation even more probable. From the point of view of economic stabilization, therefore, an NIT program may have countercyclical effects.

Although the data have not yet been fully analyzed, evidence is accumulating that the likelihood of participation by eligible households in an NIT program is highly sensitive to the tax rate and the support level. This likelihood of participation increases very sharply as the tax rate is decreased and as the support level is increased. In addition, those who do participate in the plan tend to reduce their hours of work more than those who do not choose to participate; the immediate cash benefits to be obtained from participation seem to be paramount, partly perhaps because the rules for eligibility are simple and easy to understand, unlike some of the other administrative aspects of the NIT plans.

In addition, there is growing evidence that an NIT plan can affect various other aspects of a household's behavior, mostly in a positive direction. Thus, school attendance of the younger members of the household seems to increase, as does nutrition, and many households seem to make some effort to improve their housing accommodations. An increased rate of marital dissolution seems to accompany an NIT program, however, possibly because the additional income provides participants with the financial resources to take action they otherwise cannot afford.

Some of these results could have been predicted from economic theory, but others could not. The fact remains, however, that the findings from the NIT experiments not only provide the necessary support but also furnish a basis for making empirical estimates of the extent of participation and the cost of alternative national programs, varying with the particular sets of treatments that are imposed. They offer the intriguing possibility of eliminating poverty among such families in exchange for a reduction in their labor supply of perhaps 5–10 percent, or about 1–2 percent of the total labor supply and a fraction of 1 percent of total production.

Some of the findings from the cash housing allowance experiments are not very different from those of the NIT experiments. Perhaps the most striking similarity is that the effect of the housing allowances seems to be most pronounced when the housing market is soft. When it is tight, families treat the housing allowance not as a means to improve their housing situation but as a way to supplement their consumption in other ways. In such a situation, homeowners are in a better position to improve the quality of their housing than are tenants.

Where families receive housing allowances, the quality of housing generally seems to be improved, even to some extent in a tight housing market. Questions arise, however, about the significance of these improvements because, as noted in Chapter 9, the improvements are generally of such a limited nature that one may question whether the housing standards used have much meaning. If something can be repaired with relatively little cost, it is done; if not, it is not at all clear that the necessary repairs will be made.

An especially puzzling factor in the housing allowance experiments is the very low rate of participation. Despite the best efforts by the experimenters, not much more than half of the eligible families in an area elected to participate in this program. Whether it is because most economists are not good at marketing (and there is evidence of this fact in the reports on the experiments) or because certain types of people will not accept a free good regardless of the circumstances is not clear. In any event, it is somewhat surprising to find from the housing Supply Experiment that the housing allowances seemed to have no effect on housing prices or on the functioning of the housing market in the areas studied. Then again, housing quality was improved very little. Altogether, it is a highly debatable point whether the same findings would remain valid if a similar program were instituted on a national scale and with sufficiently effective communications as to ensure a much higher participation rate of eligible households.

Interesting results have also emerged from the experiment on supported work, but it is too early as yet to judge the final effects. Thus, it is not surprising that in the few months after enrolling in the program the experimentals do considerably better economically and socially than the controls. Still, if the experimentals are able to obtain and hold jobs afterward, the benefits of the program may outweigh the costs. In terms of cost–benefit analysis, however, there is the knotty question of how to deal with the fact that nearly 40 percent of the ex-addicts and half of the ex-offenders drop out in a very short time.

What we are not likely to get from the experiment is information as to the efficacy of the different components of a supported work

program. Thus, to what extent peer support as distinct from graduated stress affects the success of such a program for a particular type
of group and for a specific sort of job training will be very difficult to
determine because of the lack of any experimental treatments on
these variables. The lack of standardization of procedures among
different projects will serve to further confound the problem of dis-
criminating effects due to particular types of treatments from purely
local or individual circumstances.

The weakest of the major experiments covered in this monograph
are those on electricity peak pricing. Carried out by more than a
dozen independent groups in different ways, with virtually no overall
coordination, the comparability of the results is highly questionable.
In addition, some of the individual studies were so poorly designed,
as noted in Chapter 8, that any findings reported from them will be
highly suspect. The very subjective methods of sample selection frequently used, combined with the very short time horizons, raise serious questions as to whether the results can be given much credence
(for example, preliminary results from some studies that substituting
peak-load pricing for declining-block rates would not yield benefits
in excess of costs).

Two major caveats have to be kept in mind in interpreting these and
other results of these experiments. One is the restricted scope of the
experiments, both geographically and otherwise. As a rule, the populations covered in these studies have been limited sharply in terms of
feasibility. Even for these populations, one of the pervasive findings
is that, contrary to expectations, people do not rush to accept a free
handout. In some of the experiments, only a small fraction of the
eligible population seems to have been included, thereby raising
some very difficult questions of representativeness.

Second, the results of a demand experiment have to be interpreted
in light of the supply situation, and vice versa. As noted earlier, for
example, in the housing Demand Experiment participant households
seemed to use cash allowances in accordance with the purposes of
the program when housing supply was ample; but in a tight housing
market, these housing allowances tended to be treated simply as additional income. In a similar manner, labor supply response to an NIT

program needs to be interpreted with regard to the demand for labor at that time. As noted earlier, one may well expect that the labor supply response to an NIT program, relative to control families, will vary inversely with the tightness of the labor market, ceteris paribus.

Pitfalls of social experimentation

The idea of measuring changes in policy variables by controlled experimentation on human populations remains a sound one. Economists have found, however, that the implementation of this idea is fraught with pitfalls. These pitfalls range from the basic design of the experiment to its implementation in the field and to the interpretation and generality of the results. It is on these three aspects that we focus our comments in this section.

Basic design

In discussing the basic design of an experiment, we are referring to two different notions of design. One has to do with the definition of the particular social policy to be tested. This policy may in practice represent a minor change or a major change. Thus, the Colorado experiment mentioned at the end of Chapter 5 deals with the change in the frequency of income reporting by AFDC families and is therefore a minor change. On the other hand, the experiments with negative income taxation provide an example of a proposal that would effect a major change. In this case, further decisions have to be made concerning which elements of the program will be fixed and which, if any, will be varied. Thus, as mentioned in Chapter 4 in connection with the New Jersey Experiment, most elements of that NIT were fixed at the outset, and only the guarantee and the tax rate were varied across the sample population. Other elements, however, such as the definitions of income, family unit, and income accounting period, could have been varied. There is little doubt that variations in such rules could have substantial effects on labor supply.

The second notion of design of the experiment has to do with the survey design, the sample size, and the adequacy of the data needed to test hypotheses concerning the experimental variables. This aspect raises all the questions dealing with the design of a longitudinal operation, including the design of the data collection instruments, field operations, and overall administration of the experiment. It is here that many of the social experiments have been flawed, due no doubt to the fact that the economists and statisticians who plunged into social experimentation were, in the main, not very experienced in survey research. On the one hand, they brought a fresh perspective to the problem of modifying survey methods to fit the experimental designs required by these experiments. Instead of adopting the standard analysis of variance–type models so characteristic of experimental design with sample surveys, they applied econometrics and quantitative methods to develop new types of models for measuring response effects with high reliability, based on a priori notions of the general shape of response functions and of the nature of the control and response variables.

On the other hand, one should not lose sight of the fact that many of these refinements would be unnecessary had the experiments been designed to permit simple random allocation so that effects could be measured by means of analysis-of-variance models. The fact that a wide range of treatments effects were sought, that samples had to be truncated, and that stratification frequently involved the use of endogenous variables (usually a measure of income), necessitated the development of these much more complex models. A basic question is whether one should seek in such experiments to evaluate the effect of a wide range of treatments with less reliability in the measurement of each treatment or to focus on a very few treatments and obtain greater reliability of response effects by means of larger sample sizes, and simple randomization.[1]

One major finding of the social experiments that became clear only in the later stages of some of them was that at least as much effect on the response variables may be due to the method of administration as to the treatments being tested. Thus, the method by which an experimental plan is promoted and communicated to the potential participants may have as much influence on response as what is being communicated. One can hardly expect much response to changing conditions if an experimental family does not understand the rules of the experiment.

The fact is that methods of administration can also be tested in an experimental context, as in the Colorado experiment. To judge by the importance of these methods of administration to the results of a social experiment, more such tests would seem highly desirable, even though they will not lead to broad new social policies. Nevertheless, such tests not only can be highly cost-effective in themselves but also may serve as the basis for the design of much more effective social experiments.

Implementation

Where the lack of survey experience hurt the experimenters is in the implementation of these designs. The lesson that seems to be learned repeatedly is that, although social experiments can be designed in a rigorous manner to answer a specific set of questions, the quality and scope of the results are severely limited by practical exigencies. Sample-size specifications obtained from a theoretical model are of little value if the necessary numbers of families with particular characteristics cannot be obtained, or if the estimates of the number of households that need to be contacted to fill these quotas are repeatedly too low.

The problems of implementation seem to be essentially of two types, those related to the research aspects and those related to the administration of the experiment. From a research point of view, sample recruitment and data collection are major problems. The final sample in most experiments constitutes such a small part of the original sample (and even of the eligibles in the original sample) that one has to wonder about the representativeness of this group, or about the applicability of the usual statistical tests of significance. Where response rates have been fairly high, this has usually been accomplished by discarding that part of the population that would be difficult to contact, as was done in some of the electricity peak-load pricing experiments.

Related to the recruitment problem is the continuing failure to deal with eligible families who will not accept a free good. Inability to deal with this problem seems to have vitiated much of the work carried out in connection with the cash housing allowance experiments and, to a lesser extent, with the Health Insurance Study. To what extent the inability to obtain cooperation from such households in the experiments may have influenced the resulting samples to be unusually homogeneous, and hence bias the results toward rejecting the null hypothesis, is a moot point.

The reliability of the data has been another sore point in the implementation of these experiments. The NIT experiments seem to have suffered particularly from data problems, some so serious that part of the data in one experiment (New Jersey) had to be discarded, and, as noted previously, there is serious doubt, because of these data problems, about the validity of much of the labor response results from the Rural Experiment. Although the later social experiments seem to have benefited from this early experience, there is by now wide awareness that it is one thing to outline what sort of data should be obtained and it is a very different matter to actually obtain them with the necessary reliability. This is particularly true of personal financial data, which frequently are a cornerstone for evaluating experimental response.

Interpretation and generalization

Possibly the trickiest aspect of all relates to the interpretation and generalization of the results of a social experiment. Based on a small sample over a limited period of time and with the sample split among the various treatments, making any clear interpretation of the results becomes very difficult. A major problem is that the experiment being conducted in a natural setting has some of the drawbacks of a laboratory experiment, confounded with the fact that the pure conditions of the laboratory cannot be maintained, to an extent that is frequently not clear. Response to a new social policy will be influenced by changes in personal circumstances as well as by broad economic events affecting an entire area, and neither of these can be foreseen. Though multivariate techniques aid considerably in holding constant the effects of these external forces, their presence nevertheless introduces a great deal of additional random variation in the error variance that serves as a basis for assessing the significance of the treatments.

In addition, with the relatively small samples used in these experiments, the desire to estimate the response surface for a particular social policy by applying a variety of treatment combinations leads to dilution of the sample size and consequent further increase in sampling variances. Still another factor contributing to the error variance is the frequent lack of comprehension of the rules of the game on the part of the participants. By its very nature, an experiment with a social program in a particular area is not subject to the wide coverage in the media that would be true of the same social policy implemented on a nationwide basis. Indeed, in some instances it is considered desirable not even to attempt to obtain much media coverage for fear of sensitizing the participants. Although the social experimenters have made valiant attempts to educate the participants in more private ways (literature, personal conversations, group meetings), there is ample evidence that many of the participants seem to have only the most general understanding of the rules to which they are being exposed. Indeed, in some of the experiments, such as in the rural NIT program, it would be hard to reject the hypothesis that the response to the treatments was as much a function of the participants' understanding of the rules of the game as of any other variable.

All of these factors act to increase the error variance and to bias the results of a social experiment toward acceptance of the null hypothesis. For this reason, some might argue that it would have been preferable in at least some of the NIT experiments to test only one treatment (one tax rate and one guarantee level) against one control group, in order to provide more adequate cell sample sizes and hence a better estimate of the effects of that particular social policy.

The generalizability of the results is equally controversial even with the best-conducted experiment. For one thing, the sample invariably constitutes not only a very small segment of the population but a segment concentrated in a very few cities or rural areas. Because, as noted earlier, the response rates encountered in these studies are usually very low, a question arises regarding the generalizability of the sample even for these areas.

Whether the same results can be generalized on a nationwide basis raises further questions with regard to representativeness, in view of the restricted groups often studied and the particular areas covered.

In addition, certain nontechnical questions arise that have major ramifications for any new social policies. The huge amount of publicity and information that very likely would be provided in the media and by the federal government with regard to a nationwide program simply does not exist in the case of a small experiment limited to one or two areas. A good indication of the differential effects of national publicity as opposed to local publicity is provided by the 1980 Census of Population and Housing. In the pretests for that census, response rates obtained on the mail-back questionnaire were in the general range of 20 percent to 40 percent, even with considerable local publicity. In the census itself, however, the response rate nationally was over 80 percent, and even in the local areas where the pretests were conducted (which were usually the more difficult survey areas) the response rate on the mail-back questionnaire was about twice that obtained on the pretest.

The social utility of social experimentation

Our overall conclusion has to be that, although social experiments offer unique opportunities for estimating the effects of new social policies, they also carry with them a unique set of problems. Much remains to be learned about this technique, learning that so far seems to have taken place more through bitter experience than through methodical study and research. Social experimentation is a very useful addition to the economist's kit of analytical tools, but it is a very expensive tool that needs to be used judiciously. Indeed, in view of the large amount of time and the great expense that can be involved in a social experiment, it is best used only after other techniques, such as econometric analysis of existing data and one-time surveys, have been tried and found wanting. Social experimentation, though, can also be a very costly tool, if relied upon by politicians merely for the sake of postponing a decision.

To a large extent, the use of social experimentation is perhaps best considered in a manner analogous to that of surgery – to be undertaken only after other techniques have been exhausted. Moreover, like surgery, social experimentation is best undertaken only after exploratory work has been done to make clear the nature of the problem and the best way to deal with it. That analysis of available data and some exploratory survey work should be undertaken is perhaps self-evident. What may not be self-evident is the desirability of prior field work, such as a demonstration project or a pretest of the actual experiment, to obtain experience with the types of problems that will be encountered in the implementation of the experiment.

Indeed, if the problems of implementation are especially serious, the primary focus may perhaps best be placed on the demonstration aspects, on gaining experience with the best means of implementing the policy. It seems hardly worthwhile, for example, to conduct an NIT experiment in a rural area until a workable set of guidelines has been developed for the treatment of farmers' income and assets and for ascertaining that such information is being obtained with sufficient reliability. If the necessary procedures cannot be developed in a demonstration project, that fact would be sufficient unto itself to indicate the likely ineffectiveness of a social experiment.

NOTES

Chapter 1. Introduction

1 The different ways in which social experimentation may assist in policy formation, at least in theory, are discussed at some length in Robert F. Boruch and Henry W. Riecken, eds., *Experimental Testing of Public Policy* (Boulder Colo.: Westview Press for the Social Science Research Council, 1975).

2 It must be realized that most of the funds are transfer payments – about 40 percent in the health insurance experiment and an even larger percentage in the housing allowance experiments, to be discussed in Chapters 7 and 9.

Chapter 2. Nature of social experimentation

1 R. F. Boruch, "Problems in Research Utilization: Use of Social Experiments, Experimental Results, and Auxiliary Data in Experiments," *Annals of the New York Academy of Sciences* 218 (June 1973): 57–8.

2 Fritz J. Roethlisberger and William Dickson, *Management and the Worker* (Cambridge, Mass.: Harvard University Press, 1939). In fact, the validity of the original experiment has been disputed because of deficiencies in the experimental design; see, e.g., Alex Carey, "The Hawthorne Studies: A Radical Criticism," *American Sociological Review* 32 (June 1967): 403–16. In the sense of panel conditioning, however, there is ample evidence that such an effect does exist, though not in all circumstances; see James M. Carman, "Consumer Panels," part B, chap. 10, in Robert Ferber, ed., *Handbook of Marketing Research* (New York: McGraw-Hill, 1974).

3 On the other hand, given the relatively small sample sizes that were feasible in that study, its planners could, and did, argue that to broaden the definition of eligibility would have introduced another set of vari-

ables that could easily have confounded the measurement of any effects on labor supply of the experimental treatments. See Joseph A. Pechman and P. Michael Timpane, eds., *Work Incentives and Income Guarantees: The New Jersey Negative Income Tax Experiment* (Washington, D.C.: Brookings Institution, 1975), pp. 28 ff.

4 G. L. Kelling et al., *The Kansas City Preventive Patrol Experiment* (Washington, D.C.: Police Foundation, 1974).

5 B. S. Mahoney and W. M. Mahoney, "Policy Implications: A Skeptical View," in Pechman and Timpane, *Incentives and Guarantees*, p. 197.

6 Robert G. Spiegelman and Richard W. West, *Feasibility of a Social Experiment and Issues in Its Design* (Menlo Park, Calif.: Stanford Research Institute, 1976).

7 Conversation with Terrence L. Connell of the U.S. Department of Housing and Urban Development, June 6, 1977.

8 Actually, this underreporting may not have been deliberate; it could have reflected in part a mistake made at the start of that study in not making clear to families that they were to report gross income, not take-home pay. See Harold W. Watts and John Mamer, "Analysis of Wage-Rate Differentials," chap. 15 in Harold W. Watts and Albert Rees, eds., *The New Jersey Income-Maintenance Experiment* (New York: Academic Press, 1977), vol. 3.

9 Albert Rees, "The Labor Supply Results of the Experiment: A Summary," in Watts and Rees, *The New Jersey Income-Maintenance Experiment*, 2: 6–8.

10 G. G. Cain and H. W. Watts, eds., *Income Maintenance and Labor Supply* (Chicago: Markham, 1973).

11 Ibid., pp. 332–3.

12 Ibid.

13 Ibid., p. 338.

14 Summarized in ibid., "Toward A Summary and Synthesis," p. 339.

15 Daniel Weiler, *A Public School Voucher Demonstration* (Santa Monica, Calif.: Rand Corporation, R–1495–NIE VI, June 1974); and Roger L. Rasmussen et al., *Organization, Management, and Incentives in the Alum Rock Schools* (Santa Monica, Calif.: Rand Corporation, WN–0244–NIE, May 1977, pp. 1–7).

16 There does not seem to be any complete listing. For a partial listing, see Henry W. Riecken and Robert F. Boruch, eds., *Social Experimentation: A Method for Planning and Evaluating Social Intervention* (New York: Academic Press, 1974), pp. 279–323.

17 Alice M. Rivlin, "How Can Experiments Be More Useful?" *American Economic Review* 64 (May 1974): 346–54. From a logical point of view, it is also not clear whether the latter two types are not really variants of the same type of experiment, as both involve the use of incentives to alter the behavior of large public institutions.

18 Because income maintenance programs also affect the purchasing power of respondents, they affect the demand for goods and services. Of par-

ticular interest on the demand side is the extent to which increased purchasing power is applied to luxuries.

Chapter 3. Challenges posed by social experiments

1 Peter H. Rossi and Katharine C. Lyall, *Reforming Public Welfare: A Critique of the Negative Income Tax Experiment* (New York: Russell Sage Foundation, 1976), chap. 2.

2 A more detailed explanation of this model is provided in the appendix to Chapter 4.

3 For a general discussion of panel and longitudinal-type studies, see Seymour S. Sudman and Robert Ferber, *Consumer Panels* (Chicago: American Marketing Association, 1980). For a more specific discussion of panel operations in a social experiment, see David Kershaw and Jerilyn Fair, *The New Jersey Income-Maintenance Experiment*, vol. 1: *Operations, Surveys, and Administration* (New York: Academic Press, 1976).

4 Jerry A. Hausman and David A. Wise, "Attrition Bias in Experimental and Panel Data: The Gary Income Maintenance Experiment," *Econometrica* 47(1979): 455–74.

5 There is at least one notable exception to this statement, as will be discussed in Chapter 5.

6 For the results of one attempt to ascertain errors in income data, as applied to the Denver–Seattle Income Maintenance Experiment, see Harlan I. Halsey, "Data Validation," chap. 2 in Philip K. Robins, et al., eds., *A Guaranteed Annual Income: Evidence from a Social Experiment* (New York: Academic Press, 1980).

7 The New Jersey Experiment may have suffered particularly from this problem simply because it was the first of the major social experiments. As a result, there was considerable publicity about it in the newspapers, attempts were made to interview families in the experiment, and, in addition, hearings were being held by Congress on possible income maintenance legislation at a time when the experiment had been underway for only about one year. For a very good brief summary of these problems, see Rossi and Lyall, *Reforming Public Welfare*, chap. 8.

8 To deal with the danger, only a portion of the families at each site were given the initial medical examination, which seems fine from the point of view of experimental design; see J. P. Newhouse et al., *Measurement Issues in the Second Generation of Social Experiments: The Health Insurance Study* (Santa Monica, Calif.: Rand Corporation, P–5701, August 1976). This procedure deals with the experimental problem but raises certain ethical questions.

9 This feature was included to avoid the more serious problem of creating different treatments, based on whether the family was formed prior to or during the experimental period, for otherwise identical families.

10 There is some evidence from the Gary Negative Income Tax Experiment that subjects may be quite sensitive to the length of an experiment and

that, in this instance, some of the subjects timed their nonparticipation in the labor market to coincide with the last period in which the subsidy payments were offered; see John F. McDonald and Houston H. Stokes, "Time-Series Analysis of Labor Supply in the Gary Income Maintenance Experiment" (Chicago: University of Illinois at Chicago Circle, Department of Economics, March 1980).

11 Charles E. Metcalf, "Making Inferences from Controlled Income Maintenance Experiments," *American Economic Review* 63 (June 1973), and "Predicting the Effects of Permanent Programs from a Limited Duration Experiment," in Watts and Rees, *The New Jersey Income-Maintenance Experiment*, 3: 375–97.

12 Robert A. Moffitt, "Selection Bias in the Estimation of Experimental and Quasi-Experimental Effects: The Gary Income Maintenance Experiment" (Princeton, N.J.: Mathematica Policy Research, Working Paper E-30, 1976).

13 *New York Times*, February 5, 1979, p. D1.

14 For safeguards that might be taken in such instances, see Ronald P. Abeles, "Government Audits of Social Experiments," *Items* (Social Science Research Council) 32, nos. 3–4 (December 1978): 47–51. For a review of the issues by the GAO, see U.S., General Accounting Office, *Federal Program Evaluation: Status and Issues* (Washington, D.C.: PAD–78–83, 1978).

15 Constance Holden, "Ethics in Social Science Research," *Science* 206 (November 2, 1979): 537–40.

16 In this connection, the experience in medicine is interesting. Bernard Barbar reports that in the trade-off between scientific progress and ethical concern for research subjects two researcher characteristics tip the scale away from ethical concerns. Struggle for scientific priority and recognition dominates over ethical considerations, particularly among investigators who have published but were seldom cited and among investigators who were underrewarded. See Bernard Barbar, "The Ethics of Experimentation with Human Subjects," *Scientific American*, February 1976, p. 29. It should also be noted that, partly in response to complaints about overregulation, the U.S. Department of Health and Human Services (formerly HEW) relaxed in 1980–81 the regulations governing the use of human subjects in research, especially social research.

17 Ibid., p. 30.

18 Walter Williams and Richard F. Elmore, *Social Program Implementation* (New York: Academic Press, 1976), pp. 5–6.

19 For a discussion of the types of problems that can arise in determining eligibility and payment levels, see Donald E. Dickson, *Certification: Determining Eligibility and Setting Payment Levels in the Administrative Agency Experiment* (Cambridge, Mass.: Abt Associates, 1977).

20 For a description of the many activities involved in such a program, see David N. Kershaw and Jerilyn Fair, eds., *Operations, Surveys, and*

Administration: Final Report of the New Jersey Graduated Work Incentive Experiment, vol. 4 (Princeton, N.J.: Mathematica, 1973).

Chapter 4. The start: the New Jersey Experiment

1 The original idea was outlined somewhat earlier in Heather Ross, *A Proposal for a Demonstration of New Techniques and Income Maintenance* (Washington, D.C.: United Planning Organization, 1966). It was also discussed at about the same time in G. H. Orcutt and Alice G. Orcutt, "Incentive and Disincentive Experimentation for Income Maintenance Policy Purposes," *American Economic Review* 58 (1968): 754–72.

2 The "official" results have been published in three volumes: Kershaw and Fair, *The New Jersey Income-Maintenance Experiment*, vol. 1; Watts and Rees, *The New Jersey Income-Maintenance Experiment* vol. 2: *Labor-Supply Responses*, and vol. 3: *Expenditures, Health and Social Behavior; and the Quality of the Evidence.* Two very good critical evaluations of this experiment are Pechman and Timpane, *Incentives and Guarantees*; and Rossi and Lyall, *Reforming Public Welfare.*

3 These levels are based on the estimates of poverty income by the U.S. Bureau of the Census, which are based on a poverty index developed by the Social Security Administration. For the methods used to estimate poverty levels, see U.S., Bureau of the Census, *Current Population Reports*, Series P–60, no. 102, "Characteristics of the Population below the Poverty Level, 1974," App. A (Washington, D.C., January 1976). Revised estimates for later years are published as part of this same series. For a broader discussion of the issues involved in the explanation of poverty levels, see U.S., Department of Health, Education, and Welfare, *The Measure of Poverty: A Report to Congress* (Washington, D.C.: Government Printing Office, 1976).

4 John Conlisk and Harold W. Watts, "A Model for Optimizing Experimental Designs for Estimating Response Surfaces" (Proceedings of the Social Statistics Section, American Statistical Association, 1969), pp. 150–6; reprinted in Watts and Rees, *The New Jersey Income-Maintenance Experiment*, 3: 430–40.

5 A detailed exposition of the application of this model is provided in the appendix to this chapter.

6 This was done by James Tobin, who was brought in to resolve the dispute among the researchers over sample allocation. For a "blow-by-blow" summary of these events, see Rossi and Lyall, *Reforming Public Welfare.*

7 Kershaw and Fair, *The New Jersey Income-Maintenance Experiment*, pp. 172–5.

8 Ibid., p. 18.

9 Actually, these costs refer to the second year of the experiment, when it

was running relatively smoothly. If start-up costs were included, the expense per family would be much higher.

10 The control group was augmented by 141 families added in October 1969 in Trenton and in Paterson–Passaic.

11 Kershaw and Fair, *The New Jersey Income-Maintenance Experiment*, chap. 7.

12 Ibid., p. 20. The increased earnings were apparently spurious, due to the fact that the experimentals learned sooner than the control group that gross earnings were to be reported rather than net earnings.

13 For this reason, little significance can be attached to the significant coefficient of earnings per week for black families in Table 4.4. Data in this table show results of only one of a series of models estimated in the course of analyzing these data, and the significance of the coefficients for the black and the Spanish-speaking families varies considerably with the type of model used.

14 Watts and Rees, *The New Jersey Income-Maintenance Experiment*, 2: 86 ff.

15 John F. Cogan, *Negative Income Taxation and Labor Supply: New Evidence from the New Jersey–Pennsylvania Experiment* (Santa Monica, Calif.: Rand Corporation, R–2155, 1978).

16 The Seattle–Denver section is based on the report by Michael C. Keeley et al., *The Estimation of Labor Supply Models Using Experimental Data: Evidence from the Seattle and Denver Income Maintenance Experiments* (Menlo Park, Calif.: Stanford Research Institute, Center for the Study of Welfare Policy, Research Memorandum 29, August 1976). The New Jersey section is based on Harold W. Watts and David Horner, "Labor-Supply Response of Husbands," in Watts and Rees, *The New Jersey Income-Maintenance Graduated Work Experiment*, vol. 2.

17 No specific allowance is made for saving, though within the context of this model it could be treated as another type of good.

18 As the authors note, this method is subject to the limitation that the individual is not likely to be on the linearized budget constraint at the final equilibrium point. Moreover, it is not clear whether the assumption of linearity is reasonable.

19 It seems rather odd that the change in the net wage rate should be based on the assumption that the gross wage, w, is unaffected by the experiment. Although this simplifies the estimation problem, it assumes away one of the basic questions that such experiments seek to answer, namely, whether an individual's choice of work (and of wage rates) is altered by the experiment.

20 Boldface type is used to represent sets of variables (vectors).

21 This set included dummy variables for normal income level, hours worked per week prior to the experiment, city of residence, age, race, number of family members, number of children under six years of age, amount of AFDC in the quarter prior to the experiment.

22 This choice of a linear arithmetic form is admittedly arbitrary. It was

selected apparently primarily for convenience, and no attempt seems to have been made to justify its use.

23 Watts and Rees, *The New Jersey Income-Maintenance Experiment*, 2: 401–10.

24 Ibid., p. 78.

25 This grouping was made on the basis of how much each plan would pay an "average" experimental family. Thus, the high plans include the following three combinations of g, t: 125/50, 100/50, 75/30. The medium plans are: 100/70, 75/50, and 50/30. The low plans are 75/50 and 50/50. These plans in fact paid almost nothing over the relevant range and were dominated by the public assistance support levels for most of the period of the experiment.

26 Watts and Rees, *The New Jersey Income-Maintenance Experiment*, 2: 90–3.

27 This section is based in part on Michael C. Keeley and Philip K. Robins, *The Design of Social Experiments: A Critique of the Conlisk–Watts Assignment Model* (Menlo Park, Calif.: SRI International, Research Memorandum 57, November 1978). Also, by the same authors, "Experimental Design, the Conlisk-Watts Assignment Model, and the Proper Estimation of Behavioral Response," *Journal of Human Resources*, 15(1980): 480–98.

Chapter 5. The other negative income tax experiments

1 If we consider those families interviewed at the screening stage, only about 7 percent of those living in the target areas in the New Jersey Experiment met these criteria.

2 The latter stratification was used because only families inside Model Cities areas were originally eligible for the day care subsidy. See Kenneth C. Kehrer et al., *The Gary Income Maintenance Experiment: Design, Administration, and Data Files* (Mathematica Policy Research, August 1975), p. 13.

3 For the details of the sample selection procedures, see D. L. Bawden and W. S. Harrar, "Design and Operation," and comments by David N. Kershaw and Robert G. Spiegelman, pp. 23–54 in John L. Palmer and Joseph A. Pechman, eds., *Welfare in Rural Areas* (Washington, D.C.: Brookings Institution, 1978).

4 The 12 combinations of tax rates and support levels are combined with two time horizons (three years and five years). Those in the experiment for three years were also allocated to three alternative training subsidies, and those in the experiment for five years were allocated to only two training subsidies (the experimenters being unwilling to provide full reimbursement for tuition if those in the five-year program should choose to go through four years of college).

5 For a detailed description of the sample design for this experiment, and the allocation process, see J. Conlisk and M. Kurz, *The Assignment*

Model of the Seattle and Denver Income Maintenance Experiments
(Menlo Park, Calif.: Stanford Research Institute, Center for the Study
of Welfare Policy, Research Memo 15, July 1972). Also M. C. Keeley
and P. K. Robins, "Experimental Design, the Conlisk-Watts Assignment
Model, and the Proper Estimation of Behavioral Response," *Journal of
Human Resources*, 15(1980): 480–98.

6 Binna Mararka and Robert G. Spiegelman, *Sample Selection in the Seattle and Denver Income Maintenance Experiments* (Menlo Park, Calif.:
SRI International, Center for the Study of Welfare Policy, Technical
Memorandum I, July 1978). See also Michael C. Keeley et al., "Design
of the Seattle/Denver Income-Maintenance Experiments and Overview
of the Results," chap. 1 in Robins et al., *Guaranteed Annual Income*.

7 Kehrer et al., *Gary Income Maintenance Experiment*, pp. 21–35.

8 Kenneth C. Kehrer, *The Gary Income Maintenance Experiment: Summary of Initial Findings* (Bloomington: Indiana University, March
1977), p. 82.

9 As Finis Welch has pointed out, this inclusion represents double counting of income because the farmers were asked to report income directly
and then, in addition, had 10 percent of their net wealth added to this
figure. See Finis Welch, "The Labor Supply Response of Farmers," in
John L. Palmer and Joseph A. Pechman, eds., *Welfare in Rural Areas*
(Washington, D.C.: Brookings Institution, 1978). The only basis on
which such an addition might be made is as a possible adjustment for the
very likely understatement of farmers' incomes, but this was not considered in this calculation.

10 As an example, see Finis Welch. "The Labor Supply Response of Farmers," in Palmer and Pechman, *Welfare in Rural Areas*, pp. 77–100.

11 Bawden and Harrar, "Design and Operation," pp. 38–41.

12 Kenneth C. Kehrer, John F. McDonald, and Robert A. Moffitt, *Final
Report of the Gary Income Maintenance Experiment: Labor Supply*
(Mathematica Policy Research, November 1979). An abridged version
appears in Robert A. Moffitt, "The Labor-Supply Response in the Gary
Income Maintenance Experiment," *Journal of Human Resources* 14
(1979): 477–87.

13 John F. McDonald and Donna C. Vandenbrink, "The Effect of Income
Maintenance on the Employment Status of Husbands: Tests of a Model
of Dichotomous Choice," (Chicago: University of Illinois at Chicago
Circle, Department of Economics, June 1980). Many of these results are
also contained in the Fall 1980 issue of the *Journal of Human Resources*,
which focused on an evaluation of the various aspects of this experiment.

14 Philip K. Robins and Richard W. West, "Labor Supply Response Over
Time," *Journal of Human Resources*, 15(1980): 524–44. These and
other results from this experiment are brought together in Robins et al.,
Guaranteed Annual Income.

15 Philip K. Robins and Richard W. West, "Program Participation and Labor Supply Response," *Journal of Human Resources* 15(1980): 499–
523.

16 John F. McDonald and Stanley P. Stephenson, Jr., "The Effect of Income Maintenance on the School-Enrollment and Labor-Supply Decisions of Teenagers," *Journal of Human Resources* 14 (1979): 488–94.

17 Yoram Weiss, Arden Hall, and Fred Dong, "The Effect of Price and Income on Investment in Schooling," *Journal of Human Resources*, 15(1980): 611–40.

18 M. C. Keeley, "The Effect of a Negative Income Tax on Migration," *Journal of Human Resources*, 15(1980): 695–706.

19 Marcy Avrih, *The Impact of Income Maintenance on Utilization of Subsidized Housing* (Menlo Park, Calif.: SRI International, Research Memorandum 54, July 1978).

20 Lyle P. Groeneveld, Nancy B. Tuma, and Michael T. Hannan, "The Effect of Negative Income Tax Programs on Marital Dissolution," *Journal of Human Resources*, 15(1980): 654–74.

21 Ibid. Also, Michael T. Hannan, Nancy B. Tuma, and Lyle P. Groeneveld, *Income and Independence Effects on Marital Dissolution: Results from the First Three Years of SIME/DIME* (Menlo Park, Calif.: SRI International, Center for the Study of Welfare Policy, Research Memorandum 63, July 1979).

22 Alan M. Hershey, Robert G. Williams, and Nancy L. Graham, *Colorado Monthly Reporting System: Design and Operations* (Denver: Mathematica Policy Research, 1978).

Chapter 6. Labor force experiments

1 The five agencies are the Employment and Training Administration of the U.S. Department of Labor; the Law Enforcement Assistance Administration of the Department of Justice; the Office of Planning and Evaluation and the National Institute on Drug Abuse of the Department of Health, Education, and Welfare; and the Office of Policy Development and Research of the Department of Housing and Urban Development.

2 Manpower Demonstration Research Corporation, *Summary of the First Annual Report on the National Supported Work Demonstration* (New York, 1976). p. 1.

3 Manpower Demonstration Research Corporation, *Second Annual Report on the National Supported Work Demonstration* (New York, April 1978), chap. 4.

4 Manpower Demonstration Research Corporation. *Summary and Findings of the National Supported Work Demonstration* (Cambridge, Mass.: Ballinger, 1980), pp. 28–30.

5 MDRC, *Second Annual Report*, p. 30ff.

6 "Others" included primarily ex-alcoholics and mentally disabled in a very few sites, as shown in Table 6.1.

7 MDRC, *Second Annual Report*, p. 18ff.

8 Ibid., pp. 90–112.

9 Ibid., pp. 132–8.

10 MDRC, *Summary and Findings*, pp. 46–7.

11 Ibid., chaps. 4–7.

12 Ibid., chap. 8. Also, Orley Ashenfelter, "Estimating the Effect of Training Programs on Earnings," *Review of Economics and Statistics* 60 (1978): 47–57.

13 As a matter of fact, the employment rate differential between this group and the control group at the end of 27 months had been declining for the past 9 months, and the difference was statistically significant only at the .10 level. The data in the final report are presented in such a way that it is impossible to ascertain the frequency distribution of the participants by the months they had been in the program and their subsequent experience. See, e.g., Table 4.1, p. 59, in MDRC, *Summary and Findings*.

14 Ibid., p. 37.

15 Manpower Demonstration Research Corporation, *The Youth Entitlement Demonstration Program* (New York, 1979).

16 Manpower Demonstration Research Corporation, *The Youth Entitlement Demonstration: Second Interim Report on Program Implementation* (New York, March 1980), p. 70. Also, George Farkas et al., *Early Impacts from the Youth Entitlement Demonstration: Participation, Work, and Schooling* (New York: Manpower Demonstration Research Corporation, 1980).

17 MDRC, *Youth Entitlement Demonstration: Second Interim Report*, pp. 96–7.

18 Joseph Ball, David M. Gerould, and Paul Burstein, *The Quality of Work in the Youth Entitlement Demonstration* (New York: Manpower Demonstration Research Corporation, April 1980).

19 MDRC, *Youth Entitlement Demonstration: Second Interim Report*, p. x.

20 MDRC, *Youth Entitlement Demonstration Program* (New York, 1979), p. 42.

21 Sheila Mandel and Loren Solnick, *A Preliminary Estimate of the Impact of Youth Entitlement on School Behavior* (New York: Manpower Demonstration Research Corporation, October 1979).

22 Farkas et al., *Early Impacts*, p. xxxiv.

23 It would be interesting to reinterview all the youth at such a time to ascertain, for example, whether those who had completed their high school education while in the program may have decided to proceed even further.

Chapter 7. The Health Insurance Study

1 A fee-for-service system is one in which the consumer pays for each service as it is rendered (the traditional system), whereas a prepaid group practice is a system in which an insured pays a group of doctors or a clinic in advance (usually monthly) in exchange for a prescribed list of medical services as they are needed.

2 "Deductibles" are the initial amounts the insured has to pay on his own, before the insurance begins to pay part of the cost. Thus, "$50 deductible" means that $50 is deducted from the bill before insurance payments are calculated. "Coinsurance" relates to the percentage of the price or the cost of particular services that are to be paid by the insured. Thus, "25 percent coinsurance" means that the participating household pays 25 percent of the cost of a particular medical service.

3 J. P. Newhouse and R. W. Archibald, *Overview of Health Insurance Study Publications* (Santa Monica, Calif.: Rand Corporation, no. 6221, November 1978), pp. 1–2.

4 J. P. Newhouse, "A Design for a Health Insurance Experiment," *Inquiry* 11, no. 1 (March 1974): 10.

5 Ibid., p. 11.

6 "Physiological health" pertains to the condition of the organ system of the body, whereas "physical health" is concerned with the response of the organism to the condition of its organ system.

7 "Mental health" usually relates to four constructs: anxiety, depression, positive well-being, and self-control. Robert H. Brook et al., *Conceptualization and Measurement of Health for Adults in the Health Insurance Study*, vol. 8: Overview (Santa Monica, Calif.: Rand Corporation, R–19878–HEW, 1978).

8 Ibid., pp. 9–10.

9 K. N. Williams, *Plans of Analysis for Health Status and Quality Care* (Santa Monica, Calif.: Rand Corporation, AR–1804–HEW, July 1978), p. 102.

10 J. P. Newhouse, *Insurance Benefits, Out-of-Pocket Payments, and the Demand for Medical Care: A Review of the Literature* (Santa Monica, Calif.: Rand Corporation, May 1978), p. 6134.

11 The sites are Dayton, Ohio; Seattle, Washington; Fitchburg, Massachusetts; Franklin County, Massachusetts; Charleston, South Carolina; and Georgetown County, South Carolina.

12 The Medicare system provides those 65 and over and eligible for social security with a basic program of hospital insurance. In addition, by payment of a fixed monthly premium such people can also obtain supplementary medical insurance to the Medicare system. Medicare benefits are generally equal throughout the United States, whereas benefits under Medicaid, the federally supported program operated by the states for the benefit of certain low-income populations, vary by state.

13 Conlisk and Watts, "Model for Optimizing Experimental Designs."

14 Carl Morris, "A Finite Selection Model for Experimental Design of the Health Insurance Study" (Proceedings of the Social Statistics Section, American Statistical Association, 1975), pp. 78–85.

15 Rand Corporation, *Health Insurance Study, Annual Report, July 1, 1978–September 30, 1979* (Santa Monica, Calif.: AR–2256–HEW, November 1979).

16 Rand Corporation, *Annual Report of the Health Insurance Study, July 1, 1976–June 30, 1977* (Santa Monica: AR–1804–HEW, July 1978), p. 59.
17 Ibid., p. 62.
18 Ibid., pp. 1–7.
19 For example, "in the first year of operations in Dayton, the one percent of persons with the highest expenses accounted for 28 percent of all expenditures." Ibid., p. 3.
20 J. Hester and I. Leveson, "The Health Insurance Study: A Critical Appraisal," *Inquiry* 11 (March 1974): pp. 54–7.
21 J. P. Newhouse, "The Health Insurance Study: Response to Hester and Leveson," *Inquiry* 11 (September 1974): p. 236.

Chapter 8. Electricity peak-load pricing experiments

1 Not included in this chapter are various other electricity pricing experiments which, though they were carried out on human populations under normal living conditions, did not manipulate electricity rates but sought to introduce price considerations through bonuses for reduced electricity and through similar devices. One such experiment, with references to a number of others of a similar nature, is reported in Raymond C. Battalio et al., "Residential Electricity Demand: An Experimental Study," *Review of Economics and Statistics* 61 (1979): 180–9.
2 James G. Boggis, "Some Practical Aspects of the British Experiment with Electricity Pricing," in C. J. Cicchetti and W. K. Foel, eds., *Energy Systems Forecasting, Planning, and Prices* (Madison: University of Wisconsin Press, 1975), pp. 375–81.
3 Much of the material in this section is based on D. J. Aigner and D. J. Poirier, "Electricity Demand and Consumption by Time-of-Use: A Survey" (April 23, 1979).
4 The lack of validity of many of the principles from consumer economic theory in applied work is not unusual and has been encountered also in a number of other instances. For a review of this area and of the principal empirical work undertaken to test the theoretical assumptions, see Angus Deaton and John Muellbauer, *Economics and Consumer Behavior* (Cambridge: Cambridge University Press, 1980).
5 A review of such procedures is provided in Robert A. Pollak and Terence J. Wales, "Demographic Variables in Demand Analysis" (University of British Columbia, Department of Economics, Discussion Paper 78–48, December 1978).
6 D. J. Aigner and J. A. Hausman, "Correcting for Selection Bias in the Analysis of Volunteer Experiments in Time-of-Day Pricing of Electricity," Electric Power Research Institute, Workshop on Modeling and Analysis of Electricity Demand by Time of Day, San Diego, Calif., June 12–14, 1978.

7 C. W. J. Granger et al., "Residential Load Curves and Time-of-Day Pricing," *Journal of Econometrics* 9 (January 1979): 13–32.

8 Compensated price elasticities involve measuring the response to a price change when that price change allows for a compensating income change so that the consumer is left no better (or worse) off on account of the price change.

9 Lester D. Taylor, "Modeling the Residential Demand for Electricity by Time-of-Day," *Journal of Econometrics* 9 (January 1979): 100–2.

10 Willard G. Manning, Jr., Bridger M. Mitchell, and Jan P. Acton, *Design of the Los Angeles Peak-Load Pricing Experiment for Electricity* (Santa Monica, Calif.: Rand Corporation, R–1955–DWP, 94P, November 1976); and Jan P. Acton et al., *Lessons to Be Learned from the Los Angeles Rate Experiment in Electricity* (Santa Monica, Calif.: Rand Corporation, R–2113–DWP, July 1978), p. 40.

11 Conlisk and Watts, "Model for Optimizing Experimental Designs," pp. 150–6.

12 Acton et al., *Lessons to Be Learned*, pp. 19–20.

13 Morris, "Finite Selection Model."

14 Acton et al., *Lessons to Be Learned*, p. 26.

15 Boggis, "Practical Aspects of the British Experiment," pp. 375–81.

16 Acton et al., *Lessons to Be Learned*, p. 28.

17 H. Donald Burbank, "The Connecticut Peak-Load Pricing Experiment"; William H. Hieronymous and William R. Hughes, "Residential Load Forecasting with Time-of-Day Rates"; and C. W. J. Granger et al., "Long-Term Residential Load Forecasting" – all in Anthony Lawrence, ed., *Forecasting and Modeling Time-of-Day and Seasonal Electricity Demands* (Palo Alto, Calif.: Electric Power Research Institute, EPRI FA578–SR, December 1977), pp. 1.1–1.101.

18 Hieronymus and Hughes, "Residential Load Forecasting with Time-of-Day Rates."

19 Granger et al., "Residential Load Curves . . ." pp. 13–32.

20 Burbank, "The Connecticut Peak-Load Pricing Experiment."

21 Scott E. Atkinson, "Responsiveness to Time-of-Day Electricity Pricing: First Empirical Results," *Journal of Econometrics* 9 (January 1979): pp. 79–95; Taylor, "Modeling the Residential Demand for Electricity," pp. 97–115.

22 Willard G. Manning, Jr., "Comments," in Lawrence, *Forecasting and Modeling Electricity Demands*, p. 1.198.

23 Boggis, "Practical Aspects of the British Experiment," pp. 375–81.

24 Conversation with G. H. Burchnell and J. G. Boggis in October 1978. During these conversations, two further interesting statements were made. Boggis, who was in charge of the work in 1966–73, emphasized the importance of having continuous support for the undertaking. He commented that he often found himself "naked," that he felt the experiment could lead to an uproar with his superiors unwilling to back him

up. The second interesting statement was that no one in the United Kingdom had taken notice of the work and that there had not been a single inquiry about it. This holds not only for the Treasury or other governmental departments but also for scholars in the United Kingdom. All the interest had come basically from the United States.

25 Jan P. Acton and Bridger M. Mitchell, *Evaluating Time-of-Day Electricity Rates for Residential Customers* (Santa Monica, Calif.: Rand Corporation, R–2509–DWP 38P, November 1979).

26 Ibid., p. viii.

27 A more realistic approach from this point of view was followed in the Oklahoma peak-electricity pricing experiment. As part of one of the treatments, a group-metering scheme, names and addresses of the group members were supplied to all the households so they could communicate with each other if they wished. See Jack J. Kasulis, David A. Huettner, and Neil J. Dikeman, "The Feasibility of Changing Electricity Consumption Patterns," *Journal of Consumer Research*, 8 (December 1981), forthcoming.

28 Daniel McFadden, "Comments," in Lawrence, *Forecasting and Modeling Electricity Demands*, pp. 1.65–1.66.

Chapter 9. The cash housing allowance experiments

1 Housing Act of 1949, para. 2, 63 Stat. 413, as amended, 42 U.S.C., para. 1441 (Supp. V, 1970).

2 The larger sample sizes in the middle three cells reflected an attempt to secure representation on an a priori basis from three different income levels. In contrast, the high-payment cell ($a = 0.6$) was meant to include only the lowest-income families, and the low-payment cell ($a = 0.2$) was meant to include only families at the upper end of the income scale among those eligible.

3 For a description of the sample design, see Abt Associates, *Second Annual Report of the Demand Experiment, December 4, 1973–December 31, 1974* (Cambridge, Mass., February 1975), pp. 124–32.

4 Ibid., p. 129. The gross sample size was 50,938 in Pittsburgh and 48,333 in Phoenix, which, after allowing for vacant dwelling units and similar types of noneligible units, reduced to 45,132 and 39,578, respectively. (Personal communication from David Hoaglin of Abt Associates, July 18, 1978.)

5 U.S., Department of Housing and Urban Development, *A Summary Report of Current Findings from the Experimental Housing Allowance Program* (Office of Policy Development and Research, April 1978), pp. 12, 19.

6 This lack of macroeffect seems to be corroborated by the results of the Supply Experiment, as discussed later in this chapter.

7 Abt Associates, *Second Annual Report*, p. 137.

8 Joseph Friedman and Stephen Kennedy, *Housing Expenditures under a*

Housing Gap Housing Allowance (Cambridge, Mass.: Abt Associates, May 1977).

9 R. Atkinson and A. Phipps, *Neighborhood Change in the Housing Allowance Demand Experiment* (Cambridge, Mass.: Abt Associates, 1977).

10 Stephen K. Mayo, *Housing Expenditures and Quality* (Cambridge, Mass.: Abt Associates, 1977).

11 In a sense, this aggregate figure is meaningless because it represents an average of the estimated adjustment for the nonmovers (between 7 and 10 percent per year) and for the movers (between 50 and 66 percent per year). Moreover, the speed of adjustment for the nonmovers is undoubtedly underestimated for very likely some of these people would move in the following two or three years if the housing allowance program were continued.

12 Department of Housing and Urban Development, *Summary Report of Current Findings*, p. 14.

13 For a broad overall description, see Ira S. Lowry, ed., *The Design of the Housing Assistance Supply Experiment* (Santa Monica, Calif.: Rand Corporation, June 1980).

14 Rand Corporation, *Third Annual Report of the Housing Assistance Supply Experiment, Executive Summary* (Santa Monica, Calif.: February 1977), p. 5.

15 Ibid.

16 Ibid., p. ix.

17 In August 1977 eligibility rules were relaxed to allow enrollment of nonelderly (under 62) single individuals, partly apparently to offset sharp drops in enrollment caused by high turnover in the program.

18 Rand Corporation, *Fourth Annual Report of the Housing Assistance Supply Experiment* (Santa Monica, Calif., May 1978), pp. xxv–xxvii.

19 Ibid., p. xxvi.

20 Ibid., p. xxiv.

21 The $146 estimate for income transfer administration may be compared with 1976 costs of $295 per case served by the national program of Aid to Families with Dependent Children (AFDC). The latter costs vary greatly by state because of differences in procedures, but only 6 of the 50 states reported costs per case under the HAO average.

22 Rand Corporation, *Fourth Annual Report*, p. vii.

23 Ibid., p. 101.

24 Ibid.

25 Ibid., p. 103.

26 C. L. Barnett, *Expected and Actual Effects of Housing Allowances on Housing Prices* (Santa Monica, Calif., January 1979), pp. 16–22.

27 Rand Corporation, *Fourth Annual Report*, p. xi.

28 Rand Corporation, *Sixth Annual Report of the Housing Assistance Supply Experiment* (Santa Monica, Calif., 1980), pp. 26–7.

29 Rand Corporation, *Fifth Annual Report of the Housing Assistance Sup-*

ply Experiment (Santa Monica, Calif., 1979), p. xviii. See also Michael G. Shanley and Charles M. Hotchkiss, *The Role of Market Intermediaries in a Housing Allowance Program* (Santa Monica: Rand Corporation, December 1980).

30 Ibid., p. xiii.

31 Rand Corporation, *Fourth Annual Report*, p. 60.

32 Rand Corporation, *Fifth Annual Report*, pp. viii–ix, 46–8. Some supplementary surveys were also carried out in 1979, however.

33 Jean MacMillan, William L. Hamilton et al., *Outreach: Generating Applications in the Administrative Agency Experiment* (Cambridge, Mass.: Abt Associates, 1977).

34 William L. Holshouser, Jr., *Report on Selected Aspects of the Jacksonville Housing Allowance Experiment* (Cambridge, Mass.: Abt Associates, May 1976).

35 Dickson, *Certification*.

36 Marian F. Wolfe and William L. Hamilton, *Jacksonville: Administering a Housing Allowance Program in a Difficult Environment* (Cambridge, Mass.: Abt Associates, February 1977).

37 Ibid.

38 William L. Holshouser, Jr., et al., *Supportive Services in the Administrative Agency Experiment* (Cambridge, Mass.: Abt Associates, February 1977).

39 Ibid., App. D.

40 Ibid., pp. 20–1.

41 David W. Budding et al., *Inspection: Implementing Housing Quality Requirements in the Administrative Agency Experiment* (Cambridge, Mass.: Abt Associates, February 1977).

42 W. L. Hamilton, David W. Budding, and William L. Holshouser, Jr., *Administrative Procedures and Housing Allowance Program: The Administrative Agency Experiment* (Cambridge, Mass.: Abt Associates, March 1977).

43 Charles M. Maloy et al., *Administrative Costs in a Housing Allowance Program: Two-Year Costs in the Administrative Agency Experiment* (Cambridge, Mass.: Abt Associates, 1977), chap. 6. The same agencies did not uniformly have the lowest or the highest unit costs for all activities, so this range is undoubtedly overstated. Also, the specific period of reference varies by agency, the dates generally referring to cost experience in 1973 and 1974.

44 Ibid.

45 This the Urban Institute has attempted to do in Raymond J. Struyk and Marc Benedick, Jr., eds., *Housing Vouchers for the Poor: Lessons from a National Experiment* (Washington, D.C.: Urban Institute, 1981).

46 David B. Carlson and John D. Heinberg, *How Housing Allowances Work: Integrated Findings from the Experimental Housing Allowance Program* (Washington, D.C.: Urban Institute, 1978).

47 Ibid., p. 48.

48 Harvey S. Rosen, "Housing Behavior and the Experimental Housing Allowance Program: What Have We Learned?", National Bureau of Economic Research, Conference on Social Experimentation, March 5–8, 1981.

Chapter 10. What have we learned?

1 For a discussion of the advantages of the latter approach, see Jerry A. Hausman and David A. Wise, "Technical Problems in Social Experimentation: Cost versus Ease of Analysis," National Bureau of Economic Research, Conference on Social Experimentation, March 5–8, 1981. It might be noted that in either case problems dealing with sample biases still remain, such as recruitment and attrition.

BIBLIOGRAPHY

Abeles, Ronald P. "Government Audits of Social Experiments." *Items* (Social Science Research Council) 32 (December 1978): 47–51.

Abt Associates. *Second Annual Report of the Demand Experiment, December 4, 1973–December 31, 1974*. Cambridge, Mass., February 1975.

Acton, Jan P., and Mitchell, Bridger M. *Evaluating Time-of-Day Electricity Rates for Residential Customers*. Santa Monica, Calif.: Rand Corporation, R–2509–DWP 38P, November 1979.

Acton, Jan P., et al. *Lessons to Be Learned from the Los Angeles Rate Experiment in Electricity*. Santa Monica, Calif.: Rand Corporation, R–2113–DWP, July 1978.

Aigner, D. J., "The Residential Electricity Time-of-Use Pricing Experiments: What Have We Learned?", National Bureau of Economic Research, Conference on Social Experimentation, March 5–8, 1981.

Aigner, D. J., and Hausman, J. A. "Correcting for Selection Bias in the Analysis of Volunteer Experiments in Time-of-Day Pricing of Electricity." Electric Power Research Institute, Workshop on Modeling and Analysis of Electricity Demand by Time of Day, San Diego, Calif., June 12–14, 1978.

Aigner, D. J., and Poirier, D. J. "Electricity Demand and Consumption by Time-of-Use: A Survey." Paper, April 23, 1979.

Ashenfelter, Orley. "Estimating the Effect of Training Programs on Earnings." *Review of Economics and Statistics* 60 (1978): 47–57.

Atkinson, R., and Phipps, A. *Neighborhood Change in the Housing Allowance Demand Experiment*. Cambridge, Mass.: Abt Associates, 1977.

Atkinson, Scott E. "Responsiveness to Time-of-Day Electricity Pricing: First Empirical Results." *Journal of Econometrics* 9 (January 1979): 79–95.

Avrih, Marcy. *The Impact of Income Maintenance on Utilization of Subsidized Housing*. Menlo Park, Calif.: SRI International, Research Memorandum 54, July 1978.

Ball, Joseph; Gerould, David M., and Burstein, Paul. *The Quality of Work in the*

Youth Entitlement Demonstration. New York: Manpower Demonstration Research Corporation, April 1980.

Barbar, Bernard. "The Ethics of Experimentation with Human Subjects." *Scientific American*, February 1976, pp. 25–31.

Barnett, C. L. *Expected and Actual Effects of Housing Allowances on Housing Prices*. Santa Monica, Calif.: Rand Corporation, January 1979.

Battalio, Raymond C., et al. "Residential Electricity Demand: An Experimental Study." *Review of Economics and Statistics* 61 (1979): 180–9.

Bawden, D. L., and Harrar, W. S. "Design and Operation," and comments by David N. Kershaw and Robert G. Spiegelman. In J. L. Palmer and J. A. Pechman, eds., *Welfare in Rural Areas*. Washington, D.C.: Brookings Institution, 1978.

Boggis, James G. "Some Practical Aspects of the British Experiment with Electricity Pricing." in C. J. Cicchetti and W. K. Foel, eds., *Energy Systems Forecasting, Planning, and Prices*. Madison: University of Wisconsin Press, 1975.

Boruch, Robert F. "Problems in Research Utilization: Use of Social Experiments, Experimental Results, and Auxiliary Data in Experiments." *Annals of the New York Academy of Sciences* 218 (June 1973): 56–77.

Boruch, Robert F., and Riecken, Henry W., eds. *Experimental Testing of Public Policy*. Boulder, Colo.: Westview Press for the Social Science Research Council, 1975.

Brook, Robert H., et al. *Conceptualization and Measurement of Health for Adults in the Health Insurance Study*. vol. 8, *Overview*. Santa Monica, Calif.: Rand Corporation, R–19878–HEW, 1978.

Budding, David W., et al. *Inspection: Implementing Housing Quality Requirements in the Administrative Agency Experiment*. Cambridge, Mass.: Abt Associates, February 1977.

Burbank, H. Donald. "The Connecticut Peak-Load Pricing Experiment." In Anthony Lawrence, ed., *Forecasting and Modeling Time-of-Day and Seasonal Electricity Demands*. Palo Alto, Calif.: Electric Power Research Institute, EPRI FA578–SR, December 1977.

Cain, G. G., and Watts, H. W., eds. *Income Maintenance and Labor Supply*, Chicago: Markham, 1973.

Carey, Alex. "The Hawthorne Studies: A Radical Criticism." *American Sociological Review* 32 (June 1967): 403–16.

Carlson, David B., and Heinberg, John D. *How Housing Allowances Work: Integrated Findings from the Experimental Housing Allowance Program*. Washington, D.C.: Urban Institute, 1978.

Carman, James M. "Consumer Panels." Part B, chapter 10, in Robert Ferber, ed., *Handbook of Marketing Research*. New York: McGraw-Hill, 1974.

Cogan, John F. *Negative Income Taxation and Labor Supply: New Evidence from the New Jersey–Pennsylvania Experiment*. Santa Monica, Calif.: Rand Corporation, R–2155, 1978.

Conlisk, John, and Kurz, M. *The Assignment Model of the Seattle and Denver Income Maintenance Experiment*. Menlo Park, Calif.: Stanford Research Institute, Center for the Study of Welfare Policy, Research Memo 15, July 1972.

Conlisk, John, and Watts, Harold W. "A Model for Optimizing Experimental Designs for Estimating Response Surfaces." Proceedings of the Social Statistics Section, American Statistical Association, 1969, pp. 150–6.

Deaton, Angus, and Muellbauer, John. *Economics and Consumer Behavior*. Cambridge: Cambridge University Press, 1980.

Dickson, Donald E. *Certification: Determining Eligibility and Setting Payment Levels in the Administrative Agency Experiment*. Cambridge, Mass.: Abt Associates, 1977.

Farkas, George, et al. *Early Impacts from the Youth Entitlement Demonstration: Participation, Work, and Schooling*. (New York: Manpower Demonstration Research Corporation, 1980).

Friedman, Joseph, and Kennedy, Stephen. *Housing Expenditures under a Housing Gap Housing Allowance*. Cambridge, Mass.: Abt Associates, May 1977.

Granger, C. W. J., et al. "Long-term Residential Load Forecasting." In Anthony Lawrence, ed., *Forecasting and Modeling Time-of-Day and Seasonal Electricity Demands*. Palo Alto, Calif.: Electric Power Research Institute, EPRI FA578–SR, December 1977.

"Residential Load Curves and Time-of-Day Pricing." *Journal of Econometrics* 9 (January 1979): 13–22.

Groeneveld, Lyle P., Tuma, Nancy B., and Hannan, Michael T., "The Effects of Negative Income Tax Programs on Marital Dissolution," *Journal of Human Resources*, 15 (1980): 654–74.

Hamilton, W. L.; Budding, David W.; and Holshouser, William L., Jr. *Administrative Procedures and Housing Allowance Program: The Administrative Agency Experiment*. Cambridge, Mass.: Abt Associates, March 1977.

Hannan, Michael T., Tuma, Nancy B., and Groeneveld, Lyle P. *Income and Independence Effects on Marital Dissolution: Results from the First Three Years of SIME/DIME*. Menlo Park, Calif.: SRI International, Center for the Study of Welfare Policy, Research Memorandum 63, July 1979.

Hausman, Jerry A., and Wise, David A. "Attrition Bias in Experimental and Panel Data: The Gary Income Maintenance Experiment." *Econometrica* 47(1949): 455–74.

Hausman, Jerry A., and Wise, David A., "Technical Problems in Social Experimentation: Cost versus Ease of Analysis," National Bureau of Economic Research, Conference on Social Experimentation, March 5–8, 1981.

Hershey, Alan M.; Williams, Robert G.; and Graham, Nancy L. *Colorado Monthly Reporting System: Design and Operations*. Denver: Mathematica Policy Research, 1978.

Hester, J., and Leveson, I. "The Health Insurance Study: A Critical Appraisal." *Inquiry* 11 (March 1974): 53–60.

Hieronymous, William H., and Hughes, William R. "Residential Load Forecasting with Time-of-Day Rates." In Anthony Lawrence, ed., *Forecasting and Modeling Time-of-Day and Seasonal Electricity Demands*. Palo Alto, Calif.: Electric Power Research Institute, EPRI FA578–SR, December 1977.

Holden, Constance. "Ethics in Social Science Research." *Science* 206 (November 2, 1979): 537–40.

Holshouser, William L., Jr. *Report on Selected Aspects of the Jacksonville Housing Allowance Experiment*. Cambridge, Mass.: Abt Associates, May 1976.

Holshouser, William L., Jr., et al. *Supportive Services in the Administrative Agency Experiment*. Cambridge, Mass.: Abt Associates, February 1977.

Housing Act of 1949, para. 2, 63 Stat. 413, as amended, 42 U.S.C., para. 1441 (Supp. V, 1970).

Kasulis, Jack J., Huettner, David A., and Dikeman, Neil J., "The Feasibility of Changing Electricity Consumption Patterns," *Journal of Consumer Research*, 8 (Dec, 1981).

Keeley, M. C., "The Effect of a Negative Income Tax on Migration," *Journal of Human Resources*, 15(1980): 695–706.

Keeley, M. C., and Robins, P. K., "Experimental Design, The Conlisk-Watts Assignment Model, and the Proper Estimation of Behavioral Response," *Journal of Human Resources*, 15(1980): 480–98.

Keeley, Michael C., and Robins, Philip K. *The Design of Social Experiments: A Critique of the Conlisk–Watts Assignment Model*. Menlo Park, Calif.: SRI International, Research Memorandum 57, November 1978.

Keeley, Michael C., et al. *The Estimation of Labor Supply Models Using Experimental Data: Evidence from the Seattle and Denver Income Maintenance Experiments*. Menlo Park, Calif.: Stanford Research Institute, Center for the Study of Welfare Policy, Research Memorandum 29, August 1976.

Kehrer, Kenneth C. *The Gary Income Maintenance Experiment: Summary of Initial Findings*. Bloomington: Indiana University, March 1977.

Kehrer, Kenneth C.; McDonald, John F., and Moffitt, Robert A. *Final Report of the Gary Income Maintenance Experiment: Labor Supply*. Princeton, N.J.: Mathematica Policy Research, November 1979.

Kehrer, Kenneth C., et al. *The Gary Income Maintenance Experiment: Design, Administration, and Data Files*. Princeton, N.J.: Mathematica Policy Research, August 1975.

Kelling, G. L., et al. *The Kansas City Preventive Patrol Experiment*. Washington, D.C.: Police Foundation, 1974.

Kennedy, Stephen D. "Evaluation of In-Kind Transfer Programs: Some Implications from the Preliminary Analysis of the Housing Allowance Demand Experiment." Cambridge, Mass.: Abt Associates, n.d.

Kershaw, David N., and Fair, Jerilyn. *The New Jersey Income-Maintenance Experiment*. Vol. 1, *Operations, Survey, and Administration*. New York: Academic Press, 1976.

Kershaw, David N., and Fair, Jerilyn, eds. *Operations, Surveys, and Administration: Final Report of the New Jersey Graduated Work Incentive Experiment*. Vol. 4. Princeton, N.J.: Mathematica, 1973.

Lowry, Ira S., ed. *The Design of the Housing Assistance Supply Experiment*. Santa Monica, Calif.: Rand Corporation, June 1980.

MacMillan, Jean; Hamilton, William L.; et al. *Outreach: Generating Applications in the Administrative Agency Experiment*. Cambridge, Mass.: Abt Associates, 1977.

Mahoney, B. S., and Mahoney, W. M. "Policy Implications: A Skeptical View." In

J. A. Pechman and P. M. Timpane, eds., *Work Incentives and Incomes Guarantees: The New Jersey Negative Income Tax Experiment*. Washington, D.C.: Brookings Institution, 1975.

Maloy, Charles M., et al. *Administrative Costs in a Housing Allowance Program: Two-Year Costs in the Administrative Agency Experiment*. Cambridge, Mass.: Abt Associates, 1977.

Mandel, Sheila, and Solnick, Loren. *A Preliminary Estimate of the Impact of Youth Entitlement on School Behavior*. New York: Manpower Demonstration Research Corporation, October 1979.

Manning, Willard G., Jr. "Comments." In Anthony Lawrence, ed., *Forecasting and Modeling Time-of-Day and Seasonal Electricity Demands*. Palo Alto, Calif.: Electric Power Research Institute, EPRI FA578–SR, December 1977.

Manning, Willard G., Jr.; Mitchell, Bridger M.; and Acton, Jan P. *Design of the Los Angeles Peak-Load Pricing Experiment for Electricity*. Santa Monica, Calif.: Rand Corporation, R–1955–DWP, 94P, November 1976.

Manpower Demonstration Research Corporation. *Summary of the First Annual Report on the National Supported Work Demonstration*. New York, 1976.

Second Annual Report on the National Supported Work Demonstration. New York, April 1978.

Summary and Findings of the National Supported Work Demonstration. Cambridge, Mass.: Ballinger, 1980.

The Youth Entitlement Demonstration Program. New York, 1979.

The Youth Entitlement Demonstration: Second Interim Report on Program Implementation. New York, March 1980.

Mararka, Binna and Spiegelman, Robert G. *Sample Selection in the Seattle and Denver Income Maintenance Experiments*. Menlo Park, Calif.: SRI International, Center for the Study of Welfare Policy, Technical Memorandum I, July 1978.

Mayo, Stephen K. *Housing Expenditures and Quality*. Cambridge, Mass.: Abt Associates, 1977.

McFadden, Daniel. "Comments." In Anthony Lawrence, ed., *Forecasting and Modeling Time-of-Day and Seasonal Electricity Demands*. Palo Alto, Calif.: Electric Power Research Institute, EPRI FA578–SR, December 1977.

McDonald, John F., and Stephenson, Stanley P., Jr. "The Effect of Income Maintenance on the School-Enrollment and Labor-Supply Decisions of Teenagers." *Journal of Human Resources* 14 (1979): 488–94.

McDonald, John F., and Stokes, Houston H. "Time-Series Analysis of Labor Supply in the Gary Income Maintenance Experiment." Chicago: University of Illinois at Chicago Circle, Department of Economics, March 1980.

McDonald, John F., and Vandenbrink, Donna C. "The Effect of Income Maintenance on the Employment Status of Husbands: Tests of a Model of Dichotomous Choice." Chicago: University of Illinois at Chicago Circle, Department of Economics, June 1980.

Metcalf, Charles E. "Making Inferences from Controlled Income Maintenance Experiments." *American Economic Review* 63 (June 1973): 478–83.

"Predicting the Effects of Permanent Programs from a Limited Duration Experiment." In Harold W. Watts and Albert Rees, eds., *The New Jersey Income-Maintenance Experiment*, vol. 3. New York: Academic Press, 1977.

Moffitt, Robert A. "Selection Bias in the Estimation of Experimental and Quasi-Experimental Effects: The Gary Income Maintenance Experiment." Princeton, N.J.: Mathematica Policy Research, Working Paper E-30, 1976.

Morris, Carl. "A Finite Selection Model for Experimental Design of the Health Insurance Study." Proceedings of the Social Statistics Section, American Statistical Association, 1975, pp. 78–85.

Newhouse, J. P. "A Design for a Health Insurance Experiment." *Inquiry* 11 (March 1974): 5–27.

"The Health Insurance Study: Response to Hester and Leveson." *Inquiry* 11 (September 1974): 236–41.

Insurance Benefits, Out-of-Pocket Payments, and the Demand for Medical Care: A Review of the Literature. Santa Monica, Calif.: Rand Corporation, May 1978.

Newhouse, J. P., and Archibald R. W. *Overview of Health Insurance Study Publications*. Santa Monica, Calif.: Rand Corporation, no. 6221, November 1978.

Newhouse, J. P., et al. *Measurement Issues in the Second Generation of Social Experiments: The Health Insurance Study*. Santa Monica, Calif.: Rand Corporation, P–5701, August 1976.

Orcutt, G. H., and Orcutt, Alice G. "Incentive and Disincentive Experimentation for Income Maintenance Policy Purposes." *American Economic Review* 58 (1968): 754–72.

Pechman, Joseph A., and Timpane, P. Michael, eds. *Work Incentives and Income Guarantees: The New Jersey Negative Income Tax Experiment*. Washington, D.C.: Brookings Institution, 1975.

Pollak, Robert A., and Wales, Terence J. "Demographic Variables in Demand Analysis." University of British Columbia, Department of Economics, Discussion Paper 78–48, December 1978.

Rand Corporation. *Annual Report of the Health Insurance Study, July 1, 1976–June 30, 1977*. Santa Monica, Calif.: AR–1804–HEW, July 1978.

Health Insurance Study, Annual Report, July 1, 1978–September 30, 1979. Santa Monica, Calif.: AR–2256–HEW, November 1979.

Third Annual Report of the Housing Assistance Supply Experiment, Executive Summary. Santa Monica, Calif., February 1977.

Fourth Annual Report of the Housing Assistance Supply Experiment. Santa Monica, Calif., May 1978.

Fifth Annual Report of the Housing Assistance Supply Experiment. Santa Monica, Calif., 1979.

Sixth Annual Report of the Housing Assistance Supply Experiment. Santa Monica, Calif., 1980.

Rasmussen, Roger L., et al. *Organization, Management, and Incentives in the Alum Rock Schools*. Santa Monica, Calif.: Rand Corporation, WN–0244–NIE, May 1977.

Rees, Albert, and Watts, Harold W. "An Overview of the Supply Results." In Joseph

A. Pechman and P. Michael Timpane, eds. *Work Incentives and Income Guarantees: The New Jersey Negative Income Tax Experiment*. Washington, D.C.: Brookings Institution, 1975.

Reinhold, Robert. "Test in Seattle Challenges Minimum-Income Plan." *New York Times*, February 5, 1978.

Riecken, Henry W., and Boruch, Robert F., eds. *Social Experimentation: A Method for Planning and Evaluating Social Intervention*. New York: Academic Press, 1974.

Rivlin, Alice M. "How Can Experiments Be More Useful?" *American Economic Review* 64 (May 1974), 346–54.

Robins, Philip K., and West, Richard W., "Labor Supply Response Over Time," *Journal of Human Resources*, 15(1980): 525–44.

Robins, Philip K., and West, Richard W., "Program Participation and Labor Supply Response," *Journal of Human Resources*, 15 (1980): 499–523.

Robins, Philip K., et al., eds. *A Guaranteed Annual Income: Evidence from a Social Experiment*. New York: Academic Press, 1980.

Roethlisberger, Fritz J., and Dickson, William. *Management and the Worker*. Cambridge, Mass.: Harvard University Press, 1939.

Rosen, Harvey S., "Housing Behavior and the Experimental Housing Allowance Program: What Have We Learned?", National Bureau of Economic Research, Conference on Social Experimentation, March 5–8, 1981.

Ross, Heather. *A Proposal for a Demonstration of New Techniques and Income Maintenance*. Washington, D.C.: United Planning Organization, 1966.

Rossi, Peter H., and Lyall, Katharine C. *Reforming Public Welfare: A Critique of the Negative Income Tax Experiment*. New York: Russell Sage Foundation, 1976.

Shanley, Michael G., and Hotchkiss, M. *The Role of Market Intermediaries in a Housing Allowance Program*. Santa Monica, Calif.: Rand Corporation, 1980.

Spiegelman, Robert G., and West, Richard W. *Feasibility of a Social Experiment and Issues in Its Design*. Menlo Park, Calif.: Stanford Research Institute, 1976.

Struyk, Raymond J., and Bendick, Marc, Jr., eds. *Housing Vouchers for the Poor: Lessons from a National Experiment*. Washington, D.C.: Urban Institute, 1981.

Sudman, Seymour S., and Ferber, Robert. *Consumer Panels*. Chicago: American Marketing Association, 1980.

Taylor, Lester D. "Modeling the Residential Demand for Electricity by Time-of-Day." *Journal of Econometrics* 9 (January 1979): 97–115.

U.S., Bureau of the Census. *Current Population Reports*, Series P–60, no. 102. "Characteristics of the Population below the Poverty Level, 1974." App. A. Washington, D.C., January 1976.

U.S., Department of Health, Education, and Welfare. *The Measure of Poverty: A Report to Congress*. Washington, D.C.: Government Printing Office, 1976.

U.S., Department of Housing and Urban Development. *A Summary Report of Current Findings from the Experimental Housing Allowance Program*. Office of Policy Development and Research, April 1978.

U.S., General Accounting Office. *Federal Program Evaluation: Status and Issues*. Washington, D.C.: PAD–78–83, 1978.

Watts, Harold W., and Horner, David. "Labor-Supply Response of Husbands." In

Harold W. Watts and Albert Rees, eds., *The New Jersey Income-Maintenance Experiment.* vol. 2. New York: Academic Press, 1977.

Watts, Harold W., and Mamer, John. "Analysis of Wage-Rate Differentials." Chapter 15 in Harold W. Watts and Albert Rees, eds., *The New Jersey Income-Maintenance Experiment,* vol. 3. New York: Academic Press, 1977.

Watts, Harold W., and Rees, Albert, eds. *The New Jersey Income-Maintenance Experiment.* Vol. 2, *Labor-Supply Responses.* New York: Academic Press, 1977.

The New Jersey Income-Maintenance Experiment. Vol. 3, *Expenditures, Health, and Social Behavior; and the Quality of the Evidence.* New York: Academic Press, 1977.

Weiler, Daniel. *A Public School Voucher Demonstration.* Santa Monica, Calif.: Rand Corporation, R–1495–NIE VI, June 1974.

Weiss, Yoram, Hall, Arden, and Dong, Fred, "The Effect of Price and Income on Investment in Schooling," *Journal of Human Resources,* 15(1980): 611–40.

Welch, Finis. "The Labor Supply Response of Farmers." In John L. Palmer and Joseph A. Pechman, eds., *Welfare in Rural Areas: The North Carolina–Iowa Income Maintenance Experiment.* Washington, D.C.: Brookings Institution, 1978.

Williams, K. N. *Plans of Analysis for Health Status and Quality Care.* Santa Monica, Calif.: Rand Corporation, AR–1804–HEW, July 1978.

Williams, Walter, and Elmore, Richard F. *Social Program Implementation.* New York: Academic Press, 1976.

Wolfe, Marian F., and Hamilton, William L. *Jacksonville: Administering a Housing Allowance Program in a Difficult Environment.* Cambridge, Mass.: Abt Associates, February 1977.

INDEX